THE TRILOGY

THE TRILOGY

Diane Freeman

Library of Congress Control Number: 2017904928
ISBN: Hardcover   978-1-5434-1244-4
              Softcover   978-1-5434-1243-7
              eBook   978-1-5434-1242-0

Print information available on the last page.

Rev. date: 04/17/2017

To order additional copies of this book, contact:
Xlibris
1-888-795-4274
www.Xlibris.com
Orders@Xlibris.com
759822

Dedication

This book is dedicated to the One, true God of Heaven, Alejandro, who saved *my* soul, and then proceeded to teach me how to assist in saving others, lost souls, without prejudging them but rather to allow Him to make the decisions regarding them so they would not suffer eternal separation from Him.

To Him be *all* the glory, and *all* the majesty, in Heaven and on Earth, for His love will save the world's people from their enemies and from themselves as they choose Him, and then His own from the lack of knowledge of who they are, why they came here, and how they too may escape the darkness. Then shall they inherit His perfect love, His Kingdom in Heaven, and should they not have achieved their destinies perhaps He will show mercy so they will be assigned new destines to serve Him eternally.

May His name, Alejandro, His true name, which was forgotten by His people days without number while in their captivity, where they were not permitted to call upon His powerful name, nor to sing their songs of praise to Him, may He again be lifted up on the hearts and minds and in the voices of His people because in so doing is their power to call upon Him to deliver them from evil.

So be it.

Summary of Chapters

Chapter One

Wolfgang Amadeus Mozart

History has recorded the story of Wolfgang Amadeus Mozart without recording the complete truth of the origin of the music he composed. This first chapter will reveal the truth as Mozart himself realized it upon his death.

Chapter Two

Patrick Henry

Patrick Henry's allegiances were to his new found country of America, and he would fight for her freedom above all else. He reveals some hidden truths about this nation of ours and the challenges he met while serving the interests of her citizens.

Chapter Three

James Maitland Stewart

Jimmy Stewart as he was known in Hollywood as a leading man of some acclaim. What he was not known for he will discuss in this chapter as he came to me for his release to the heavens giving me some insight into the nature of Hollywood.

Chapter Four

Princess Diana of Wales

Even those who are married to The Elite can find redemption. Princess Diana found the light in the darkness which led her to confess her lack of devotion to the One, true God of Heaven. She speaks to the nature of love and its power when lifted up in the world.

Chapter Five

Jacqueline Kennedy Onassis

The wife of John F. Kennedy, Jr. opens up about the tragic loss of her husband and the nature of politics in general. She comments on the dangers of not following The Elitists orders and the loss of livelihood living under their watchful eyes.

Chapter Six

Robert Trent Jones

Robert Trent Jones, an architect and designer of hundreds of golf courses over the period of his lifetime. A golf advocate himself, he speaks of his realization that in the end of his life, the shocking thought came to him that he had never lifted up the name of the Almighty, only his own, naming countless courses after himself. How will he reconcile this with God?

Chapter Seven

Adolf Hitler

One of history's most hated and notorious, Adolf Hitler, has a story to tell the world that will shock you and maybe even cause you to feel sympathetic towards history's monster of humanity. Will God forgive him too?

Chapter Eight

Abraham Lincoln

A fine leader, well respected, noble, and patriotic indeed but would he remember who it was who first spoke of the need for all men to be free for we are all created equally? Did he truly honor the One whose idea it truly was and turn the nation back to Him? Abraham creates a new document of freedom.

Chapter Nine

Samuel Adams

A Statesmen, Samuel Adams was an advocate for freedom and liberty in the United States of America. He did fight for these to be qualities of life so that all Americans might be free. However, each of us has his own destiny which is achievable only with a continual connection to the God of Heaven. Samuel does explain this to us.

Chapter Ten

James Madison

Former President of the United States, James Madison speaks to his lack of seeking Divine guidance for the nation and the certainty that if he had, the nation would have faired better if he had done so. He takes a good look at his life without God and repents before Him.

Chapter Eleven

Abigail Adams

Abigail Adams was married to John Adams, 2nd President of the United States of America. Abigail shares insight into the workings of the President and who is controlling the voting process and the real need for reform there.

Chapter Twelve

Lee Harvey Oswald

Who was it that picked up Lee Harvey Oswald as he headed home from work that Dallas day in November 1963? What was Lee thinking as he listened to these men talking? Did he fear for his own life? Was Lee responsible for the death of our beloved John F. Kennedy, or was he just a scapegoat. Read what he says.

Chapter Thirteen

John Edgar Hoover

Edgar Hoover knew the truth about the Illuminati when he served the F.B.I. and investigated this group so why didn't he tell the truth? He tells us why at the request of the Almighty. Edgar also addresses why our votes in our elections no longer matter. Who is behind the "no-God" policy in the United States? Learn from Edgar Hoover himself who could now tell the truth from beyond the grave.

Chapter Fourteen

Arthur M. Young

Arthur Young was an author who acknowledges that he never gave credit to the Almighty in all of the books that he had written although he did write books on his theories of the Universe and the Creator.

Chapter Fifteen

Christopher Columbus

The explorer Christopher Columbus sheds new light on what he discovered when he "sailed the oceans blue" on behalf of the Queen of Spain and what she ordered him to do against his better judgment. This type of behavior of conquering occupied lands continues to create negative and destructive energy on the planet which must be resolved for peace to occur worldwide.

Chapter Sixteen

Isaac Asimov

Isaac Asimov tells me that space and time exist simultaneously so it is possible to get published in one day. I pray that it is so.

Chapter Seventeen

Ricardo Gonzalo Pedro Montalban y Merino

Ricardo Montalban was an advocate for the people of his homeland Mexico wanting to do whatever he could to lift them up and represent them while in Hollywood. He did not feel the support of Hollywood however feeling shunned by the Elite for his efforts to build bridges stating that they have turned from doing good to merely being focused on making money.

Chapter Eighteen

Benjamin Franklin

Statesmen, President and inventor Benjamin Franklin has come to speak to me about a rather lofty idea focused on my husband and I. We shall see if this is meant to be a guide for the future as to whom might serve us in these positions he speaks of or if he really does me it for myself and my beloved.

Chapter Nineteen

Albert Schweitzer

Albert Schweitzer would tell me that he was a scientist of the highest order and yet he stated that during his life he missed the most important truths. His insight from "the other side" tells him that our government is planning to decide who is treated with health care and who is not. Read more.

Chapter Twenty

Alexander Haig

Alexander Haig was appointed to serve as Chief of Staff for Richard Nixon, during the height of the Watergate affair. Why was he sent to me? He wanted to confirm the existence of the Reptilian race and their presence on the planet and to tell me that there was nothing we humans could do about it but perhaps pray for Divine intervention.

Chapter Twenty One

Elizabeth Taylor

Elizabeth Taylor a stunningly beautiful Hollywood actress was sent to me for her taste in women's attire and to give me guidance in style and beauty. She has her regrets regarding her life choices however and reveals them here.

Chapter Twenty Two

Lewis Meriwether

Lewis Meriwether of Lewis & Clark fame learned a bit late that he asked to come to earth to be an explorer and take the news of who the One, true God is to all of the new lands and people he would discover . . . and he forgot. He was Governor of the Louisiana Purchase at one time and one of his discoveries in the U.S. was that we are not alone here in the world. There are other beings here.

Chapter Twenty Three

Mark Antony

Are you ready to hear the truth from someone who served his family honor and Rome with such passion yet he forgot completely to serve the One who sent him here and this after he did promise to come here to make a difference for the Almighty? At the end of his life he found himself in a place "not fit for beggars" to quote him. Read how he reconciles with God

Chapter Twenty Four

Ronald Reagan

A man of ideals with the intention to do good as President of the United States of America was denied that privilege by The Elite who had their own intentions about how they wanted the President to lead. He would also suffer at the hands of The Elite as they attempted to assassinate him while he was in office. He would find his way home through repentance.

Chapter Twenty Five

Steve McQueen

Actor Steve McQueen was one of Hollywood's most beloved actors. He was admired by many of Hollywood's finest actors and actresses as well as by the public in America. What you will learn about him here comes directly from him before he did depart and go to the heavens. It is enlightening indeed and he speaks to his peers giving them sound advice for their careers and life choices in general. Worth your time and, for those of you in Hollywood today, Steve McQueen wanted to leave a legacy of truth for you and it is contained herein.

Chapter Twenty Six

Karl Marx

Everything you already believe about the nature of Karl Marx's teachings is true and here he will recollect what led to the origins of his early thoughts and writings and then he will repent before the God of Heaven for providing a way for that evil to enter the world.

Chapter Twenty Seven

Dr. Thomas Walker

Though not much is said about Dr. Walker today he was instrumental in providing some of the first maps and information about unexplored areas of the east coast of the Americas. Dr. Walker wants the world to know that he was a good man and yet he did not go to heaven and he wants to know why no one told him how to get there when he was in the world.

Chapter Twenty Eight

Heinrich Luitpold Himmler

Few men in history have the kind of reputation that Heinrich Himmler had for being ruthless and pure evil in his destruction of humanity. Men, women and children were all his victims of atrocities committed under Hitler. Himmler admits that he sold his soul to whatever it was that was controlling Hitler. So if you have any doubt that Hitler's regime was real and the men he trained were evil, read Himmler's confession and repentance before the Almighty.

Chapter Twenty Nine

Franklin D. Roosevelt

FDR admits to compromising himself when he served as President of the United States and says that he did *not* serve the Almighty rather he chose to serve The Elite that he would gain money, fame, success and power which The Elite promised him. But when you choose gods who are *not* gods as your god there are eternal consequences. See how he works it out before the Almighty.

Chapter Thirty

Henry Brooks Adams

Henry Adams was an up and coming historian of the ages when he gave himself to The Elite to write whatever he was told to record as history rather than the truth. This would come back to haunt him at the end of his days for he was chosen divinely to come and record history in the making of America for faith was being lifted up and freedom and liberty. He would miss his destiny but in the end, repentance leads him to an even greater destiny in heaven.

Chapter Thirty One

John Wayne

John Wayne comes back to reveal the truth about Hollywood players being sworn to secrecy as to the "rules" for celebrities. He speaks to the "show" that is now Hollywood whereas society really just wants to be entertained, not programmed to accept those who are not human through Hollywood's enactment of characters as emotionless, murderers, tactless, racist, and worthless people. They no longer represent the truth of who "we" are nor is it their intention and John Wayne wanted us to know. (go back and check the original text of John Wayne's testimony and see if there are more pages or an additional line or two that I just erased)

Chapter Thirty Two

Thomas Paine

Apparently, Elitists, whom Thomas refers to as evil, saw opportunity when the Americas were being established and they did come here too. In order to win our freedom from them at this point, Thomas does say that there will certainly be rebellion and turmoil. He recommends preparation and discusses it here.

Chapter Thirty Three

Herbert Hoover

Herbert Hoover was the 31st President of the United States of America. He struggled for success in his career as President as many of his liberal peers resisted his conservative viewpoints not supporting his ideas or proposals for a better government. He did leave a worldly legacy behind however he did not achieve his preordained Divine destiny and this we did discuss as he was anxious to depart the darkness where he was all of these years and go home to the light.

Chapter Thirty Four

Stonewall Jackson

Rather than a chapter involving the individual listed here, what we have is a statement brought forward for such a time as this as Stonewall was directed by the Almighty to do so. It concerns an upcoming battle that must be fought.

Chapter Thirty Five

Louis Armstrong

A famous trumpeter is invited to the game by the Lord Himself and accepts his new destiny with joy to serve the higher good. Louis Armstrong will bring forth the trumpet blasts heard around the world.

Part I: Breakthrough from Beyond Death

Part II: Lost Souls Follow in the Footsteps of the
Redeemed

Part III: A New Dawn for the Remnant

Part I

Breakthrough from Beyond Death

Introduction

On the morning of my husband's heart attack in January 2011, I was the same today as yesterday as our Lord is fond of saying but something happened on this day that would forever change me. As I sat next to my husband as he lay in the I.C.U. at Scripps Memorial Hospital in La Jolla, California, I would be contacted by first one departed soul after another. They wished to tell me their stories of life at the direction of our Lord Himself and then I was to assist them in their transition home from darkness.

They would each confess to Him their own shortcomings while in life as the Lord listened through my connection to them and then He forgave each of them allowing them to go home.

This all began as an act of obedience by me as I was asked from time to time by Him with His protection to assist a soul who had passed from life but without understanding of themselves and where they were to go after death or even who they were. Sometimes their own soul's Higher Self would testify against their soul in death for they had not served their Divine destinies and each had requested to be here for a Divine purpose.

When it was all said and done, months would have passed and I now had quite a compilation of these brilliant stories from those who have now passed on to glory.

Finally, we can answer a few questions that we all have as human beings.

Why are we here?

Who are we?

What are we supposed to do while here?

How do we find out these things that we are here to do?

Who is the one, true God of our world and how do we connect with Him?

By sharing these stories I think you too will find answers to these age old questions and perhaps the world can be a better place.

So with love to Him, who did show me the way to help myself and others, both living and departed, to bring glory to His name's sake, whose name is revealed here for the first time in a very long time, Alejandro. To Alejandro, a beautiful name, whose name was forgotten by His people days without number, to you Alejandro, with the utmost love, respect, and admiration. I am yours!!

Part II

Lost Souls Follow in the Footsteps of the Redeemed

Wolfgang Amadeus Mozart

January 27, 1756 – December 5, 1791

Wolfgang Amadeus Mozart was one of the first souls who came through directly to me without my asking to speak to him or more importantly after first having received Alejandro's instructions to do so. It was January 23, 2011 and as I was feeling extreme discomfort in my right foot. Originally, I thought this was due to those who could not cross over who were of a different vibration and who were beyond my ability to assist them. I had been receiving guidance from Alejandro about how souls can reach out to us.

In ignorance, I had been trying to get them to leave by instructing them to go to the light if you will. Instead I was instructed to please help these souls as they wanted my help and the heavens would be standing by to assist me in helping them one by one. I was nervous initially as I wanted to be certain that I did indeed recognize who these departed souls were and that I would hear their proper names.

The name that I heard was Amadeus. The heavens said to me, "Amadeus is anxious to get out of there. Are you willing to help him tonight?" I said that I would come back later after my husband was asleep and was told "The composer is restless and wants to come to the light".

Alejandro instructed me as to what to say to the composer Mozart when I came back into my office later that evening. What I heard was this. "We want you to ask him a few questions.

First, ask him how it is that he came to know that you could speak to those on the "other side".

Write it down. Next, ask him if he knows why it is that he ended up there? Write it down. What has he had to do while there? How is it that he could contact you? What did he do to contact you? Is he able to inspire you with some music as a thank you? Ask him? Tell him that you are going to help him and then be here in your office tonight at 11 p.m. and Diane, now you shall have some fun!"

I responded, "Very nice. I am delighted to help Wolfgang Amadeus Mozart."

I felt a pain in my right foot and immediately heard who it was, "It is Wolfgang Amadeus Mozart. I am thrilled that you have finally heard me. I have been calling to you for some time as I heard that you were able to hear the departed ones. I was not able to demonstrate to you that I was not one of the dark ones for you were not listening to me. I was so sad that you thought I was evil."

My response was that I was experiencing intense foot pain and quite honestly just wanted relief not understanding what was happening.

Wolfgang apologized for the pain that I felt saying that he saw that it hurt me but said "you must imagine my despair. I have been in this darkness with no way out. But there you were, willing to come here and rescue souls. I heard and so I thought that if I could make you hear me, I had a chance to escape this darkness."

I responded to him saying, "How wonderful that you trust me to help you. Of course, I will help you I am honored to 'meet you' as it were and I would hope that, to give me a degree of believability, that you might tell me something that others would realize that I was telling them the truth when I say, and I will, that I assisted you to the heavens. We will do it. Tonight at 11 p.m. Come back to my office then we will become friends."

"The honor is all mine dear one," responded Amadeus. He continued, "I have never seen one with such a beautiful light as your own.

You are becoming well known here among the lost and hope is rejuvenated."

I told Amadeus that he was one talented man and his music lives on among the living. Cherished, and adored, duplicated around the globe, still remembered.

Amadeus then said, "You too can be remembered Diane. We must get your message out there. Perhaps I can help you once I am free. Let's put our heads together to come up with some music for your website that will draw people to your site. I have many compositions that were given to me divinely that inspire and invigorate the soul. I will choose one for your website and you will see that men's hearts will melt to the words you are speaking. Will you look up my name on the internet and see what music comes to you there?"

"Yes, of course," I said, "Right now!" I found this one, "String quartets: No. 2, String Quartet No. 2 in D Major, K 155/134a (1772). Amadeus then said, "This was my first ever string quartet inspired by, as you say about your hearing, Alejandro. I wrote out the compilation and then found those who would play it for me. It was the most beautiful sound I have ever heard. You may use it on your site for there are no copyrights on my music."

I asked Amadeus if he was certain of that. He then indicated that I should check the truth for myself telling me to "then find the music and put it in the background on your site for those who are reading to hear the music of heaven Diane. Their hearts will be opened I assure you as was mine when I heard it first in my dreams."

"Amadeus, this is such a wonderful thing for me," I said, "I give you my heart full of thanks for wishing to assist me and I will assist you as well my friend."

The heavens came through to me then and Alejandro said to me, "Diane, tell Mozart that we are going to assist him home at 11 p.m. Prepare his heart to go home. Think of love and love only. Release all thoughts of his experience there and go with those who come for him. We are ready to take him home."

I asked, "At this moment?" Alejandro stated that "Yes, for once contact is made the darkness is stirred to intervene. We must take him immediately if we are to avoid interference."

I responded, "But I was talking with him." I genuinely was enjoying talking with him and hearing about his life."

Alejandro stepped back in to say, "We understand beloved but it is his time to go. Send him to us now. We will assist him in crossing. You have done well to assist him. Enjoy the music.

Bless him with light and here we come."

I thanked Alejandro and then told Amadeus that I had news for him. "They are coming to get you and you get to go home. I have a couple of questions for you however. Will you answer them for me please?"

Amadeus responded by saying, "Anything at all for you Diane for you are a blessing to me and to others ask away."

Alejandro was guiding me to ask him first how is it that he came to know that I could speak to those on the 'other side'.

Amadeus answered me saying, "It became known that a light had shown here in the darkness and that souls had been delivered to the light by a woman named Diane Freeman. I heard this and was given hope that perhaps I too might be freed. I looked for the light again to come and then I followed it to its origin after the souls left. I found you and have been pressing on your foot attempting to get your attention but when your foot hurt, you assumed that it was a dark entity and you would not entertain my voice. I was desperate to get out of here and I was persistent I must admit. Please forgive me."

I told Amadeus that my foot hurt even then as the energy is different than my own and it hurts.

He said, "Please forgive me but I must beg you to assist me home. This is not my home and I cannot stay here nor can others who are here. You must also help them Diane."

I thanked Amadeus and then Alejandro asked me to question Amadeus as to why he thought he ended up there? His response was "I was not cognizant of God's love as you are Diane but I knew that I was not the one composing the music which came to me for it was rich, intense, and magnificent. I was intelligent in a worldly way but this music was not from this world. My world was dark too. People were not inspired in this world but the music brought to me opened them up and they were in awe. It was seemingly from the heavens and so I allowed myself to listen to it carefully, writing it down and finding the appropriate musicians to play the compositions. The result? Not of this world as you too will hear. Play my song on your website. You will see what will happen."

Next I asked Amadeus, "What have you had to do while there?"

Amadeus answered "I have had nothing to do that has been worth noting. My life was rich with composing music. Since then, I have been lost, hopeless, full of despair not knowing what to do or how to escape this madness. Thank God for you princess."

I asked him how it was that he could contact me? He stated this, "My spirit is enthusiastic though my energy is depleted almost to nothing. I heard about you Diane as I said and I decided that it was now or never for there is talk that the earth's axis is shifting and the energy of the planet will make it impossible for those trapped here to ever leave. I could not endure such a tragedy and so I sought you out, followed your light and there you were in all of your radiance. I have been reaching out to you since then. Again, my apologies to you for causing the pain in your foot. We are different vibrations you and I."

My response of course was to tell Amadeus that no apologies were needed and I asked him to please forgive me for not recognizing the source of the intrusion. To this Amadeus simply said, "Indeed." I did however want to know how it was that he had made my foot hurt. I asked him and he told me.

"It is simple and yet it is not. I must concentrate on your physical image and imagine that my energy is reaching out to yours by pushing my energy towards you. Not to intrude too personally, I chose your foot. And you felt it, but you were not hearing my communication. I persevered even to the point of your deciding to choose my music at one point and yet you did not hear my voice. I was in despair when I knew that I had communicated enough for you to choose the music but you still did not hear me."

Again I said, "Forgive me sir."

"I am delighted that we have arrived at a communication Diane," said Amadeus, "and you are all that I imagined in a lovely woman for who would choose such a destiny as to come into the depths of despair to rescue men, women and children? It is unheard of and yet, there you were."

I thanked Amadeus once again for his kind words. Alejandro had asked me to inquire as to whether Amadeus might inspire me with some music as a thank you. I did not know this was possible and asked whether Alejandro was referring to his First String Quartet perhaps.

Amadeus asked me to look at the list of songs again which I had from the internet. He then said to me excitedly, "What about *God Is Our Refuge*? Play this music. It will inspire you. Play it often. It has a lovely sound you will like."

"Thank you. I am sorry for your suffering Amadeus. I am so sorry. I wonder if others that I have admired are there too. Patrick Henry? What about him, I asked?"

"I do not know Diane. I do not know all of the souls that are here due to the inability to communicate with others. It is not allowed in fact it is strictly forbidden."

My response to that was "Well thank the heavens above that you could communicate with me.

Glory be to the Father of heaven," to which Amadeus replied, "Amen to that".

I began, "Now let's get busy. Let me send you light enough to go to the heavens and the angelic forces will come for you. Thank you for the blessing of music Amadeus. I send you love from 2011 if you can believe it. The year is 2011."

"Glory, who could believe it", said Amadeus. "I died in the 1800's. Look it up and you will see.

It was a pleasure talking with you Diane Freeman. I look forward to meeting you in the heavens.

I will ask that support be given to you for your endeavors. I will think of you often and know that you are free to use my music for you have inspired me in ways you cannot imagine. I am yours in spirit, adieu."

I sent Amadeus off with blessings of love and peace to go with him. I thanked God for the freedom I have to assist others and for the understanding to do this job well. Adieu Amadeus and thank you for the music.

I thought that I was finished and then Amadeus came to say "One more thing Diane. I am going to send you a song from the light. Listen for it. I will ask how to send it to you and then you will hear it. Record it if you can.

I asked him whether the song would be audible. He could only say that he hoped so and asked me to find a way to record it. I will do the rest and then he said "So be it my new friend. Love to you."

I said goodbye and realized Amadeus was not gone. He said, "I can't let go yet Diane". I asked Him why not. He said that he had some regrets for not "having shown more love to God or appreciation of Him as you have and others I knew showed Him."

"You must let go of all negative feelings, all negative emotions," I told him. "They will cling to your being and prevent you from leaving. You must think only love. God forgives and loves you as he loves all who are trapped there. All can go home. Don't let the lives of the dark ones entrap. Release their energy and embrace only the light. Embrace it. Feel the love. Feel my love that I am sending. Let it lift up your being. Feel the love of God which is real and is able to lift you up."

I continued to tell Amadeus, "Remember how deep, how long and how wide, how high is the love of God to save His beloved son Amadeus? How great is His love? Forgive yourself. Let it go. It was just a worldly experience of an energy being, your Higher Self, having a body experience here. God loves you. Always has loved you and always will. You can go to heaven and all is well with your soul. Did you hear me?"

"But I am not worthy," he said.

I told him that no one was worthy. That is the point. We are just having an experience and now yours is done. Go to the light and embrace the love of heaven. It is yours for the taking. Ignore the liars and the deceivers and go immediately when you see the angelic light. Your freedom awaits you."

"But they are telling me that it is too late for me," Amadeus replied.

"Don't listen to them. They are lying. Go to the light and ignore them. Do not believe them. I do not lie. I tell you the truth from Alejandro. You are free to go home. Concentrate on love and nothing else.

Remember the story of the prodigal son? He left home. He went away. He squandered away his money but when he came home his father was so happy to see him that he threw a big welcoming feast and so it shall be for you Amadeus. Hear me. Read my light. I am telling you the truth believe me and no one else right now. Believe me. You are free. You are FREE! I once was lost and now I am found and so shall you be when you go to the light. Go with them when they come."

Amadeus then answered me, "You are a marvel to me Diane. My heart bears witness to your truth. I am free aren't I?"

I had another personal request for a song which I did ask Amadeus for and then said "Amazing was that grace the hour I first believed. Go home now Amadeus and peace be with you."

"And also with you Diane, I am letting go of you now for I can see the light in the distance coming for me. I believe you that I am free and so I will go home now to the heavens. What a glorious day! What a momentous moment. There is nothing to describe how I feel right now for it is indescribable. Thank you."

"Thank you. You are my savior in this moment from the bowels of what was hell for me. Thank you. I will send you a song. Listen for it. Ask your husband to borrow his recorder tonight and when you hear my name, get your recorder ready. Adieu."

I sent love to the heavens and to all of the ascended Masters, love from Diane Freeman.

Patrick Henry

May 2, 1736 – June 6, 1799)

It was my husband's birthday, January 28, 2011, but sadly he was in Scripps Memorial Hospital in the ICU at the time of this visitation and I was seated right beside him there in his hospital room. I was saying to this soul that I must be afforded respect as I was obviously under duress due to the circumstances I found myself in with my husband being attended to in the hospital. There were so many tubes going every which way and we really didn't know what the situation would be for him yet. But then, due to the persistence of this energy I asked for the soul to please tell me their name.

I heard this, "I was a Statesman Diane. You know me as Patrick Henry."

I asked if I was hearing correctly and he responded, "P.A.T.R.I.C.K H.E.N.R.Y."

Well I got that for sure. Patrick Henry is one of my favorite patriots of all time. I asked him to please tell me something about himself for many deceivers had gone out and were attempting to lead mankind astray from the truth. Before Patrick Henry could respond, I was interrupted by The Divine who broke through to say this, "Ask Patrick to tell you who it was that he feared that moved him so greatly to patriotism but let's get him first to let go of your foot shall we?"

Alejandro then said to Patrick, "Patrick, we are The Divine, here to assist you in crossing. You need to not fear any longer hence you may let go of Diane's foot for it causes her great discomfort.

Patrick's response was immediate, "200 years in darkness is long enough. I must not stay here. I long for liberty and freedom."

Alejandro responded, "And you shall have it. We have your frequency as it were now and you shall cross to the light. Let go of Diane's foot and we will show you the way."

I asked Patrick to read the truth in my own light. I told him that God would never leave him or forsake him now. I said, "I'm here, am I not?"

Patrick indicated that he would indeed let go saying, "I'm letting go at your request Diane. Keep me close and shine your light here for me."

"Indeed, I desired to help you Patrick for your few words, at least these words that were attributed to you have inspired me all of my life. 'Give me liberty or give me death.'"

Then my foot started to hurt so much. I said, "Oh no, let go of my foot." Perhaps the mention of his words stirred up his energy.

Patrick said to me "I did let go! This must be another soul come in for your assistance."

I had to ask Alejandro to please move this other soul for another moment. I needed to assist Patrick now. "Divine ones can you please move the soul attaching to my feet as I help Patrick please?"

I asked Patrick the following question. "Patrick, the question that I have for you is who were the people whom you feared in Virginia and surrounding areas?"

"They were Abolitionists who claimed to want the slaves to be free and yet there were quick to enslave them in other ways. It had become known that prominent men participated in the killing of black men and in order to hide this truth, these same men calculated yet another means to an end. They would work to free the slaves seemingly making laws to protect them and at the same time . . ."

"Excuse me Patrick," I said. "Divine ones please you must tell these souls to step off until I am not working for Patrick. I cannot concentrate the pain is so great. Please."

Patrick continued, " . . . freely execute them in secret. Then under the guise of being men who were for freeing the slaves they could hide their true intentions but the public would view them by their public persona, judging them by the laws they made. This making of law to hide the deeds of men whose nature was against everything I believed in caused me great anguish, and I desired to awake my countrymen to the dangers of the law and its' hidden agenda.

Unfortunately, the people were blinded by a false sense of freedom and they would not listen to me."

"And so it is today Patrick," I said. "Men such as these have gained control over God's country.

How do we prevail against them now?"

His response was swift saying, "One by one remove them from office. Choose men whose hearts are pure. You shall know them by their works, isn't it written? Then clear them energetically to serve in office. They must choose which God they will serve. The God of heaven or the God of money. Choose only those who will serve the God of heaven."

I asked Patrick how do we open a door to this beginning now? "Can you help us Patrick when you are free?"

Patrick said something then that was surprising. "Perhaps it is time for your husband to serve Diane. He can no longer serve full capacity in the law but he can protect the law of heaven by serving God as a leader in the world."

"Then doors must open for wealth to come to him for only the wealthy seem to make themselves known well enough today to be voted in to serve," I stated.

Patrick said, "Many know him now and his integrity is legendary."

I asked him to continue please.

Patrick added, "We will publish your book immediately and the first of your trilogies in order to reward your efforts and raise money for Dick to run for public office. Then we will send those with lots of money to support him."

I told Patrick that my husband would need dynamic, miraculous healing if he was to be set apart for this purpose.

Patrick responded, "And he shall have it. Ask him if he is ready yet to serve the God of heaven and leave a legacy for men. If the answer is yes, then he will need to seek God's counsel and not the counsel of men. Tell your husband he will need to pray for God's direction and then he will hear. We will pay him well in speaking engagements, books, and in your books as well Diane.

He won't have one worry about money ever again."

"Patrick", I asked, "he is just today out of the ICU. What is the timing of this question to him?"

He responded, "The sooner the better however you have a point. Wait three weeks until February 22, 2011, Washington's birthday, then ask him if he is ready to serve as the first godly President since the first one? See what he says on February 22, 2011."

I then asked Patrick to assist me in visualizing the next Godly President. I asked Patrick, "who is the next Godly President?"

Patrick began to then tell me who indeed ought to be the next Godly President saying, "He is 6'4" tall. He is a casual man and yet stately. He is handsome and lean. He has a clear resonant voice and can articulate the truth. His mind is his own and he will not cave to special interests but will seek first the Kingdom of God in counsel. Then he will seek Godly counsel with others rooting out those whose intentions are for evil.

He will have a Godly wife, beautiful who seeks Godly counsel in all things. She advises her husband and is steadfast to protect him from evil, seeing all who seek to manipulate him or to do him harm. These two will serve eight years and then retire in bliss to celebrate their children and grandchildren living into their early 90's before going to the light."

My response was "Sweet! Nice job Patrick. Now how may I assist you Patrick?"

"I want to transition home Diane, but regret lingers for I knew the dangers of these men and yet failed to expose them."

"Patrick," I said, "Regret is an e-motion, energy in motion created by you and others to show you how you felt at a particular moment in time You can send it now to the light where it will be reabsorbed. Acknowledge it for what it has taught you or demonstrated to you and let it go.

Send it in love and now regret is free. Try it. Acknowledge feeling regret and systematically send it home. Thank it for showing you that feeling for to not have felt it is to have not learned that lesson about choices we make."

"I see," said Patrick. "I can do that. I can do that."

I asked him if there was anything else keeping him stuck.

He said, "I lost at love a few times. I still feel this loss."

"Love too is a feeling and there is different love in this world. If you were able to love despite the difficulties of the world you did well. Take the love you felt as a positive and let any disappointment, regret, sadness, and send it to the light. Love awaits you in the light for all are welcomed home. You are free to re-experience God's love there. It is men who judge the lives of others, men and women who condemn us. I know for I too have suffered at the hands of men.

We must forgive them as God forgives us so we can go home to love."

Patrick heard me and said, "This is beautiful Diane and I embrace it wholeheartedly. I embrace my eternity."

I then instructed Patrick to let the love of God fill his heart but I asked him to send the world insight from heaven as men seek it for what to do to oppose tyranny. I told him that, "We need God's wisdom."

To this Patrick stated, "You shall have it when you seek it Diane. I see the light of heaven now.

Amazing grace for me and you were the light I saw in the night guiding me away from the enemy of men. I will remember you always my friend."

I asked God to give us liberty and eternal life for all those good men who love God, for the good of all.

Patrick then stated, "I will go and tell the others there of your work Diane and your husband's needs to become a Statesman, i.e., renewed health, prosperity, and renewal of faith in God and men."

I thanked Patrick Henry sending him blessings of eternal love and light and glory to our God in the Highest to which Patrick said, "Amen."

I responded, "Love to you Patrick Henry," and he simply said, "Til then. Adieu."

James Maitland Stewart

May 20, 1908 – July 2, 1997

On February 2, 2011, this time my own birthday, I was visited by Jimmy Stewart. My husband was due to be released from the hospital at Scripps in La Jolla, California and, it was my birthday. How strange that my husband would be hospitalized on his birthday and then we would still be there as my birthday arrived. I asked the soul that was coming through how I might help them and I asked for them to tell me their name please. I was excited to hear the name Jimmy Stewart for he was one of my favorite "old school" if you will actors.

"My name is Jimmy Stewart. I was an actor, movie star if you will. I spent my entire adult life making films and hobnobbing around with Hollywood types."

I asked Jimmy why he was here and "where is it you are and why do you need me?"

He said, "Diane, I am here because I forgot the essential tenets of faith, a belief in an Almighty Creator, acknowledgement of that Creator in my life, and giving credit to that Creator for the good things that came to me in life."

"I had a good run," he said, "but I neglected to give proper credit to the One who gave me life. I allowed credit to be given to me instead and here I am . . . nowhere with lots of others just like me.

We neither asked God for help us nor gave Him credit when we didn't need any help."

"So why do you think you are "stuck", I asked? "God is a forgiving and loving God. Not an evil task master."

Jimmy then said, "I cannot forgive myself for not connecting with God. Of course, I want to know God now. Who wouldn't if the alternative is to be in this hell of an existence which is apart from everything good."

I wanted to know what else he was feeling and asked him.

Jimmy responded, "Remorse for I did not serve the Kingdom of Heaven nor did I assist man in any way to make life better for others as you are doing. I served myself and when I made money for doing it, I spent that too. It was a deplorable existence."

I asked Jimmy, "Who says so?"

Jimmy answered, "The dark lords. They tell me that I was selfish, self-serving, without the love of God and without love for man."

"Is it true," I asked him?

Jimmy said, "No, but I did not think to do differently."

I asked Jimmy, "Why did you suppose that was the case?" .

Jimmy answered, "I don't know. The mention of God was left to the churches. It certainly was not part of Hollywood and in fact, it was discouraged among actors. Talking about God or serving God was a negative for an aspiring actor."

My answer to him was, "Well, there you go then. If your livelihood was acting you chose to act rather than to serve God or give him recognition. It was a choice. Acknowledge that and let it go. Send the negative controlling thoughts to the light, with love, they merely serve to show you what you were choosing of the world instead of God. In addition, there are those whose agenda is evil to keep us from remembering God. I am hearing The Divine coming through right now."

I then heard from Alejandro, "Diane, ask Jimmy what message he would wish to convey to Hollywood actors and actresses today so that at the end of life they can go home?"

I asked Jimmy if he did hear the question from Alejandro too.

He answered, "Yes, I am thinking. I would say this to aspiring actors and actresses. If you have to sell your soul to act out a part in Hollywood, it is too great a price to pay. No man should ever require you to deny yourself in order to earn a living. This usurps your authority to choose to live life in the manner of your destiny as well as robs you of your freedom as a man/woman.

The signing of contracts which limit your ability to choose which parts you would play is against your nature. You will regret doing that which is against your nature. Learn from the mistakes of others before you. Heath Ledger is one such individual who acted against his nature and was overcome by it. Learn from his story. Preserve your integrity or you too will find yourselves lost at the end of your days."

"Good", I said. "I will share this. How can you make a difference now as you head home to heaven?"

Jimmy stated, "Perhaps I can tell the truth of the men who manipulate through actors and actresses and then in showing the actions in movies in order to shape humanity."

I told Jimmy to "Open the door then for actors and actresses to believe the truth that they will not soon recover from the selling of their souls."

Jimmy said, "I can and I will do this Diane. Then a legacy will be mine too."

"Indeed," I answered. "Have you released the negative thoughts to the light and all negative energies of the world Jimmy? Send them home too. So they too can be free."

"I am looking forward to going home now Diane," he said. "I will tell the Father of Heaven to bless you and your husband for helping me to cross and for reminding me of the love of God."

I responded that it had been my pleasure to assist him. "I will see you in the light someday then sir. Many blessings to you. Now give God the glory."

Jimmy merely said, "Adieu", but then I could still feel his presence. I asked whether he was still there.

He responded, "I feel anxiety, fear, of God's judgment".

I told Jimmy the following. "God is love and does not judge His own. Send these feelings to the light in love. Let me send you light and love and read its' truth to you. I then began to push out the energy of light and love to Jimmy from within myself. "Do you see," I asked?

Jimmy stated, "I do. I am free now Diane and they are here for me. I am encouraged and delivered of fear and anxiety. Thank you."

I instructed Jimmy to go with them who were there for him in peace and God speed. Again Jimmy spoke, "I will remember your heart's love for me always."

I thought that Jimmy was on his journey home but again he was there to speak with me.

"Diane, this is Jimmy. I need to offer something to you my dear for your kindness to me in freeing me. I would like to do this on your behalf. Oprah Winfrey has a new show. I would like to open the door in heaven for you to gain access to appearing on her show. There you can tell the truth. Many will be encouraged and it will open hearts and minds. What do you think?"

"Yes, I love it. Please this might be the door to my success. Thank you, Jimmy."

His final words to me were, "No, thank you Diane. I was lost and despite your own needs and your husband's, you gave me back my freedom. I will see that it is done for you."

I sent Jimmy Stewart off with many blessings and love and waited for the next soul encounter.

Princess Diana of Wales

July 1, 1961 – August 31, 1997

Here I am and it is now February 4, 2011, having assisted various souls at the request of Alejandro in crossing to the light It is the appointed hour of 3 p.m. and I spoke to the souls clamoring for assistance that I could only assist two more souls at that time in moving on to eternity but that I must have a break after this.

I asked the soul pressing in to tell me their name as I was feeling the connection on my right. I said, "Here I am, at your service if you will. Please tell me your name."

"It is a pleasure to make your acquaintance Diane. I am Princess Diana of Wales."

Oh my gosh, I was thrilled. I had always, always admired this person and imagined her life as perfect. Not only was she young and beautiful when she first married but seemed genuinely innocent and special as a person within. I was ecstatic that I would get to help her but also sad that she had not yet crossed over. I believe that most people do know who Princess Diana was but if you do not she was married to Prince Charles of England.

"My goodness, it is a pleasure to speak with you as well even if it is after your life in the body,"

I responded." "I grieved your death as so many others did Diana. I studied what might have happened to you, reading about you and wondering why anyone would take your beautiful life.

Your example of love was far reaching and perhaps that was just too much for those who wish to rule the world through intimidation and fear."

Diana spoke, "You are exactly right Diane. The message of love is one that they are not interested in promoting particularly from England. The country has lost its love of God and given itself over to men who rule for power, greed and posterity. They do not care about the common man but merely to use them as a tool to gain more notoriety for themselves and for their own families by usurping their power and authority and using it for personal gain and control over the land. I saw much of this as I came into the role as Princess of Wales. Though I sought to do good, it was not encouraged and in fact, it was discouraged and was very disheartening to me for I wanted my sons to see how one can rule in the land to make a difference not merely to be known for his title and worshipped by the people for having done nothing at all as some have done."

I asked Diana, "What happened that fateful night? Do you know? Do you know who was behind it and why they did it? Is it as awful as we imagine and was it done to merely make an example for the dark side that the light will not rise up? What happened?"

Princess Diana told me this. "All that I am permitted to tell you Diane is that it indeed was a conspiracy and it was carefully orchestrated in an attempt to control the rise of love in the world for those who rule over such things know that the highest vibration among men is love. If love reaches all men, then there is nothing that they cannot do for themselves, others and unto God.

Love is the greatest gift one can give another as you know and have exemplified in your life under the harshest of conditions you have shown love and as such you are being chosen to a position of leadership among women."

To this I responded, "I hardly know what to say except that it will be an honor to serve the Almighty, with glory unto God, in the highest for the good of all and as it is said, "all for one, and one for all". I wonder if that is a good motto to use as it seems to hold a high vibration regardless of the Musketeers. Diana, I send you love from here and from those who loved you so much around the globe may it come through me now for you." I began to send her love.

Princess Diana then said to me, "You are too kind Diane. I would have learned much from you about how to guard myself from others whose desire it was only to harm me, to use me for their own purposes of controlling others. I was naïve as a young girl, inexperienced with men and infatuated with being a Princess no doubt. Little did I know what was in store for me and my young sons to be raised by this hierarchy without the love of their mother, it saddens me still."

I told Diana that I would love to reach out to them to assist them in knowing the truth but it is so difficult to reach anyone in a position of authority. Perhaps if my husband were to really achieve the Presidency, I would have an opportunity to meet her sons and then I would speak to them. If I did, I asked Diana "what would I say"? What would she have me bring to their lives?

"My greatest desire," said Diana, "is that they would exhibit love of humanity in their leadership in England. Love of humanity is the greatest gift they can bring to the world. Love for the lowest of the lowest in life who have no hope, no foreseeable future, no livelihood or knowledge of God. My desire is that they would remember who their mother was and desire to be like me in this one regard if no other. Love others as you love yourself. Give to those who give to you . . . love. In addition, if they treat others with respect, dignity and kindness they will leave their mark in the world as I did. To use others for no other reason than to attain some power over an enterprise or people is wrong and is not sanctioned by God. Tell them this. God will reward those who serve Him with humility and humbleness before Him. God will sanction all that they do unto Him for the good of all. This is a promise under heaven. That which you seek to do that will benefit humanity without harming another is to be exemplified and duplicated throughout the land. Do no harm. This is a worthy saying and unfortunately, it was not followed even by those I trusted."

I asked Diana if these words were merely for my benefit. I asked her if I was able to speak of any of this in my book and how would I tell her sons these things if I did not put them in my book for them to read?

She told me to do the following. "Diane, do this. Write of this to my sons, William and Harry. Put a note in a copy of your book Freedom Come and send the copies to my aunt. Tell her who you are and that you are asked to share your book with my sons by me, Princess Diana, that my sons would leave a legacy of their own of love in this world. The world desperately needs to wake up to the power of love. No other thing can change the disposition in the world the way that love can. It is the highest vibration because it is the nature of God and in the nature of God is every good thing. I want my sons to know this for they are good in their nature for they are my own and God is in them too. This would please me more than anything else that I was able to speak with you for the benefit of my beloved sons whom I was not able to kiss goodbye before my death. I will always remember them. I will also miss them until they come home to the heavens at the end of their days. They are a part of me forever. Tell them so Diane. Tell them that they can share in my legacy by being love too."

I indicated that I would attempt to contact her Aunt to share with her this truth. It would then be up to her Aunt to have the faith to believe and then to question God as to whether these words were true and then to share the message with Diana's sons, William and Harry.

Princess Diana said, "This makes me immensely joyful. I cannot tell you. I can say goodbye to my sons. They were my greatest gift to the world. I only wish that I had shared my life with someone who loved me for who I was instead of some belief in a dynasty not of God. I will remember you always Diane."

I asked Princess Diana if there was any way in which I could assist her further.

Princess Diana then said, "It is not necessary to assist me further for sharing your energy with me has allowed me to energize enough to see the truth of God's love for me and to release the pain and anguish of my life. I am transitioning even now as we speak."

I asked Diana what advice she would give to me for the work ahead of me. I stated that I could only hope that I too could exhibit the poise and grace and beauty which she had for so many saying that I hoped that I could share love with many as she did and that I might represent the God of heaven in a beautiful light so that many would be freed.

This is what Princess Diana told me to do.

"Be yourself. You are a beautiful woman with a lovely soul. You need not change your character for any reason certainly not to serve in the land beside your husband. Be yourself.

People will see the truth of who you are in your light. You need only exercise caution in speaking about those whose intentions are for evil. Rather, give the situation over to God and those who serve Him, and ask for resolution of the matters as they arise. Ask that those who are your enemies are struck down, removed, and of no consequence to the work you are doing for the good of all. Ask God to do it, in prayer, and set it in order in the heavens and so it will be according to your need. God will do it for you. You do not need to concern yourself with the ways of evil either with who they are or what they do in secret."

"Excellent," I said. "I will follow your advice. If I need a reminder from time to time, come and see me again. I think we could have been good company as I believe that you and I would have shared a love for the common good."

Princess Diana responded, "You are correct in saying so for I see your nature in your light. We are sisters of a sort you and I. How may I assist you Diane in my departure to the heavens?

May I ask after you in some manner for a provision of some kind?"

My only request was that God would give to me good grace, beauty and knowledge of how to speak publicly that I might convey His truth of love of all in an eloquent and masterful way that others might believe. This I need and a powerful, clear, voice. I told Princess Diana that I needed to have my speaking voice and singing voice released and the congestion in my chest and nasal passages removed for good.

"This is an easy one," Diana said. "I will put forth your request with my blessing upon it and you shall have it."

Princess Diana added, "Let me go then now Diane and I will go to the light. Peace be with you my sister in love. Give my love to my sons William and Harry and a hug and a kiss should you see them. They will know that I sent you by this endearing act of love."

"Peace be with you Diana. You were a lovely woman. You were a kind, generous, loving and a peaceful beauty. The world is a better place for you having been here. Blessings of love upon your soul and love to you and to your sons. I bless them with the knowledge of God and the wisdom of the love of God that they may know Him, and His love for humanity. So be it."

Her final words were, "This is beautiful Diane. Thank you. I must go now. The heavens are calling to me. Peace be with you. Adieu."

"And may peace also be with you. God be with you. Adieu Diana."

Jacqueline Kennedy Onassis

July 28, 1929 – May 19, 1994

In the night prior to February 5, 2011, things were getting a little rough as souls were desperate to leave the darkness where they were and apparently the word was getting out where they could go for help. I felt overwhelmed but was willing to listen to one soul at a time and to do what I could do to assist them in their desperation. But this soul, this one, I felt honored to be her assistant in helping her understand her circumstances and how she might change them and be able to cross to the light where she belonged.

I asked who was there to speak to me saying, "Who is here? Please tell me your name. I will listen to you and only you at this time."

And then I heard, "My name is Jacqueline Kennedy. I was the wife of John F. Kennedy, Diane. I apologize for the pain that I caused to you in coming to you but it was my time to go and so I followed the example of others to go home. I am here that you would assist me in leaving this God forsaken place. I came here upon my death and it was a disaster. The women were frightened, hopeless, without God and without an understanding of why they were here.

Myself included. I was left to my own thoughts for the longest time as thinking was not permitted by those who rule in this place. I had to question my own sincerity about how I felt about God and why would God allow me to be in this place. I had suffered greatly being married to John and his death was tragic indeed. Being in the public was difficult at best after I left the White House and I was lonely much of the time dealing with my own thoughts then as well. It helped me to begin to write about what I had experienced some of which was published, some not.

"Jacqueline," I said, "I can understand that it must have been shocking to you in many ways what happened. Were you and John aware of those who were attempting to control the government and its leaders?"

She said, "Of course Diane. They made their power known to us and were quick to step up in every situation to manipulate policy and actions that were taken by my husband. We were not allowed to speak to anyone about what was taking place behind the scenes."

I asked Jacqueline if she had ever felt that their lives were in danger to which she replied, "Not necessarily because my husband was well aware of the dangers of not following their guidance to the letter."

"Did John speak to his brother Bobby about his concerns, I asked."

Jacqueline stated that "He did. They were blood brothers and very good friends. Bobby was outraged and he began a campaign to put them in jail. Of course Bobby tried to accomplish these things in the flesh and this you cannot do. It must be done from a vantage point outside of the flesh, with God's counsel and guidance and it shall be done for you."

This was interesting and I wanted to know from Jacqueline, "Is this what you are here to tell us?"

She said, "In part. I wanted to offer my congratulations at the recovery of your husband. He will fair well and be a great leader to the country in this difficult time.. You must believe that God can do anything and He will demonstrate to you His authority and power if you just take the first steps as He directs you to do. Your husband will find this to be the case. God is greater than all of mankind in His ability to accomplish that which He wants to accomplish if it is the will of His people to do so."

I thanked Jacqueline for this advice and said that I would tell my husband. "What other things that you learned being the wife of a President that you might like to share with others", I asked?

Jackie began, "There is much to say about the responsibility of being married to a President, Diane."

"There are many women who need direction in this world. They need to know who they are and that each and every one of them carries a destiny in this world. They must be free to find it and to seek and this comes from realizing that they too come from God. You can assist many in the realization of this truth when you ask to speak at women's functions. These offers will come as the position of First Lady is a great one. Your message of strength in times of trouble with the power and unity of standing together with God's protection is just what the country needs. The people of this country who wish to return to God need a leader showing them how to do it. The women in particular need to know how to support their husbands and families with God's guidance and direction. You can tell them how to do it, how to raise leaders not followers. You can teach them how to listen for the voice of God and then how to put the things that they hear into action."

She continued, "No other First Lady has had this message Diane. You are unique in this regard and so is your husband for his training in the law is necessary to restoring the truth of the power of the Constitution to protect this nation and he must speak about this to the nation. The nation needs a reminder of the sovereign power of these doctrines to connecting us to a powerful deity whose hand is not too short to reach down and assist the nation called by His name. Remember this always as you serve together and you will go farther than any previous couple to establish truth again in the land. Together you are a united front against the evil tide against the nation under God and no one can stand against you as long as you cling together and to the connection which you have to God's truth."

"Do not allow anyone to rob you of this connection or tell you that it is not permissible to speak of God from this position of leadership. In fact, it is an abomination that God has been absent from The White House for so long. Lift up His name again and see what will happen to change the dynamics of this nation in a powerful way. You will see."

Though I did not understand how these things Jackie was talking about could possibly come about, I continued to listen to her and to document her comments to me.

"Now Diane," she continued, "for you specifically, organize yourself with help because you will need it, You will need a person whom you can trust implicitly to assist you with appointments and in scheduling them. You will have security details to work with but you have access to the heavens for the highest level of security as well Diane. Do not fail to use it each and every time you go about the nation. Call upon the heavens to set angels at your right, left, north, south, east and west and they will be there for your husband. Do not forget to do this ever."

I knew that she had more to say and she did saying, "There will be State affairs which you will assist in planning. You will want to cover the room with protection from the heavens, setting armed heavenly guards in place throughout the rooms, and blessing each and every place within the White House where others have been before you. Ask God what he would want to have occur at these functions and He will guide you down to the smallest details as you know from organizing previous functions. Invite His people. They are the ones who can learn from you who is God. You know. Many of them do not. Share it with them. Enlighten them. This is your day Diane to tell the world what you have learned about the God of Heaven and His power to change the world to be a place of peace and joy for everyone once again."

I told Jackie that I did appreciate her sharing all of this with me. I asked if she had more to say to me before we would move on.

She did. "Do not concern yourself with the workings of evil. Do not focus on it or give it your attention. God will deal with their actions upon their deaths justly. Your concerns are to work with the light for the good of all and to let that be your focus always. Work to make lives better and God will always be with you as you have seen."

I wanted to know more should these things come about that she was sharing. I wanted to know, "How do I go about selecting people and finding those to assist me?" I told Jacqueline that I wanted women who know God but who are not judgmental and restrictive in their understanding of who God is and who He allows us to be. "I want godliness to be in their nature but with a knowing of the freedom which God permits us to have in choosing who we want to be in life."

Jackie had an answer for this too saying, "All things are possible with God. Begin to pray about this now. See yourself surrounded with women of caliber but who understand the truth about the nation, God and the freedom that is available to all people. Ask God to begin to introduce you to these women who are above reproach, who have integrity, honesty, openness, and a willingness to serve the nation.

I indicated to Jackie that I would begin to meditate on these things before God and to ask Him for direction.

It was now time for Jackie to go and she stated that I should not hesitate to call upon her if I did require guidance from her related to her experience.. She said that she would come and that it was permissible for her to do so. Interesting indeed!

Of course I thanked her. I sent her many blessings asking her whether she had seen that I had already assisted John, Ted and Bobby Kennedy to go home to the light and they had all transitioned and gone home.

It surprised me when Jackie then said that she did know this already for she saw it in my "light's record". "This is a good thing," she said, "for though there was some complicity on Ted's part, it was due to those who threatened and intimidated him. However, no one deserves to die the way that my husband died."

I agreed with her for it was a time that I will never forget even though I was very young in 1963 when these events occurred. The nation was rocked and very saddened by the loss of this man. I thanked Jackie for her insight and asked that God would keep my husband and I in His arms all of the days of our lives on this earth, guiding us, teaching us, helping us to improve the lives of others.

Jackie did once again invite me to call upon her for guidance in these matters related to the work ahead of me stating that she is permitted to assist according to my needs.

I blessed Jackie for her insight to me. I told her that I would definitely call upon her as needed for her assistance in these matters where she has knowledge.

"Peace be with you Jackie and love to all in the heavens and to our heavenly Father."

Jackie said her goodbyes too.

Robert Trent Jones

June 20, 1906 – June 14, 2000

The following day after having assisted Princess Diana I again found myself dealing with souls attempting to get my attention to help them in crossing. I apologized to the particular soul who was contacting me at the moment for not answering sooner but I stated that it was becoming a problem to my sleep to have so many souls trying to get a hold of me at once. I must rest like every other person in the body I explained. I knew the name of this particular person when he relayed it to me and I was stunned that I would be assisting someone so involved with golf particularly since it was the passion of my husband's life.

It was Robert Trent Jones and he said, "It is understandable to me, for it is a matter of life and death due to the changing energy. People are afraid that they will be lost eternally here if they do not find a way out."

"I am here to help as best I can. How may I help you Robert? It is a pleasure to "meet you" as it were. My husband is a huge golf fan only due to recent health concerns he cannot play for a season while he heals."

Robert said "I see that he has a great golf game Diane and he would really enjoy many of my golf courses throughout the U.S. and Canada in particular. Tell him to try the course in Atlanta and in Spokane . He might like the properties up there as well as a retirement spot".

I did look up this information to see if it was fact and the golf course he spoke about in Atlanta is in Peachtree. I am unable to locate a Spokane property but perhaps he had a say in a redesign there rather than an original design. It is also possible that he had a favorite course there that was not his design, I do not know. Sometimes things are a little fuzzy on that side of life until the souls cross over.

"Robert, I will tell him but it is a little colder up there for my tastes. Any other spot I might like as well? There is Poughkeepsie, Alabama and several in Texas that are quite nice. I don't think either of you would enjoy the humidity of Florida or the bugs for they are large to say the least.

I looked these all up to find out if it was true. I could not even spell Poughkeepsie before he mentioned it. I found a Casperkill Golf Course in Poughkeepsie, New York. Wow! I also looked up Robert Trent Jones courses in Alabama and I did find the Robert Trent Jones Golf Trail there.

Robert mentioned Texas and so I searched that state and found Houston Country Club and Gleannloch Farms Country Club in Spring, Texas.

I thanked Robert for these references and then asked if there was a particular reason that he had come through now and not others?

"No, not really," Robert said. "but I am an innovative kind of guy and when I saw there was a way out of there, I got busy to find it.

I asked Robert to describe what that means exactly please.

Robert continued then, "Well, imagine that you are in total and complete darkness and that there are areas of concentrated energy where souls are sequestered and then there are areas that are patrolled as it were where no one is permitted to go. That is where I went in search of the light as I was not content to stay in darkness without a hope for eternity. Not after spending my lifetime in beautiful green spaces was I going to stay in darkness. What a tragedy that would be."

"And so Robert, where did you go and what did you find there?"

"I went into the area that we were told to stay out of and I found traces of energy indicating that the light had been there. It felt genuine and it felt like love. I cried when I found this energy. It felt like home. I stayed there waiting for it to come again and it did and I saw others grabbing hold of the energy and so when it was possible for me to do so, I did."

I told him that this was very interesting and that I wished that I could see this. I asked him how I might assist him today.

"I am here to find my way home Diane. I lived my life in awe of the beauty of the land and in an attempt to make a way for men to enjoy the outdoors without having to spend too much money to get a break from the routine and that would allow them to find an adventure outside in the sport of golf. It was challenging and rewarding for many men were finding it competitive to outdo the next guy on the course. It allowed them to let off some steam and to enjoy the outdoors at the same time. Very rewarding for me I might add and I did very well creating golf courses around the world. It was very satisfying."

I asked Robert why it was that he thought he was stuck there where he was.

"Though I created these designs for golf courses around the globe Diane," I did not once ask God how I might name the courses to give glory to the heavens. I did not consider where my thoughts and ideas might be coming from particularly. I just took the credit for the creations myself and allowed the courses to receive my name everywhere I went. You can attest to that Diane as you and Dick have seen my name on courses in the United States. So you can see my dilemma now can you not? As my death neared, I knew that I would stand before God without anything to bring having lived in the world and not making a difference for God."

I wanted to help Robert and so I did say, "But you did make a difference as you made living here a better experience for many who would not have had a release from the pressures of life without the beautiful golf courses which you created for them to retreat to and find some peace here. Granted, you might have done things differently, thanking God publicly for the wisdom to create, but perhaps you can think of a way to do it now."

"This is an excellent idea Diane. I can this," he said. Contact my sons Bobby and Rees and tell them this:

'To my beloved sons. I am asking Diane Freeman to speak to you in my name for she is able to communicate with me via the energy of her being connecting with my energy for the purpose of assisting me in my transition to the heavens. It is my wish that future golf courses created in the Robert Trent Jones name be created giving some of the glory to the God of heaven whom I neglected to give honor and glory to in my lifetime. If you will do this for me, I can go on to glory having done something that I can be proud of before the Father of Heaven for at this time, I have not left a legacy to Him, and for this I am feeling guilt and shame which has left me locked in a place not earth, and not the heavens. It is not due to the judgment of the Father of Heaven, but of my own judgment of myself that I am here. Fortunately, Diane is here to tell me differently, that I am forgiven, and experiencing the earth is for all of us and we need not feel guilt and shame beyond the earthly experience but rather we must release all emotional feelings before death so as to transition to the heavens free, unburdened by emotions which confound our energy fields trapping us here."

Robert continues to his sons, "As I communicate with Diane, I am learning these things and more about life on earth and who I am, and why I came here to earth. I came to bring leisure to the lives of men who were struggling in life without pleasure. I came to help to develop the land in such a way that the working man would have an activity which would challenge him and his mind in such a way that he could leave the work day behind him for a brief time. This was a noble cause but upon reaching the earth, I neglected to give God the glory, for it was God who allowed me to have this experience, permitting me to come with my plan for the people. Please hear my voice in this communication my sons for I now know what it was I was to do in my life, to assist men in being free from worry, stress and strife by providing a beautiful form of entertainment for them but I was to do it to the glory of God and I forgot. I forgot somehow.

Upon my death, I remembered. Can you imagine my guilt and my shame upon remembering?

Now, I must ask Diane to ask you to do something for the glory of God and then I will be proud that my name was not the only name lifted up on earth that provided men with a beautiful entertaining experience away from the struggles of life."

"Robert, this is very enlightening. First, men forget why it is that they come to the earth, and then at death, they remember. If they remember and emotions attach to their energy field, it can confound them and cause them to remain in between life and the transition to eternal life. It is this that mankind must understand. We must awaken to our true callings, giving glory to God for who we are and what we do and then upon our deaths in the body, we can transition home nicely."

"Well said," Robert replied. "I will ask that my sons receive my message understanding its' truth for it is the best gift that I can give to them now. Perhaps they will remember their true callings before the end of their days and they will go home to the heavens with their heads held high having given the glory to God for all of the good which they have done on earth."

I told Robert that I would find their addresses and do the best that I could to forward this communication to them. I asked him to do whatever it is that he could do to open that door so that his sons would listen to me instructing him to find the door that will permit them to hear this truth and then to open it when he gets to heaven. This he could do for both of us so they would have to hear him and me.

"This I can certainly do Diane for I am good at navigating the landscape and finding a good way to go."

"Robert this is excellent," I responded. "Bless you Robert and thank you for you have given me a new appreciation of golf courses and what they can do for my beloved husband for life is full of stress and he needs an escape each week. Thank you. Now, you can still tell God in heaven how much you appreciated the guidance and the abilities given to you for what you were able to create on earth. Do it now. He is listening. I will wait." Then I began waiting quietly for his response thinking myself at this time of the width, depth, breath of God's love for His own.

Robert came back saying, "I am overwhelmed by the light of love you are demonstrating Diane to me of God's love for me and for His people. Allow me to demonstrate back to God how grateful I am for His gift to me of creating golf courses. One moment," I said, as I again waited as Robert began conveying to God directly his thankfulness for these things.

The next thing I heard Robert say was, "I can hear a heavenly choir Diane. I can hear it. I know that I am being heard. I know it. Thank you for your assistance as you have shown me in love, with love, God's love for me and forgiveness. How can I thank you enough?"

I again asked him to "open the door in heaven which allows your sons to hear the truth and while you are opening doors, open the door for my husband to know that His calling is yet upon him.

Help him to know that God calls him His own to do His will. We are not here just for our own purposes. Open the door to my husband understanding God's will for his life and then you will have done well by the United States of America my friend."

These things may or may not come to pass. Only God knows what the future holds for His own.

Robert told me to "Consider it done" and he said, "tell your husband to join one of my golf courses when he is President. I will make certain that he receives the best of treatment there. He may like my course in Virginia. Look it up Diane. And the Greenbriar course is lovely too."

I did look this course up on the internet and found Lansdowne Resort in Leesburg, Virginia and also the Robert Trent Jones course in Gainesville, Virginia.

Finally I thanked Robert for this bit of information and said "May God bless you and receive you with love, as He will, and may your sons hear the truth and embrace it and give glory to the God of Heaven so men will again, give thanks to the Almighty accordingly."

Robert said amen to that and told me that he must go. He thanked me for my assistance in shining my light in the darkness. "Others wait for you too," he said. "Help them as you have helped me and more blessings are sure to come your way. Until then Diane, adieu."

Adolf Hitler

April 20, 1889 – April 30, 1945

I would invite my readers here to read the entire chapter before making any decisions as to whether or not this could possibly be true once you have read the name above. Believe me when I say that it was a shock to me when I heard his name and I sat motionless almost afraid to move when this soul identified themselves to me. There were no words to describe how I felt at the moment thinking that perhaps it was a mistake and that he had somehow broken through to me inadvertently. But it was apparent, he was here and not leaving, of course not, if it were me, and I was lost but found a lifeline, I would hang on to it too. Because I do not judge those who are sent to me or those I am sent to assist, this was no exception. This soul was sent to me to bring forth revelation in the process of my assisting him. I encourage you to read this chapter and to pray for wisdom and understanding. Here we go.

I felt the presence of yet another soul and asked for identification of who this was that wished to speak with me. How in the world could this person possibly be saved? I asked a second time for the name. This time the soul spelled his name out for me.

"A.d.o.l.f. H.i.t.l.e.r."

As I heard this, I paused, not wanting to hear it. Considering what to do, I then heard Alejandro speaking to me.

"The name you heard is correct. We are here to confirm it. What will you do?"

I responded with my own question. "What would you have me do," I asked?

Alejandro instructed, "Clear this energy from the planet . . . . once and for all time."

That was all I needed to hear. My job was to assist in helping the people of the world for good.

I spoke to the soul who had identified himself as Adolf Hitler. "I am here Mr. Hitler. I am hearing from Alejandro that the name which I heard is correct. What do you want from me?

Why would you come to me?"

What comes next may change the world's view of Hitler and what power God has to forgive.

"I am here for forgiveness for massive crimes against humanity," Hitler said. "I know that I am the least deserving of forgiveness from God for that which I have perpetrated against the nation of the Jewish people but not only them, all people. I set an example of horrid atrocities against all men, women and children and for that, I do not deserve mercy and yet, when I heard that there was a glimmer of hope that God was willing to set men free for their crimes against Him, I thought I would try myself to see if God is who He says that He is before men."

My answer to Hitler was that "God is the same today and yesterday and as always. It is not God whose character changes in time, it is man's nature which takes on another characteristic when living in this world. Rather than continuing to exhibit the characteristics of a loving God, we assume the nature of emotions we are exposed to and this is the tragedy of men in this world. Many do not hold fast to God nor do they seek Him when faced with evil. What happened to you Adolf Hitler?"

"I was the worst of the worst if you must know then for I sought to understand the nature of evil and it consumed me completely," he said. "I read all that I could find about evil, and it came in like a flood to move me to action in crimes against humanity. I could not even stop myself after a time certain, it was no longer me in charge of my body but something else."

I asked, "What something else?"

Hitler then said, "You don't want to know Diane. It is best not to know this evil. Best to leave it unknown to your nature and focus on the character of a loving God instead as I should have done. I wanted to be a leader of men. I sought to have power over men. I researched how to manipulate men into following me. This is where I made my mistakes."

I asked Hitler why was he now willing to admit to his mistakes? I asked him, "When did you come to the conclusion that you even had made any mistakes at all. Most ego maniacs do not admit when they make mistakes because in their minds, they are perfect, incapable of error. I asked him when did he realize that he had acted in complete violation of God's will for him in this world and against his nature.

Sadly, his response was one I have heard before. "Not until my death," he replied, "for as long as I was in the body, I was no longer my own. I had given myself over to a nature of evil.

"I commented, "In everything I saw, you seemed consumed by anger."

Hitler responded, "You are partially correct but there was more, much more."

"Do you now understand the evil that you perpetuated against humanity," I asked, "and how do you think that you can make amends for this now that you are no longer in the body? How will you explain yourself to God? Have you tried to do so?"

Hitler responded, "I have sequestered myself away from others for their hatred of me was too strong for me to endure."

"And the other questions I asked? How do you answer them Adolf?"

"I suppose that I cannot because I do not see any way possible for a loving God to accept me for all of the atrocities that I committed against His people, the innocents, the families, and all the rest that I did without regard for life, country or God Himself. I was without regard for myself or anyone else. I did everything evil in my sight to do and more. All of it, I did it."

Incredible.

I asked Hitler. "Why did you pursue evil rather than pursuing a loving God?"

His response was "I had no introduction to God but I did have access to publications about evil and there were those willing to instruct me in the ways of evil."

"Every man has access to God" I told him, "simply by speaking to God in their hearts and minds."

"But I did not know," he responded, "and why would God speak to me? I was a nobody."

"God is no respecter of persons Adolf. All men may approach Him, seek Him, and request an audience with Him. This sounds like an excuse for what you did."

To this Hitler said, "It is not. I was ignorant of the things of God and so I chose what I did out of curiosity and when I got too involved, it was impossible to extricate myself for evil came in and I was doomed."

"A lesson for all men I suppose," I responded. "Do not seek after evil for it roams the earth seeking whom it may devour. How is it that you are speaking English to me?" It occurred to me that I was having a discussion with a man who had been a German speaking man when alive.

Hitler's response was classic. "I don't know exactly, but I suppose the energy is translated as needed in the manner necessary for understanding."

I asked Hitler what was it that he wanted me to do for him?

"I came because I saw many being set free by the light. I was hoping that in your light I would find the answers to the nature of God's forgiveness. I was hoping that the God that you speak of is a God big enough to forgiven even the likes of me."

"Well, He is, a God big enough to forgive the likes of you for God is not like us. The people of the world fear men like yourself who would destroy life without any regard for the souls within those bodies, without any fear of God or other men and for no apparent reason other than for control and power. This drives men to fear. Do you know why you did what you did other than that you sought knowledge of evil?"

He told me this. "I gave my mind over to evil in order to sustain power over men. I was no longer my own but evil ruled me."

"This is radically insane," I said. "Truly, and now, what do you want?"

"I want to know if the God of heaven can forgive me? I want to know if there is redemption for a person like me or must I remain in solitude in darkness for all eternity?"

I asked Hitler if he was prepared to ask God to forgive him. "If so, you must put aside all the dark thoughts, the negative controlling emotions which drove you to do what you did, you must not think them but you must release them, sending them to the light and nowhere else. You must understand that God's love is greater than the greatest sin of an and that perhaps, in returning to God, the lessons you learned in what you did to humanity can serve the highest beings in such a way as to prevent such an evil from EVER happening again on this planet to any people. Are you willing to set aside these evil thoughts and send them to the light, in love, for they will be transformed too?"

"I never attempted to do such a thing before," Hitler said, "to not think these thoughts was beyond my control. But to send them way as I hear them, this is a novel idea and I will do it now."

I told Hitler that I did not want to know what these thoughts of his were because I wanted to stay free of evil and its control over men. "Keep these thoughts silent and send them to the light," I instructed. "Do it now. You must acknowledge them and send them each to the light for they were there to demonstrate to you the behavior which you were exhibiting which was not love, not the nature of men and yet you embraced them and they changed you."

"I see this Diane for I was not born evil. I was a normal child. It was my desire to control others that changed me. I am releasing these thoughts of evil even as we speak for my desire is to be transformed by the light myself, to be that which I was created to be, not the evil that everyone has said that I am.

"This is not what I want to be anymore and I am sorry for the evil that was perpetuated upon the earth because of me. I shall ask the Father of Heaven . . ."

I wanted Hitler to know that the Father of Heaven that I know forgives every soul if they are sincere in asking for forgiveness. God can see the heart of a man and know whether or not he is sincere. It is not possible to make a fool out of the Creator for He created all and knows all. Do you understand this? He knows all."

This man didn't cease to surprise me with his comments. "Then he knows that I too have suffered for the deeds that I have done. I too have suffered in my misery knowing that I have contributed more evil in one lifetime than all of the men born on the earth, ever! How can a soul live with that legacy? How? I cannot and yet I am doomed to relieve it for I cannot escape it here. I am reminded day and night as it were of my atrocities by those here who tell me that I am evil."

I had to ask him and so I did ask him. "Are you willing to ask for God's forgiveness? Do you understand that God is able to forgive all for His love covers over a multitude of sins? He is pure light and in Him, is no darkness at all. If you return to God, He will forgive your sins, and you will be free but do not mistake His nature. He sees all in your energy field and if you do not let go of evil, you shall not see heaven."

Adolf was quick to respond saying, "I have seen enough evil to last a thousand lifetimes. I never want to participate in evil again. I will relinquish the thoughts of evil gladly if it will allow me to see God again and to receive his forgiveness. What shall I do?"

"Do the things that I have laid out for you. Let go of every evil thought sending it to the light for it served to show you, and mankind, the worst that men can be if they so choose to be. Let it go.

Let the love of God heal your heart, mind and soul. Confess your desire to be free of evil and ask God give you a new heart, a heart of love for men, for God, and for His people. Do it."

He responded to me that he was indeed saying, "I will. I am."

I offered a prayer for him in accordance with the will of God for him.

Hitler thanked me. He said, "I doubt that anyone has ever prayed for me but rather that I would rot in hell."

"Well then," I said to him, "let that thought go to the light too for men say things without understanding the damage that they do. I can imagine when I learned about what you had done that I was none too happy with you either. But I do know that the Spirit of God did stop me from studying the evil men as yourself have done on the planet and that is a good thing and I listened to what the Spirit guided me to do. So, have you stated your position before God, Adolf?"

Adolf commented, "I believe that I have Diane. I have asked his forgiveness for the evil that I did against His people and people who did not know God for what man could know God while I was torturing them? There was no example of a loving God in that action against men certainly.

And what man could know God's nature in my advancing my armies against other nations taking and destroying their homes, their livelihoods, their money and food and clothing? What could men learn from that about God's nature? Nothing! I served no purpose in my life except to drive men away from God for they would cry to the heavens, "why would a loving God allow this to happen to us?". In fact, most men would never believe that God would forgive such a person as me Diane."

"Then most men do not know God sadly for His love is for all men and if we repent, He is faithful to forgive us our sins", I told him. This is a true saying. God is faithful to forgive us our sins. So have you asked him to forgive you completely?"

Hitler indicated that he had asked for God's forgiveness, "Completely, for I have nothing now to offer Him except the truth that I did evil in the eyes of God and that I am sorry for that and I cannot change the evil that I did. I cannot correct it. I cannot ask forgiveness of the people I harmed, who died because of me, their children and grandchildren, who died because of me. I am humbled before God for I am considered the most evil of all men. What a legacy I have on earth? It is tragic indeed. And just like other men, in death, I became aware of what I was, what I had done, and what I did not do to honor God. The knowing of all of this was indescribable."

I asked Hitler then if he was prepared in his mind to let go of all of the negative experiences of earth, to take the knowledge of what he did to the higher beings that they may learn from it how these tragic things happened in order to perhaps prevent it from occurring again. I told him that God does not judge him but that he judges himself more harshly than any man.

His answer to me was this. "I am humbled by your willingness to share the truth of God's love with me. I do not deserve it yet you speak with me as if I am the same as anyone in Gods eyes."

"Because one sin is the same as another with God," I told him." "If he judges you, than he must judge all. Do you see? If you repent, ask for forgiveness, and let go of all of negative feelings and emotions, and the connection to evil, you are forgiven and can go home to freedom."

"This is great news then," he stated. "I have nothing to show for the evil that I did on earth. I did not bring glory to the God of Heaven and I am so sorry for the choices which I made while alive. I ask for forgiveness for all of my evil deeds and for the example of evil which I demonstrated to others who followed me. Please forgive me. I accept the truth of God's love for me despite the evil that I did for Diane's light shows me the truth of God's love. But I must make good to His people of earth for the evil that I did." Hitler then began to make a statement for me to record for God and others to read.

In his words, "This is what I, Adolf Hitler, would like to offer the earth. I would like to ask God in heaven, when I get there, to open the door to healing of the planet for the evils that I perpetuated upon it. I will ask God to clear the energy of the evil perpetuated against the Jewish people, the German people, the Polish people and even across the globe where German soldiers took refuge and brought their negative influence abroad. I will ask God to heal the world and to bring new energy of love to the planet in its place. It is the least that I can do. I receive my forgiveness and I will respond in kind towards the people of the earth Diane. You have my word that I will ask these things in heaven in return for my freedom."

"Praise be to the God of heaven for this promise," was my response after I heard him. "I will hold you to it as will the people of earth for this healing is needed to clear the earth of much negative energy and much fear that such a tragedy would occur again. It is time to clear this energy. I send you forth to the heavens then as those come for you that you have repented. Pray for peace on earth for it is long overdue. Many have lost the opportunity to experience their destinies. It is time for healing."

Adolf's final statement to me was, "I thank you for not hating me too Diane for I know that it was difficult for you to speak to me at first but the nature of God is truly within you to love those who are the most hated among men. Adieu."

This was the time to say goodbye to Hitler, once and for all time here on earth. I told him "Go in peace then and keep your promise. God will hold you to it."

Abraham Lincoln

February 12, 1809 – April 15, 1865

I was asked today on February 8, 2011, to assist a soul who apparently was contacting me in the night in order for them to cross but I did not feel this soul. The heavens told me they would encourage this soul to return later and that I should wait for it.

The following day, I made my contact as I usually do and said that I was here and available to assist the soul which came to me in the night, or early in the morning whichever it was and invited them to come and make themselves known to me. I offered to help them now. I then felt the presence of energy and asked who it was that was there. Nothing could prepare me for the name that I heard as he was quite a famous person in life and since then has been very respected and admired. But let me say this, it is clear in the scriptures that people of faith follow that only God knows the heart of a man. We cannot judge nor should we what the condition of a man's heart is for it is not given to us to do so. Nothing is impossible for Him.

"My name is Abraham Lincoln. I was the 16th President of the United States of America."

I apologized for not hearing him earlier and said that I am always a bit shocked when I do hear correctly. "It is good to meet you Mr. Lincoln," I said, "but I am wondering why it is that you are here for I understood that you were a man of faith."

"In some ways, I was a man of faith," he answered. "I recognized that there was indeed a deity to which we owed a measure of respect and yet in serving the Presidency, I neglected to turn the nation to Him directly when they were in consideration of such things such as the right to own or not to own an individual as a slave. I was given an opportunity with this one particular issue to be of service to the

Nation in a great way by advocating that all men are created by God and as such, have access to God for determining the affairs of men. If each man would consider in his heart before God what it is that God would want from each of us, all things would be decided in accordance with the will of God thus making the world a much more peaceful place. My greatest regret is that I did not turn the country towards the God of heaven when I had the opportunity rather I allowed it to be attributed to me, that it was my own idea to all men should be free. Of course, this is not the truth and it has been made abundantly clear to me that this was not my idea nor was it of my creation. God created all men to be free under heaven and upon the earth. It is man's idea that it should be otherwise with men slaving in work towards the goals of other men who wish to made rich upon the backs of others."

He continued, "It is time for this notion to be overturned. All men are created in the image of God and as such, are given certain unalienable rights of life, liberty and the pursuit of happiness and it was outlined as such in the Declaration of Independence which set apart this nation from all others under God. This document was God breathed before men of faith and should be upheld by those whose faith is in the One, true God of heaven. As a Statesman who was fond of writing, it is upon me to give your husband some ideas as to how the new document ought to be written. Are you ready for this Diane?"

I indicated that I was still here listening and ready to follow. Mind you, while these things are happening to me, life was continuing around me and I was frustrated that my husband was not following doctors advise to not drive his car only two weeks after surgery. Interestingly, it was Abraham who said to me, "Leave him to the heavens Diane. God knows how to get the attention of those he wishes to use before men. Ask Moses, who also thought that he was not able to speak well enough to serve as a leader of God's people."

"This is an excellent idea. I just may ask Moses if I am allowed to speak with him."

Mr. Lincoln was ready to go and said, "Now let's get down to business shall we? Concentrate on what I am about to tell you and record it for historians everywhere. Upon this day in history, man is called in this nation of the United States of America, to consider a new document of freedom. This document shall be a document of emancipation of a new era, a document of freedom and liberty to the people who wish to serve the One, true God of heaven. No other document of its kind has been given to mankind prior to this day for it is upon the nation, whose God is the Lord, to accept responsibility for its turning away from God to serve other Gods, as it were, the Gods of greed, lust, love of money, sex, and many others."

"It is upon the people whose God is the Lord of Heaven, to decide this day, who they will serve.

Will you turn from your ways of serving men, following their insurrection against the God of Heaven, or will you now, turn back to the God of Heaven, whose hand has been upon this nation to this day, protecting you from your enemies, both foreign and domestic, preserving your people and your children's children? What will you say to this question? Your God is listening to your answers in every home of the United States of America. Your God is listening."

"What you say now to the heavens shall decide the fate of your country. You shall either maintain your country as a nation under the God of Heaven, or you will be reduced to a nation without a God, like so many other nations before you, where your God is yourself or those who lord over you because you have no God any longer but the God of your own choosing.. The nation's future hangs in the balance at this juncture in time. What will it be then people of God?

Whom will you serve?"

"As Joshua once asked the people of his nation, "Choose this day whom you will serve", you too must decide for God is able to hear your prayers and to offer a solution to your quest if you are willing to return to Him and to lift up His name in your lives, your families, your businesses, and your nation. It is no longer acceptable to the God of Heaven to be ignored while His people go astray after other gods, which are not gods, of this world for the God of Heaven is the same today as yesterday, is He not, and is it not written?""

"You will have 100 days in which to decide what it is that you will do people. After that, your nation will be turned over to the desires of the hearts of its' people. This is a true saying and it is advisable that you not test your God who is able to restore your nation to its former glory. And when you decide, consider what it means to be a Nation under God. What are your responsibilities to other nations? Are you to conquer other nations in all your glory? Or perhaps are you to share the love of God with other nations? Not in a proselytizing kind of way but in a leadership kind of way. People will come to know God through the actions of your leaders. You need not beat them over the head with the love of God for they will see it in your actions towards them as a people. Help them each to build their own nations without sending men of war there at the same time. This is a conflict of interest and confusing to people of other nations. How can you love and hate at the same time? It is incongruous to them. You must separate acts of war from acts of kindness for they have nothing to do with one another but serve only to weaken the nation whose economy is paying for rebuilding a nation they also destroyed."

"Additionally, allow men and women to use their monies to give as God shows them to give to the nation of their choice for each man has his own destiny for which he came to earth. Some may give to the country of their origin, and others to another. This is as it should be for God has given it to each man to know what is his own destiny in life and to each to have the freedom and liberty to explore his destiny

64

DIANE FREEMAN

within the confines of a loving environment protected by people of faith and the God whom they serve."

"As the people are liberated to choose whom they will serve, and to give as they deem fit and necessary, to those whom they will, the world will flourish and men will find true happiness. It is not given to men to dictate the desires of another man's heart for this is tyranny. God Himself will offer the guidance necessary to show a man how to achieve his destiny without overburdening his heart to disease, that is, if he is willing to follow God's direction for his life."

"This is the truth which must again be given to the men of this nation. All men are created equally, with a sovereign purpose under heaven, to know God, to seek God's will for their lives, and are to be blessed by God for the purpose of achieving their Divine destinies under Heaven.

This opportunity must be restored those who seek Him. For this reason, a new set of documents must be prepared which outline the reasons for such a document t such as was done by the original Declaration of Independence."

"This document shall set apart the men, women and children whose God is the Lord. It will separate them from those whose God is themselves, their chosen dictators over them, or some other controlling force not human which they have submitted themselves unto which will destroy their souls."

Abraham stated that this document need not be complicated but can be simple by stating the following:

"Upon this ___ day of _____, 20__, I choose this day to serve the God of Heaven, the ne, true God, the Creator of all things in my personal life, family, business, and in my nation, that His name, and only His name, Alejandro, be lifted up as sovereign deity over the land. I submit myself, and my life, to Him for the purposes of restoring the land unto those likeminded individuals whose God is also the Lord Himself. I give my sacred honor to serve according to God's hand upon my life and as such, He will protect me, my family and my nation from my enemies both foreign and domestic. Attested to this ___ day of _____, 20__ by two witnesses below, I declare myself the Lord's. So be it."

_____

Declarant

_____

1st witness

_____

2nd witness

"Let this document be circulated throughout the land and signed by all of those whose desire it is again to be free from tyranny. It will be seen by the heavens and honored in accordance with God's will. God's will is that all of His people would be free."

Abraham addressed me again here saying "Now Diane, you will have to take the bull by the horns and see that this document is circulated. Send it to the churches. Distribute it as you will to those you know of faith. Tell them what God is willing to do. Tell them that God is watching what His people will do with His word to the people of this nation. Will they respond or will they reject the notion that God is able to speak to His people in their time of need? It remains to be seen and a cloud of witnesses are watching to see what they will do. Send it to Rush, Glenn, Michael Savage and others. Let's see if they will believe that God is the same today as yesterday who will honor the faith given to such a simplistic agreement."

I was very grateful for this and told Abraham so. "I pray that Glenn has read my previous message to him given by other Statesmen. Can you see? Has Glenn read it?"

"Not yet Diane," he replied, "you may have to fax it to his studio. Then he cannot ignore that you have persevered to get this message to him. See it you can locate a fax for Fox News in New York City where Glenn is located." (At the time of this book preparation, Glenn is no longer in New York).

I would like to insert here a comment as I type this that it is not easy to contact those people that I am told to contact by the heavens because many of these people who have become "famous", surround themselves with Secret Service or perhaps handlers are assigned to them so the light doesn't reach them or perhaps they have protection or whomever that runs interference for them so even those who do hear divine messages are not able to deliver them. However, I did thank Abraham and told him that I would press on with this.

"May the God of Heaven richly bless you Abraham Lincoln and see your love for Him now.

May the God of Heaven have His name lifted up in the nation for a revival of truth, love and hope, freedom and liberty for all, not just for some, but for all, and then ALL will be reunited in the love of God."

Abraham answered, "Indeed, it is the heart of God to see all men using these gifts and talents for the good of all."

"Then I must get busy to do my part," I said.

"Perhaps so," he said. "Do not worry so much about the body. Do the work given to you and the body will perform nicely for you."

I am not sure exactly what that meant but I asked if there was anything else?

Abraham wanted me to record something here for my husband. I will include it here for it may be that it is intended for all to read to know the truth of who it is that God wants to see leading His people and how He wants to see it done regardless of whether my husband is able to follow through with the encouragement here from others to step up and lead.

"Let me say this to your husband," said Abraham. "Richard, my name is Abraham Lincoln. I was the President of the United States of America during a difficult time. It was not easy to rule for there were factions against the rule of God whose intentions were for evil, to rule with tyranny over the lives of other, for their desires were for evil and not for good. I did the best that I could under the circumstances and yet, still, I could have done better. If I had turned the hearts of men towards the God of Heaven, He would have shown each man individually how they could serve too and the burden for me would have been lessened. I could have focused more on what my particular role was rather than on how to demonstrate to the whole nation what their roles were to be free. It is not for the President of the United States to equip each person with the knowledge or wisdom for each of their individual lives."

This is to God, and to God remains the glory in each life for what a person is able to achieve based upon their adherence to God's will for their lives. What is expected of the President of the United States of America, as a representative of the nation under God, is to remind its' people, who is the Supreme leader over men, and who is able to bring about their destinies in life."

At this time, I had to interrupt Mr. Lincoln for I was receiving a Divine communication intended for me to listen to immediately. I heard this, "Diane, ask Abraham, what one thing he learned in his dealings with men that would serve Richard if he were to accept Gods call to serve as the nation's leader? What would serve Richard greater than any other advice you could give him today? Proceed."

Abraham who did hear the question through me, as that is how the energy transmission works when you are connected to a soul and Alejandro comes through, said this. "I would have to say this Diane, do not align yourself with any particular group to achieve their personal goals in the country. You must always, always, remain aligned only with the God of Heaven. You must first and foremost, seek God's will for your life, the nation, and her people. This means, regardless of the pursuit of you by men to accomplish their fiendish goals, you must submit to God and ask what is His will and then you must be willing to implement it, regardless of the consequences to you via criticism from those whose desire it is for greed or manipulation of the highest office in the land. God is no respecter of persons and He will uphold His will with the man who is willing to uphold Him. You will find everything you need is provided as long as you submit to God and submit to His will for His nation. This you must do with regular prayer and meditation despite your weariness, regular prayer and meditation for God cannot lead through a man who is not submitted to Him. That is all."

"Thank you Abraham and I will pass this on too. May God's will be done for our family and for the nation."

"This is good Diane. Perhaps something good will come from this for the nation. Submit the word to the churches, to their pastors, to the leaders of conservative talk radio. They too must awaken to whom it is that has allowed them to speak to the nation at this time. Let's see what they are made of shall we? Send the message today."

As a side note, I did send this information and I have shared the truth of it so many times with others. I did not hear back from any churches, any of the talk radio personalities or anyone else I sent the information to at the time. I do not know what happened with the truth of it.

I did ask Abraham if he was free now to move on to the heavens or whether he was already there and speaking to my from the heavens.

Abraham indicated that "sadly, I was not there as yet but I am able to return home now for I have given God the glory here, in this message and I am free to go home now. Thank you for allowing me this opportunity to make a contribution to the nation I loved Diane. You too are making a difference but always, always remember who it is you serve."

"May it always be so in my life until the end of my days here on His beautiful Creation."

Samuel Adams

September 27, 1722 – October 2, 1803

I learned early on that the departed have no sense of time and they do not think twice to come to you either in the middle of the night, during your dinner, or to interrupt your date night at the movies. They come whenever they can get through. In this case, it was 10:00 p.m. on February 6, 2011. I asked who was it there on my left side and was surprised, if I can be surprised any more, to hear "Samuel Adams, I too was a Statesman."

I immediately looked up on the internet to see if there was an image there of Samuel Adams so I could picture him more clearly and when a biography popped up and I opened it, I felt a tingling on my left hand, as if he was acknowledging that I had the right name. Truly amazing!

I told him so saying, "Samuel, I felt your energy on my left hand when I opened the biography.

Did you see your name there?"

To which he said, "Yes. I saw it which is why I touched your fingers to acknowledge it."

"Wonderful Samuel", I said. "How do you do sir?"

"Not so good as I am here and not there in the world, nor have I moved on eternally. I would suggest that I am somewhere in between the two, unsatisfactorily I might add."

I asked Samuel Adams how it was that he came to find me. I wanted to know who sent him?

"Needless to say," said Samuel, "I have been searching for some time to find a way out of this place yet there has not been a glimmer of hope that it would ever be possible . . . until you came Diane."

"Alejandro is the one responsible for teaching me how to accept the fate of those who were without love, lost, and the like. It was the will of God that I learn how to do this and so it is that it was inevitable that I would be sent to help those who were trapped in the darkness. God is not without a remedy in any situation particularly when it involves those He loves and I surprise myself really for not giving Him even more credit in stating how it is that I am here myself able to speak to you. It was through Alejandro's training that you might be saved."

"Amen," Samuel agreed. "I agree with you that without God's love for the lost we would remain lost so I must be certain to give credit where credit is due however it is always the choice of those of us called to a thing to choose whether or not to do it, so to this, I give you credit and thank you. You chose to come and that is why I am speaking to you now."

"Thank you, Samuel. It is my pleasure to be of service to those whom God loves. How many I help you Samuel? Tell me something about yourself."

"I was one of many who were interested in the cause for freedom and liberty within the United States of America. We fought long and hard to be free but where there is liberty, there will be those who fight against it for nothing more than the desire to rule over the destinies of men. It is a tragedy really for all men ought to seek after their true destinies without fear of peril in doing so, at least they should not fear peril from men seeking to stop them from doing so. I see that this nation of ours is in some danger of losing its freedom altogether Diane."

"Yes, apparently so, without a return of the people of faith in the One, true God, whose nation it is, we would suffer the way that other nations have who have turned their backs on God and God's will for the people an d their nations. It is my desire to see the people return to God but without someone to teach them, the people falter. Without a Godly leader, they lose their way.

They need someone with wisdom to bring forth the truth in an understandable way which resonates the truth of God's nature and for God."

"Well said, Diane. I would like to assist you in formulating a plan for how to reach the people in great numbers with the truth. It is quite a task considering the numbers of people in the nation at this time, but it is possible. It is quite a task considering the numbers of people in the nation at this time, but it is possible. Where there is a dynamic message, it will resonate in the hearts of men and men will share its truth. Let's think about this for a moment. What kind of message will the people listen to today that is unlike anything they have heard before about God's love?"

Samuel continued with this thought. "Let me suggest the following. All men know that they are free to be who they desire to be, but what they are missing is that God will support them in their efforts in finding their destinies and asks only very little in return. Do not deny your God. All things come from God and are given to men for the sole purpose of serving God in this world that all men may find their destinies. But in the midst of this journey are obstacles to getting there if one does not stay connected to the One, true God. You will never ever find your destiny if you get off course and disregard the God who made this journey here possible. God is the compass you need to weather the storms of the world and He has the capacity to show you the way through every and any circumstance which you encounter while here. But if you desert Him, you will become lost in this world unable to navigate through the storms that life will bring you. It becomes too difficult to understand the reasons for what happens to you in this world without God. It is hard enough with God to know why you experience that which you do while in the world."

"Much of what you experience in this world is prechosen by you for purposes of bringing about a profound learning experience for your soul. In order for you to have the requested experience, your journey must not be interrupted but at your request, when you ask God to help you, and even then, it must be decided if helping you will interfere with your desire to have the experience and the anticipated outcome from the experience. Do you see now why many things that are attributed to God, are not His doing, but it was the soul itself which asked to have the experience and God will not intervene with personal choice but at the request of the soul."

"Wow! This information will come as a surprise to many people on earth who do believe things happen by accident and without a reason and they believe that God has forgotten them, or even cursed them in some instances for they experience many hardships."

Samuel began again, "It is understandable to believe that because God is love that He would not allow bad things to happen to good people but consider this, what if the person themselves chose to have the experience at any cost? What then? Should God interfere and change the outcome for the soul by His interference?"

My question back to him was this, "What happens when one soul affects many others as with what occurred with Adolf Hitler, Mussolini, and others like them? The actions of these men affected the possibilities available to other souls in this world by the very hateful actions of these men upon so many people in the world."

"Indeed when one man sides with evil much can be done to circumvent the good will of others,"

Samuel responded. "Perhaps now that this energy of evil is being released from the earth plane, it will not reappear for years to come again and men will be able to enjoy the planetary experience without this type of interference."

"I can only pray to God so for it is time for peace in the land and for men to be reminded of who they are, their connection to God, and the joy of life in the body."

"I could not agree with you more Diane," said Samuel. "Shall we make a plan to clear the earth's energy then of all evil leadership such that men can live to their full potential in search of God and His will for the good will of men?"

"I am thrilled to agree with you, Samuel, for such a plan for earth and her people."

Samuel stated, "Then so it is. We can agree for the good of all men and God will do it that His name may be lifted up among men and praised.

"I shall be the first to lift it up right now and to praise Him. Glory be to God in the highest this February 8, 201, and may His name be reinstated among men in the United States of America and to Him be the glory, and the praise, as men remember where they come from and from whom, as God, the Creator of all things, to Him, be the glory in the land and His leadership over the people of the United States of America."

Samuel concurred and said, "Amen".

"Now where do we go," I asked him?

"First," he said, all men must not bow down to foreign Gods, for there is only One, true God, and He is a jealous God. Give glory to His name then and no others. Second, God is the leader in the land and chooses whom He will to serve Him. He will make known His choice for leadership of the Nation called by His name. Then you are to seek Him for confirmation that this is the person of His choice. Third, give God the glory for the richness of the land, the bounty of the land, and for the blessings of children, for it is God who gives to His people faithfully and no other. Give Him the glory and He will continue to bless the land accordingly. Fourth, make an offering to the God of heaven by offering Him a tithe of your earnings. Now what does this mean exactly? God has no need of your money Himself but there are those who serve Him who do need monies to do the work of the Kingdom of Heaven. If you are being given a service which blesses your life and frees you to pursue your destiny, give a tithe to the person who has assisted you in obtaining your freedom so that the work of freeing others may continue. You will know these people as you have need of their services."

"Fifth, God does not require that you worship Him. Understanding is needed here. The God of Heaven is not an egotistical maniac and is not needy nor does He need your worship but rather that you would love others as you love God and in this is worship of God. Do unto others as you would have them do unto you. This is a worthy saying. Sixth, God has formed a man and a woman for purposes of bearing children in the world for this is the greatest gift of all, creation of life. It is not possible without a male and a female but man has attempted to create on his own without God and this is an abomination to God. That which God creates, He blesses. Seventh, the time has come for the understanding of the matter of coveting that which does not belong to you. When a man or woman, desires to own that which does not belong to them, nor did they work to own it, evil is created in the form of greed, jealousy, animosity, murder, theft, mayhem, and other forms of evil for in the desiring of that which does not belong to you, you invite every wicked thing. This cannot be overstated for man was created with the opportunity to reap what he sows. It is not God's will that another man would plunder that which does not belong to him for the sole purpose of owning that which belongs to another. It is wrong and will no longer be tolerated. Men must earn that which they wish to own for themselves for this is as God created it to be. Eighth, all men are created equally with equal opportunity to achieve something of measure in this world. What is different, are the obstacles chosen by men before coming into the world that would have to be overcome before the destiny would be achieved. God will not interfere with a man's choice unless there is the possibility that the man would lose his life before he could achieve his destiny and this only if the man asks God for assistance before his death occurs. Few do however for men always that that they are capable of handling every situation on their own. It is an anomaly."

"Ninth, God's will shall be the highest goal for every man at all times in his life on earth for God has chosen what is good and right in allowing men to experience the earth in all of its' glory, therefore, me are to seek God's will for their lives here on earth. This is to ensure the greatest good for all is achieved for the planet and her people. Finally, no man shall impose his will on another without their consent. This is against God's will for God does protect us from evil. That which is done against our will by another is considered evil in the eyes of God. All men reserve the right to protect themselves from that which they do not wish to participate in at any time while experiencing earth. This is God's will."

I asked Samuel if this as all and what was I to do with these ten items.

He indicated, "We are finished with these ten tenets of faith for they set out what is God's will for His people so that they remain free to live and breathe and have their being without control or tyranny over them. God's will is for men to live freely in the land according to His will. These tenets of faith ought to be distributed to God's people that they are reminded of what it is that God has said about the experience which humanity was to be given here on earth."

"Much mocking takes place when one such as myself attempts to tell "God's people" anything at all for they do claim that God has spoken once to all the prophets and then He did not speak again, and it is in the bible, in His word, which they have you know, the King James version of His word."

Samuel listened and then he responded, "This is true that they say they have His word in the King James' version but they did not know the King. The King was power hungry. He lorded it over the people to control them so that they would not know God in the manner in which God wanted to be known for if the people knew God, they would be free. This is why the people who sought God wished to go to the new frontier, to find freedom to seek God in the manner of their choosing and many did leave England for this very purpose, including myself."

My response was that, "It seems you were followed by the King's men".

"Indeed," he replied. "So it seems and so it was and you know the story for it is being played out in full theatre right before your eyes. Godless men lording it over a Godless people for many have had their eyes closed for centuries not seeing the glory of God for He is hidden in your churches as though He were not able to do miracles today."

"This I do know for I have been in those churches and seen what it is that they do and say. They will take your money however and with it, they will go to Africa or elsewhere and preach some more while our own people and her children languish here at home not knowing God. False teachers are corrupting His word. They are teaching against the truth of God's word and His ten commandments. Instead they teach a false truth that all things are okay and that God does not have a standard. But still our loving God would have us take the truth into the churches as long ago there were those deceivers who crept into the churches as leaders to undermine the truth and to compromise God's will for His people. These deceivers occupy churches today all over the globe.

Then Samuel asked me a question. "Will you do it, Diane? Will you go into the churches and let the love of God shine?"

My question back to him was this, "Does it require my talking to them or just going? I can go the churches, but they don't always like me."

He then asked me, "Who DO they like?"

"Good question. God knows."

Samuel announced, "I will tell you who they like, the compliant ones, who sit and do not make a fuss, who tithe without question. These are good servants of the church you know."

"I enjoy talking with you Samuel and I wish that I had been able to meet you and many of the men whom you knew who were like you, patriots of the country, who loved God and wished to see liberty and freedom established in the land. I have always admired the Statesmen who took a stand in coming here whose hearts were intent on finding freedom for themselves, their families and for a nation. I long to see this again in America and I pray that it will be so. God willing, it will."

"I trust that you will not give up," he said. "You have much to do yourself in getting your message out and God will give you the opportunity yet Diane. You will see. Hold fast to Him and to the truth which has been imparted to you by those who you have assisted in crossing to the light."

"Thank you Samuel. I will hold fast to the truth. I have in spite of much criticism and condemnation from others. We just need to see many more men awakened to the need to resist the tide of evil in the nation and to return to God. I pray for it. I ask God for it. I ask those who return to God to open the door for men to remember who they are and to return to God. Can you assist us in this way when you return to heaven Samuel? What might you do there to assist the cause here?"

Samuel was quick with his ideas saying, "Perhaps I can appeal to the Almighty that a door be opened to assist you in getting your message to the churches Diane. If the people who are seeking God can be reawakened to the truth, then the message can go farther, faster for they are the ones who will pray to God for assistance."

"Yes, they are but there are also the false teachers in many churches leading the flock astray, not to believe in a God who can speak into their lives, guiding them, doing miracles, and such."

"I will ask God to open the door for the truth to come back into the churches as God is the same today as yesterday and able to speak to His own. Then we will bring the message to the churches of what He is saying to them today."

"This is excellent," I told Samuel. "Thank you Samuel. You are a blessing to me and to our country even now. Thank you. May hope arise again in the land and God's will for His people, who He loves. I will do what I can when the door is opened unto me to assist. Tell God to show me the way and the timing for it."

Samuel stated that it was "time for me to go now Diane. I see that it is late for you as well.

Adieu."

"May God's blessing of love be upon you and may His will be done on earth as in heaven. Love to all, to you Samuel, especially. God speed. Love to you. Diane."

James Madison

March 16, 1751 – June 28, 1836

Growing up in Virginia, this soul's name was one that I of course had heard and in fact there is a college in Virginia named after him. I wish that all Americans knew these names and who these people were and what their contributions to our early history had been. I believe it is an intentional insidious act that is occurring by controlling factions in the world that is keeping the truth of man's struggle to preserve individual freedom and liberty and to excel and succeed in this world. The reason for hiding the truth of our history I believe is because we do learn from our own mistakes and the mistakes of our leaders what not to do for ourselves and our country. Without a record, we repeat the mistakes of the past over and over.

"Here I am to do a little soul seeking, seeking souls as it were. Here I am. Who is with me to my left," I asked? "What is your name? James Madison? Is this correct?"

"Yes, this is my name, James Madison."

I had taken a photograph from the internet and printed it out as we were talking and I asked him if this photo was of him.

"Diane, this is my photograph, not as a young man however and I look a little worse for wear as you are fond of saying."

"Hello James. It is a pleasure to make your acquaintance."

"I thank you for taking the time to speak with me Diane. There is quite a stir here as to what has been happening with the transitioning of so many of my colleagues. Naturally, I would want to join them for I have been here, in this no place for quite some time without a possibility of going anywhere."

"Strange how this is and I cannot say that I understand completely why it is so. Do you have any ideas as to why it is that men's energy is trapped in that place?"

"As human beings we are exposed to certain energies which mimic our choices of behavior back to us. When we do not acknowledge and then release these energies their constant presence deters us from becoming that which we come to the earth to become, primarily enlightened. If we die in the body without having released these energies, their presence continues preventing a release of the soul to eternity. This is the dilemma being experienced by myself and others. We are trapped by the exposure to energies of the world without a way to release them. Your coming here allows us to be exposed to a higher vibration which then moves these energies out of our energy fields, permitting us to see beyond ourselves once again and releasing us to the promise of eternity."

"This is a wonderful thing to participate in as long as all of the glory of this possibility is given to God for without the Spirit of God, I would not have understood that God loves all people, all things, and this allowed me to accept that I could love those too who were trapped where you are. On my own, I was not able to grasp the depths of God's love, but by His Spirit, He demonstrated the power of love to heal me, you, all men, and the earth experience. All you need is love."

"Love is the answer," James then added. "It is too often lost in the political realm I can attest to that. One gets caught up in the notion that all you need is brilliant ideas and that it is sufficient to solving all of a nation's problems but without love for God and His people, many mistakes in judgment are made. I for one, made many mistakes in judgment for I did not seek God's voice in providing direction to me as President of the United States of America. I wish to make amends for this for I might have continued to guide His people had I sought His counsel in leading His people. This is a trait highly necessary if one is to assume leadership over a Nation under God. Its leaders must be willing to seek God for direction and then, and only then will he people hear from God for the people do not seek after God as you do Diane and they do not hear him as you do. They fear Him rather due to the direction that they are going in their lives. It is easier for them to say that God does not speak than to risk being admonished by Him for the things that they are doing rather than seeking after God."

I said that I understood this very well. James continued saying, "In order for a Nation under God to continue as such, God must be able to choose a leader who is willing to listen to Him on behalf of the people. This can happen in a number of ways within the current system of government which is in place in the United States of America. It can happen through the voting process if the people themselves submit themselves in asking God what is His will for the nation.

If they are willing to fast and pray unto Him for direction in choosing a leader over them, the Spirit of God is able to show the people God's choice for leading them to prosperity and freedom as a Nation. If the people are lost in their connection to God, God is still able to raise up a man or a woman and lead them to know His will for the people and thus lead the people from the top down back to God. This is the only possibility left at this time for America for the people have turned their backs on God for days without end and they worship themselves as greater than God."

I asked James the following question, "How does God plan to do this for 2012?"

"God will need to draw your husband to Himself and this He must do Diane. You cannot do it yourself so don't try. You may watch as it is done before your eyes, but you will not be able to do it. God knows the heart of a man, if you will. He knows what it is that a man thinks, does He not? He is able then to draw a man to the truth about God Himself without having to require another individual's assistance to get there. Just be there when it happens and know that God's will shall be done despite the man himself."

"I absolutely believe that God is able. Praise be to God who is able."

"Indeed, He is able. Now I am going to do something here for you and for your husband. It is apparent that in order to run for the President of the United States your husband will require quite a bounty. It is not possible in these days to get even a Divine message out without a supportive group of people and a treasury of available funds to get the job done. I would like to go to heaven on behalf of the Freeman household requesting that a bounty be laid before you for the purposes of accomplishing God's will for your husband. What do you think of that idea Diane?"

"I am in favor of it. Thank you."

"I will ask God to please open the door for money to flow into your household in order to support the work of spreading the truth about the nature of man and the nature of God throughout the land. In addition I will ask that a bounty be laid before you that will allow you to become debt free, so that no judgment will come your way as to your debts, and that money will pour out from the heavens to free your husband for the purpose of serving God in the land by traveling to make His name known to those who have forgotten Him."

I said that I was in favor of this also for due to the manipulation of the country's banking and lending systems, many, like ourselves, are under water with household debt.

"This is known Diane, and so I will appeal to the heavens on your behalf," he said.

"Thank you very much for your willingness to assist James. I bless you expressly with love for you, and to the God of Heaven, who is merciful and mindful of man's needs to accomplish God's will and even our own destinies under heaven. So be it according to God's will and for the good of all James."

"So be it. I concur and so it shall be done for you in heaven to the glory of God and I will mark it in the history books that God once again is being lifted up under heaven due to your name and your work Diane."

"Thank you. Bless you James."

Amusing as James stated, "I see that smiling face."

"What may I do for you now James," I asked?

"Nothing for your light tells the story Diane for my benefit. I am free to go home as it were and I will now that I have been able to make amends before God for not lifting up His name in a definitive way under heaven. I want to bless you myself Diane, that you may have the honor you so deserve for assisting men like myself to find our way to glory. May y our destiny be bestowed upon you and may you always remember whom it is that you serve, never forgetting that it is God who gives to men according to their need that they may be enriched, rewarded, and given the opportunity to serve Him."

"I will be headed home then now Diane. I pray that America rises again to her former glory, dedicated to the cause of honoring God in your homes, your schools, libraries and history books.

May God's name be given a place of honor in your government buildings again, not relegated to the back room storage areas where lawless, and Godless men do store such things. I pray that children again may sing of God's love unpunished bringing a blessing upon the land in that energy of love as only out of the mouths of babes such as these can come such blessings. "Peace be with you Diane."

"And may peace also be with you James and love for you and the heavens and to ALL the great ones there. Thanks be to God. Take my love to Him. Help me to do what I am to do dear God.

Help me to do it and to not back down."

"The heavens are here to receive me Diane. Adieu."

"Adieu James".

Abigail Adams

November 11, 1744 – October 28, 1818

Today is February 9, 2011, and I must say that this person is someone that I was not entirely familiar with though I did know her name from history and that she was the wife of one of our former Presidents, hence a First Lady. Speaking to this person would provide some new and interesting insight for me for I had never known one of our country's First Ladies. I was making my availability known to the souls at the appointed time and asking who was present seeking my assistance by telling them I was here in accordance with God's will that they may return to eternity in the heavens. I was about to meet Abigail Adams.

"I am here. Please make your name known to me so that I may assist you. I am aware of a soul on my left. What is your name please?"

I heard this. "My name is Abigail Adams. Yes, I was married to John Adams. My position was that of First Lady in The White House, as I served next to my husband John who was the 2nd President of the United States."

"Blessings to you Abigail. Blessings of love. How nice to meet you. Did you see your photo there as I opened the internet," I asked?

"Yes, yes, I did! I was surprised to see the gold coin with the representation of me on it. What an honor I suppose however I would rather it was the glory of God which were given recognition particularly now in your nation for men worship every desire of their heart but not the God of Heaven. It is disappointing for so many of our peers were intent on keeping America free."

"Yes, Abigail, however there is a resurgence of resistance to the status quo throughout the land. Perhaps men and women need a reminder of who it is that has given the liberty and freedom expressly under a Nation under God, then perhaps they can return to Him, and in all of their ways acknowledge Him for His blessings. What would you like to tell me about yourself Abigail, or your husband, or your duties as a First Lady, pray tell?

"First, I want to thank you for allowing me to present myself here for life here has been hell for sure. There is no "life" here if it were to be known. No one is permitted to be anything at all but quiet, in their minds, and in their expressions of energy. Nothing is allowed here. It is like a prison and yet there are no bars for there is nowhere to go even if one were permitted to go about this space. There is nowhere to go."

"Why do you say this Abigail?"

"For the emptiness of the space where we are is apparent to all who are here and so it is that seeking to go somewhere else does not happen. One merely stays where they are doing nothing, saying nothing, and unless it is done against the will of those who lord over us, thinking nothing at all. This in itself is a task almost unbearable for the mind wanders constantly to think, to solve the problem of entrapment, and yet, it is not permitted."

"What is the punishment for thinking thoughts?"

Abigail answered, "Isolation. If it is determined that a soul is thinking or contributing thought to the others, they are sequestered away from all others and a deep sense of loneliness and sadness overcomes you. Imagine it if you will for a second. You are alone in the pitch of night as it were, without the comforts of any light, or God, or others who may wish to offer you comfort.

You are not permitted to cry, to call out, or to otherwise ask for assistance."

My question to her was, "What if you do cry out?"

"The punishment is a longer isolation and since there is no sense of time or space such as you have here Diane, it seems an indeterminable amount of time that one must suffer."

"Abigail, it is such a tragedy due to lack of truth being told to men that all men and women and children are free. We have come to the earth to experience a destiny, with the help of God at our disposal, as we ask for it, and when we complete our destinies, we are free to go home to eternity, to return home is the goal. It is also known to me now that God does not intervene or interfere in man accomplishing his destiny, unless it is absolutely necessity and help is desired by the soul having this experience for to intervene is to perhaps circumvent the entirety of the lessons the soul wishes to participate in by being here. Does this make sense?"

"It makes perfect sense to me," said Abigail. "I can see where my husband needed much more the assistance of God in his role as President for there were many who were bent on establishing their own authority over the domain of the Presidency for their own wealth and power. A little more of God's will and power would have sustained us nicely. I can only say that it was difficult at best to serve as President over all men when some men were in constant conflict with the idea of their countrymen being free to pursue their own destinies. This was not a welcome idea to men who were used to controlling the liberties of others. We did our best at a time when men were rising up against the new government in America. The King's men, as they were, were here to create unrest. They were here to secure a hold on the wealth of this new nation and they would do it at any cost regardless of the time that it would take to secure its wealth for England. We knew this. Many men who served the God of Heaven knew this and yet, the battle continued to against us."

"What was life like for you inside The White House while men sought to destroy the power of the Presidency, and to rob men of the newly established liberties and freedoms under the Constitution?"

Abigail began, "I found it difficult to trust those who were in our care, who assisted with the work of The White House. I felt certain that there was whispering and eavesdropping going on behind the walls of The White House. It seemed that there was no place to hold a private conversation or confidential conversation outside of the ears of those who might subjugate our freedoms. I yearned to have a private area where no one could enter or listen in on any conversations with my husband. The help was not to be trusted."

I wanted to know whether Abigail sought God's counsel to hire those who knew Him who would be trustworthy and noble to serve His nation and is Godly leaders?"

"Though I was a minister's daughter, I did not know how to speak to God as you do. I did not see God as a personal friend, or one who might entertain my personal requests. Why would He?

I was merely a woman who by circumstances ended up married to the President of the United States of America. But individually, I was merely Abigail Adams."

"Abigail, perhaps you know now that God is no respecter of persons. All may approach Him equally and with respect for He listens to all of His children for in this is love demonstrated, love of God, that you would come to Him with your concerns and allow Him to offer solutions to them."

"This is lovely, Diane," she said. "I wish that I had known these kinds of things about our Creator. Perhaps my own life would have gone differently as well. I left all decisions to my husband not offering much to the process."

"And what would you recommend to me, Abigail? Let me ask this also, how is it that your husband decided to run for President? Did he choose it on his own? Pray tell."

"Let me start with the question as to my husband's desire to be President. It was not his idea alone. There were many of his constituents who urged him to run for President for he was passionate about liberty and he was willing to take a stand for freedom. They assisted him in making himself known to the public."

I asked Abigail if the elections were honest at that time. "Were the votes counted without deceit," I queried? "Do you know?"

"I dare say so that there was much trickery," said Abigail, "for men did not take the process lightly but there were those who watched over others who counted the votes in an election. It took time too so the dedication to overseeing the process had to be real."

"I wish that I could say that the vote was calculated honestly today for I believe that there are those whose intentions are for evil who adjust the vote to suit their agendas, here and abroad, sadly."

Abigail said that this was unfortunate saying, "The will of the people cannot be upheld if there is dishonesty in the voting booth whether it be at the beginning or at the end of the vote."

"And there is more," I said, "men create manipulative language in an attempt to confuse the voters who are voting on particular issues. If the people cannot even understand what a particular proposition is, much less what it would do or what it will cost the taxpayers, how can they vote on it with a good conscience? It is difficult to hear the Spirit of God within a voting booth to know which way to go, and as I said, the language is often written poorly deliberately to deceive the voter. It is apparent, that those wishing to gain access to voters' monies for a particular project, expect a certain number of people to simply vote "yes" when they do not understand the question being posed to them, or when the author of the proposition has manipulated the language to make it appear that the expenditure of the money is for the good of all. In fact, many times, it merely benefits those who are putting forth the proposal and no one else. Add up of those votes and they have their project in their hands and they can say, the public voted for it."

"I see," Abigail responded, "This is a problem for in order for freedom to advance its cause, there must be an honest voting practice in place which assures that the will of the people is enacted in the land."

"Exactly, and so it is, that perhaps you can help us with this one, Abigail. Perhaps when you get to the heavens, you might explain this situation to the powers that be, and ask that God would move His hand to expose all of the improprieties of the voting process, in order to ensure an honest election and if the people who love God do hear His will for the next leader, that we need the blessed assurance that God's will shall be done, for the good of all through an honest and fair electoral process."

"This is a great idea Diane and I am feeling privileged to be able to present it to the heavens for consideration. This nation still belongs to the Kingdom of Heaven despite those whose desire it is to deceive its people into giving up that covenant with God and so it is, that God will do what is good and right for His people."

"Must we have others putting forth this request or do you suppose that it is good enough that you and I agree, as I agreed with Samuel about some issues before God, for Him to move His hand, on behalf of the people of God within this country and under His name."

Abigail reminded me then, "If two or more people come together in agreement, God is with us to hear our prayers and to give to us according to our need. It is needed that honest elections again can be held in the land. We must ask that all of those who oppose honest elections be removed from the process permanently. We must ask that Godly men and women rise up to again look into these things such that honesty is the highest priority in the election process. We must ask that God Himself will oversee the process and expose those who wish to usurp the freedoms of men to choose whom they will serve under God. Now, something else we might do, before God and His Kingdom, is to ask that God will deliver this country from evil. We do ask that he will return the nation to its' standing as a Nation under the One, rue God, and that He will again bless the land by blessing its people, with truth, understanding and wisdom in the knowledge of God's way as it is said that God's ways are not our ways."

"I agree Abigail, 100%, before the Almighty, let the hand of God Himself be upon our requests.

I ask in the power of the light and the Authority of the Divine that these petitions be heard in the throne room of God for it is said, that whenever two or more are gathered in My name, I am there in the midst of them, and if they should ask anything in My name, it shall be given unto them. So be it to the good of all, pressed down, shaken together and overflowing. Let it be done. Praise be to the God of Heaven that our electoral process would be restored as a blessing unto God and unto the freedoms of men.

"This is so heartfelt Diane and I agree with you before God that His will shall be done in the land. We stand together in this one Diane, two women desiring what is good and right for the people of this nation."

"Amen, thank you Abigail. We have accomplished something good today. Thank you. I will remember this meeting. Now is there something that I might do for you Abigail. Do you understand the transitioning process? First is to acknowledge God, His love for you, and it is for all men to let go of all negative feelings, emotions, judgments of this world as they are merely to teach us about our choices that are apart from God's nature? Do you see this in my light or were you already in the light?"

"I was not for I had not sought God's counsel in all things and I did not give God the glory either for the things that I possessed, or the position that I was given in life. Rather I allowed these things to be as if I had created it myself, not recommended I might add for the end of things, one has only what he has done in the name of God to be rewarded for and all else fades away. This is the way of things Diane. Something to think about isn't it?"

"Yes," I told her, "I will pass this on to those I am privileged to share with in life. Abigail, is there anything else you wish to share with me today?"

Abigail then said that it was upon her to ask if there was something that she might do for me when she returned to heaven. "How may I assist you," she asked?

Aside from taking me with her, I asked that a door in heaven be opened to faith to be restored in God for My two children, Brian and Ashley, real faith, so that they may again know and love God for though it may have seemed so God did never leave me nor forsake me. He showed me the error of my own ways in understanding Him, and He showed me my lack of understanding of the ways of men who portend to serve Him, and many other things which I needed to learn, and He did not leave me even in the most difficult times of my despair about the way in which men treat those who love God. I wish to see God reintroduce Himself to my children. Am I allowed to ask this on behalf of them or must they seek Him themselves?"

She said, "Let's do this. We will ask. It is all we can do. We will ask and then if it is God's will, it will be done."

"Correct, of course. May God's will be done for my children. I bless them with the understanding of God's ways, for they are not our own. I bless them with God's love for it is immeasurable, for it is so deep, wide, long and reaches into the depths of our souls to demonstrate the love of God. I bless them with the desire to know God for God is love."

"That is all you can do," said Abigail. "Pray for them. Bless them. Encourage them without judging them in the ways of God. They will find Him in their time of need. Right now they are searching things out in the world just like we all do."

"Thank you Abigail. Love to you and to the heavens and to my God. Thank you dear God for giving me this opportunity to speak with those you love. Thank you for sharing with me these bits of wisdom. May they reach the rest of your people and open their hearts to return to you."

Abigail indicated that she must go now too. "Rejoice in that you are beloved of God Diane for few are chosen as you know. Few are chosen."

"Blessings to you. God speed. Open the door to honesty my friend and integrity in the election process too."

"You have my word Diane. Adieu."

Lee Harvey Oswald

October 18, 1939 – November 24, 1963

I had to make apologies to the next soul who was contacting me. I was due at an engagement related to my husband's business and yet this soul required my attention. I asked for them to please tell me their name. What I was about to hear from this person did not come as a complete surprise for I had suspected for some time that certain factions at work in our country would stoop to anything to undermine what was good and right about America. The darkness has an agenda after all and it is to destroy all that God has had a hand in and to keep people from turning to Him, for in doing so, we have power to change our circumstances. The soul coming through however was helpless in his circumstances to protect his life and as such was absent from his body but not present with the Lord.

"Lee Harvey Oswald."

"I asked who he was saying, "who were you in the world?"

"I was the one accused of assassinating John F. Kennedy, Jr. but I am here to tell you the truth of the matter."

"Ok, do you want to tell me something Lee?"

"Yes, I do. Though I was accused of murdering two people, one of who was the President, it is a lie! I did not do these things but I was framed for it."

"Why do you suppose you were framed for this murder Lee?"

"Because I was thinking of moving to the Soviet Union. I had family there but I certainly was no spy."

"You were thinking of moving to the Soviet Union Lee?"

"Yes, I spoke of it but nothing was set in stone. I had not made any arrangements to do this.

I really had not looked into it much at all. Something about it intrigued me."

I asked Lee to tell me what happened on the day of November 22, 1963. "I was just a third grader but I do remember this day well. Tell me what you do know."

Lee began, "I was at work that day but there was much going on related to the President being in town. At the time of his arrival, of course, there were not many customers in the restaurant where I worked."

I asked him to help him hear him better and then I asked him, "Where did you work?"

"I was a dishwasher in a restaurant near where the motorcade was passing. I had this job as additional work to support my growing family. I obviously was more qualified than what was required to do this type of work, but I needed the money for bills that I had accumulated."

I then asked him what happened on November 22, 1963.

Lee started talking again, "I went up to the sixth floor of the book store to see the commotion below. You could see some of what was going on from there but it was not a perfect view. was not anti-American nor did I have a vendetta against the President He was a normal guy from all that I could see with a taste for the ladies from what I heard. I wanted to see what I might see from up there."

"Please tell me more," I asked.

"It was a fairly uneventful thing. I went up to take a look, stayed a few minutes or so, and left. I thought that I might be able to leave work as there really wasn't much going on due to all of the hoopla with the President there. Many wanted to see him and they were not interested in visiting the shops or restaurants in town."

"Where did you go Lee," I asked?

"Well, I got into my car and attempted to drive home but was stopped a short distance after leaving work. I cannot recall the reason used for stopping me. It was all very confusing. I knew that they wanted to arrest me but for what, I was unsure of that. They were not normal police who stopped me because they were plainly dressed. This seemed odd to me as I expected police officers in uniform due to the siren that they had. They bullied me out of the car and said that I was being investigated for the assassination of the President. This was rather incredulous to me because I had not been down to see him driving by. How could I have done such a thing? I was certain that I would be cleared but little did I know that they had an agenda to blame me for the President's murder. Perhaps it was because my wife was Russian and I had lived there for a time but I brought her home to America with me. We had our family here. I had hopes and dreams for us here. I would not have done anything to destroy my position as the father of my girls.

They were young and needed me to support them. It was very confusing but I knew that they meant business. I was not going to be released it appeared that they had fabricated a story about me as a Communist sympathizer. I may have been married to a Russian woman, but my heart was in America.

I asked Lee if anything had been revealed within his hearing of those who had arrested him that indicated who was behind this senseless murder?

"Yes, I could hear the men speaking close to me and it was obvious they needed a scapegoat.

They would not allow me to speak to the press, or to my family. This was being discussed.

They would keep me away from anyone who might corroborate my story of where I had been.

It seemed that it was a setup to convict me without a jury, without a trial, and without any chance of learning the truth from others. They would make sure of that. They were going to see that I was killed. I knew it in my heart. My life was over. I knew in that moment that I was not going to see my wife or my girls again. They had chosen me to bear the brunt of whatever grand scheme they had to overthrow this Presidency and so it was that I would be sacrificed for their greater cause.

"Wow. What thoughts went through your head Lee?"

"How do I get out of here? Is there a chance anyone will come for me? Will anyone even know that I am here? How will they pin the murder on me without evidence? I was a Marine and had served our county and yet they would let me be the fall guy for President Kennedy's death so they would be rid of him and his brother Bobby who were creating trouble for them."

I asked if he had any idea who these men were.

"They seemed like mobsters to me. They dressed like it. Spoke like it. Acted like it.

Very tough guys. Very businesslike in a manner of speaking but in a "I am going to kill you" kind of way."

"How would you describe what you were feeling Lee?"

"I was shocked and I felt at a loss to do anything to save my life. I knew that it was over. I just knew it. They had me and I was chosen to pay the price for their deeds. That was it!

Game over! They didn't need to beat me up. I wasn't resisting as I thought they had made a mistake. Why resist? I wasn't even sure why they arrested me in the first place so why would I resist? Mistaken identity perhaps but I knew that I would be cleared, at least I thought so in the beginning. As time went by, and I overheard a few things, it became apparent that my life was over."

"Why would anyone believe this story Lee?"

"Because I was not a violent man. Ask anyone who did know me. I was not a violent man.

There were instances in the service where I did not wish to participate in the drills because it seemed to me to be unnecessary violence. This is verifiable. However there is probably no one to tell the truth now. No records kept on me being a more docile man were likely kept to corroborate the truth that I was nonviolent. They needed a different truth and they began spinning their story the moment they arrested me. When I heard what it was they wanted to accuse me of, I was sick to my stomach. I felt so sad for what my wife and daughters would have to deal with as a result of their accusations against me and I also knew that it was likely they would kill me. As far as I knew, this kind of crime would be punishable by death and this was going through my mind as I waited on them to explain to me what was happening."

"They had done their homework researching my Marine career and my travels. They knew where I had lived. They knew that my wife was Russian. They knew that I needed work and was working extra jobs and they knew where I was working. How? Because I had attempted to get my wife's documents in order so that she could stay in the country with me. She was Russian. This got their attention. They needed a scapegoat."

I asked Lee if there was anything that he could tell me that would be something they did not know that could be proved that might point to someone other than him as the murderer?

Lee's response was simple and honest. "How about I did not do it?"

I did not respond.

"I know. They don't care if I say that I did not do it because the criminals who set me up, set me up good."

I asked Lee if I had the information correct that he was a dishwasher in a restaurant on the day of the assassination?

"No, I was working in an office nearby though and I went over to the depository to check out the procession. The building was empty as everyone was outside watching the procession. I wanted to see it too."

I told Lee that I would need to look up the job that he had at that time, and its location. I was thinking maybe I had it confused.

Lee said, "I told you that it was nearby, near to the depository."

"Well, it is a sad thing indeed when the government participates in setting citizens up, however, I just went to the Wiki site again and it says that you were photographed holding weapons, rifles, that were like, or similar to what was used to kill JFK and that your wife said she took the photo."

At this same moment, I was being contacted by The Divine. I was told to ask Lee Harvey Oswald this, "Ask Lee Harvey Oswald what he was doing with guns at this home and why was he being photographed holding them if he was a peaceful man? Ask him Diane."

"Did you hear this question Lee?"

"Yes, I did. I had my wife take the photos to demonstrate that I was a tough guy. I knew how to use weapons but I was not a murderer. Don't you know young men who have liked to have their photos taken with a weapon in their hands? Men like to pretend to be what they are not. I had no idea that those photos would seal my fate as a murderer even in my wife's eyes."

I had to ask Lee to hold onto my energy as I went with my husband to our commitment elsewhere telling Lee I would pick back up with him at around 9:30 p.m. I asked him if this was acceptable.

"My pleasure as I appreciate your sharing your light with me Diane. I will wait for you."

"Don't worry Lee. We will get you home. I also want to hear about your love of God."

God has told me that every soul whom I contacted or who contacted me has been freed from the darkness due to my spending time with them as the light that is mine does illuminate the truth for them, and they are freed. So it was with Lee Harvey Oswald.

Lee Harvey Oswald did confess his sins to Alejandro and was forgiven though we are not recording them here.

Lee was adamant to Alejandro that he would serve Him to expose those in the Mafia who do take the lives of the innocent. It is this which he is called to in Heaven.

He was not a monster as portrayed by those in the higher ranks of government but rather he was rather an ordinary man who loved his country, America, where he lived with his wife and two daughters whom he adored. However, he had the connection to Russia that could be used against him to draw attention away from those who are responsible for *much* death and destruction in our country and around the globe.

Their day is coming!

John Edgar Hoover

January 1, 1895 – May 2, 1972

It was the evening of February 26, 2011 and I knew that there were at least two souls present who wanted me to assist them. I had a trip coming up in the morning and indicated that I can only help two souls this evening but offered to do some work while I was out of town yet I still reached out to see who was there. I had not known much about this person's life unfortunately and blame that to some extent on the condition of our nation's schools. I believe that the nation's people ought to be learning about our previous and new leaders in the course of our educations for this is true history. Instead, we tend to be teaching our children a lot about social issues and radical personal choices which affect their personal lives much more than they affect the nation, that is, unless we give them power over all of us and allow them to force us to accept that which is anti-God and anti-faith and anti-personal choice. Unfortunately, it looks like we are allowing national programming to do just that. But back to the soul at hand.

I asked the name of the first soul to my left and heard "John Edgar Hoover".

I asked if Edgar Hoover was the correct name I had heard as I wrote it down for him to see.

Mr. Hoover responded that "Now you do", as I had written John Edgar Hoover originally.

"How may I assist you Mr. Hoover? First, let me say, nice to meet you. I do not know much about you or your life. There are too many people to know unfortunately."

Mr. Hoover stated "I am here at the request of The Divine and I see they are here again."

Mr. Hoover was speaking of The Divine whose presence I did feel too.

"Ask Mr. Hoover what it is that he learned about serving as Director of the FBI that may have caused him some concern. What did he know that was not told to the people of this nation. Why was it kept secret? See what he reveals to you Diane."

"Mr. Hoover," The Divine has asked a question here do you see it?"

"I do," he responded, "and I see there is yet another question."

"We also want you to ask Mr. Hoover why he did continue with the FBI once he learned what it was that was going on and the lies being told to the public?" Why didn't he tell the truth?"

I stated to Mr. Hoover that there were several questions here for him to answer before we proceeded.

"I know precisely what it is that God wishes to have me reveal for it was a great controversy during my time as Director of the FBI. I will tell you Diane so listen carefully. When I was Director of the FBI, there was an investigation into the goings on of the Illuminati. It was started by the Bureau to determine what evidence there was of those who belonged to this organization meddling in the affairs of the United States of America. It was evident that other countries knew about this organization and we were intent on educating ourselves as well for purposes of protecting our own interests where this organization might be concerned."

"And, so what happened," I asked him.

"The evidence was overwhelming as to their involvement with the banking systems of the world for one. In addition, they were very involved with governments around the world. Money is a great manipulator, don't you know Diane? Money can't buy you love the song says, but it can buy you a lot of influence and a lot of politicians. What we found was compelling evidence against them."

"What did you do with it?"

"Nothing, I am afraid," Hoover stated. "And this is why God must want to have me speak to it now. I did nothing. I did not bring it to the public's attention for to do so would have been fatal for me, and many others who did the research. This organization is notorious for doing whatever it takes to silence those who pry into their affairs."

I wanted to know for myself and others and so I asked it. "How are they at handling God's power to dismantle their abilities to destroy what is good and right?"

"I can imagine they would not stand up to the Almighty," Hoover said.

"Why did you stay with the FBI after you found out the truth? What were the lies being told to the public?"

He responded, "First, I will address the issue of why I did stay with the FBI after learning what the truth was and the involvement of the Illuminati in the United States government. I feared for my life and the lives of those I loved. The extent of their influence is widespread. They have a network that is worldwide and they fear no one."

"Okay then, so you were afraid. What about the lies told to the public?"

"They were too many to list here I am afraid of that too. Too many to list."

I said one thing, "try".

"For instance, the people believed that their votes matter in the public election. This is not true for the voting is controlled by those at the top . . . and I mean the top . . . not the President of the United States of America. This is why your current President thinks that he is the Sultan because he was chosen by the Illuminati to rule the United States but he was not chosen for the reasons that he thinks. He was chosen to further enslave the people of this country into greater poverty, loss of their earnings, savings, retirement funds and even their right to good healthcare.

Additionally, he was chosen to continue to pull those who follow him into greater dependence upon the government for those who depend on government are not free. This program has been in motion for such a long time Diane. You must understand something here. This has been going on for a few generations and some. These people are very patient to gain control over the planet. It is not merely a human interest group that you oppose to controlling the planet and her people, but beings of another sort. As long as those who wish to control the planet and her rich resources cooperate with these beings, they have all that they could ever wish to own but in the end, the world suffers, and her people for no one can give the people back their freedom at this time but God."

"What do you know about these "beings"? They are not of God?"

"No," he said, "they are not". They are a warring faction and the wish to use the planet for themselves but in order to do so, they must control its people while destroying the belief in God of Heaven for if the people believe in their deity, they become empowered against those who wish to dominate them. Thus they are strictly enforcing a no God policy in our government, our schools, businesses, and even soon, in the churches. They already have those who cooperate with them inside the churches to mislead the people, to believe a lie about God and not the truth.

This was not hard to do for there are few seeking to lead the churches anymore, haven't you noticed?"

"What can be done to stop them and to have a proper election of the people for 2012 then?

If the Illuminati control the world's governments and voting processes, what hope do we have of regaining our freedoms, our liberties, and our destinies," I asked Mr. Hoover?

Mr. Hoover said, "Remember I said that only God can restore the freedoms of the people and liberate the earth from those who came here on the heels of men."

"Ok, so what is the message for this book about what you are revealing to me? Am I to write about this in this book of the crossings of men from obscurity to eternity? What purpose is there in telling me this if these men are wicked and evil and will stop at nothing to keep the truth from the public?"

"The Divine asked that I tell you. You will have to ask them what their intended purpose was in having you know the truth."

"So what other lies were told to the good people of this country Mr. Hoover?"

"I am at liberty to say just this one thing about that Diane. When Martin Luther King died, it was not a random shooting at all for those who desire to eradicate God from public life are serious about their work. He did not have a chance but let me say this, God is not mocked!! God is now ready to take a stand for His people on earth. There are rumblings in the heavens now as people have been leaving the darkness for the heavens and the truth has been revealed of the deeds of men against God. God will not be mocked. It is certain that a day of reckoning is coming soon. Your husband will make a fine leader in this country and you can be sure that God will protect his life, as long as his heart remains open to God. This is essential for any leader for egos tend to grow wildly when men rise to power and authority over others. Without the Spirit of God to temper a man, it is difficult to control that ego. It is essential for a man to continue to seek God's will for himself, the nation which he represents and for the people and then to listen, as you have learned Diane, God expects obedience in His own. This is for a reason for what man can see that which God can see and what man can know what God can know for what man has lived as long as God and seen as much as God has seen?

There is none. The counsel of God is necessary in order to rule over men justly."

"I agree. I do wish to see Godly leadership restored in the land, for the people cry out and ask, 'what can we do' but there is no one to tell them as they do not hear God."

Mr. Hoover responded, "This is duly noted Diane and God is reconciling Himself to mankind as we speak due to the revelation of souls of what evil men have done to deny Him and to impugn Him in this world in an effort to keep men from Him. The reign of these men who have sided with evil is coming to an end quickly, you will see."

"What would you like to say here to God," I asked Mr. Hoover?

"I am making my peace with God now, in asking for forgiveness for I did not serve Him, nor my country, with honor. I failed to reach my destiny Diane for I did not honor God in serving as a leader in His nation. This is a tragedy for no man can reach his destiny apart from God. This is something for you and your husband to tell your children. No man will ever reach his destiny if he separates himself from God, for God has established each man's destiny prior to adding the energy of life to their dna, and without God, it cannot be known to them what is their destiny.

God reveals it at the right time to be known to them and only when their hearts are open unto Him."

"Now I will go to heaven and I will ask God to open a door to end the reign of the Illuminati on the earth for men are repenting and asking for their freedom again around the world. Men no longer wish to serve evil men who rule with an iron fist. This era is ending and you are seeing it now. Do not believe that this is a bad thing per se Diane. It is good to see men beginning to desire their freedom. It is a start is it not? Now, if they can be impassioned again about freedom, perhaps they will be more open to the truth about who they are and why they desire freedom with their whole being."

"This makes sense Mr. Hoover and I do understand."

"Next, I will ask that God open the door for your understanding as to when to begin preparing for what is ahead for you both. There will be much to do and you will need to connect with other Godly leaders, not men who merely say they love God, but by their actions, you will know that they have loved God. This is who God will show you to work alongside with you both.

No mistakes this time for God will enthrone Himself over this administration of Godly leadership and there will have been nothing like it ever before."

"The time for this is coming . . . and you will see it and in fact, you will participate in it. Perhaps even your son will remember God in time to serve Him in this administration. Your husband could appoint his own son to a position of authority over the banks to oversee their actions as unto God."

"This I would love to see happen," I mused. "our son remembering His God, His first love."

"It will happen, Diane. For love is going to pour out on the earth. You requested it. It will happen. In thirty days' time. At the end of March. Watch for it."

"Now I must go," Mr. Hoover stated, "and so must you. Be safe in your journeys. Speak to no one about the plans for your husband yet and particularly about what I have revealed to you.

Do not speak of it at this time."

I needed to know and so I asked, "Is it to go in the book?"

"Yes," he said, "but the book will not be ready for a season and by then, love will reveal those who are not His own for they will not receive Him."

"I hesitate to ask what that is going to look like. Mercy!"

"Peace be with you then Mr. Hoover, and love to all in the heavens, to Our God in Heaven, the Most High, we send you love, gratitude, thanksgiving for all that we have and are, in this world. We give thanks."

"You have nothing to fear for you are well protected by the heavens Diane. If only you could see the armed angels standing near you even now. No harm shall come to you or yours. You are beloved of God Diane for no one has served Him with such passion in some time on this earth denying themselves food for extended periods of time simply to know His name. No one ever did such a thing and so it is that you are favored of God."

"This is a wonderful thing," I said. "Now, if I could live in peace from these men who lust, murder, steal, hate, destroy, and every other evil thing and who destroy the lives of men just because they can, stealing all that a good man can earn in his life, stealing it, just when the men are old enough to take a rest from work. It needs to stop."

"I agree and stop it will. Wait for it. See it coming. Peace be with you Diane. They are here for me and I must go."

"Peace be with you Mr. Hoover, and love to all of the heavens, to Our God in Heaven, the Most High, we send you love, gratitude, thanksgiving for all that we have and are in this world. We give you thanks."

Arthur M. Young

November 3, 1905 – May 30, 1995

Before I begin to share the story told to me by the individual who is named above, I want to state emphatically that I had never heard of him before this day. I had to look up his name to verify that it was indeed a person of note. I was soon going to find out his importance in the world and yet, again despite his work and accomplishments in the world, he too did not achieve his Divine destiny.

I was contacted by a soul whose energy I felt and I asked "what do you want me to do?"

It was simple. He said, "I want you to help me".

"Please tell me your name and I will assist you at best I can. Tell me plainly your name while you were in the body."

He answered, "My name is Arthur Young."

I found a photo of Arthur Young and asked if this was him.

He said, "Yes, that is my photo, can't say that I aged greatly but you can see that I still have some spunk in my eyes can you not?"

"I do see that Arthur. Tell me why you are here. I do not know your name nor do I know anything about you."

I did a quick search on the internet and found a bit about Arthur Young. There were some essays he had written. I asked Arthur if he could tell me where he was now.

"Indeed I can Diane. I am here with the rest of lost humanity I am afraid. Though I thought that my understanding of things might propel me into the light and beyond. I was mistaken.

It takes more than that apparently. I was an author of many topics and I lived a long time.

Unfortunately, in all of my writings, I neglected to acknowledge that my information came from above, not from myself, but through me, for the greater understanding of all humanity. I did not give all of the glory to the Almighty as I might and as such, I can't say that one person is better for having read what I have written for if they did not find Him through reading my books, what good are they? There is much written about random topics in this world but not enough written about how to reach and connect with the Almighty. This is what humanity needs to know. They must reconnect to their power and their freedom and liberty. All else is in vain. No one can achieve their destiny without this Divine connection for in it is the Deity's wisdom and reminder of why you chose to come here. Without it, you are a soul on a mission of no consequence to anyone but perhaps yourself."

"Now Diane, I was chosen to come and speak with you for two reasons, one is that with your light, I can go home but not without redeeming myself before the God of Heaven. I must tell you a few things about life. First, you must get a couple of my books about the Universe and about the Creator which I did write. Though they are centered differently than your own, they do give you some insight as to how things are in the Universe. Get my book about theories on God, and my book about the Universe."

I asked Arthur if the book he was speaking about was called *The Reflexive Universe* book.

He answered, "Yes, Diane, this is the book that you must read. It will give you greater insight about the Universe."

I indicated that I would try to find the books and order them for myself.

Arthur said that his was a good idea then. "You must read this and ask for Divine guidance and understanding when you do read them."

"Got it," I said. "I will order these books or essays. Thank you for the suggestion."

"Next I am to tell you that you must seek Him daily for guidance in the preparation of all of the work that is before you. You cannot do all of this without His guidance and He wants you to seek Him to know what to do."

I asked Arthur if he was saying that I needed to set a specific time for meditation.

"Yes, of course, for you are representing Him are you not? If you are representing Him, you need to connect directly with Him. Though you are hearing Him throughout your communication with others, this is one thing. To seek Him directly for the pleasure of communicating with Him for yourself is quite another," Arthur stated.

I responded that this was true. "I need more energy, more time to perform the work in front of me. More help. More everything and as soon as I have a minute, souls keep coming to me asking for help."

"Though it seems that they are coming to you for help, and indeed they are, they are also coming to you at the direction of the Almighty, for it is His will that you receive the insight which you need, the open doors which you need, and the opportunities presented, which you need, in order to bring forth His truth. He is doing it for your benefit as much as you are doing it for the benefit of others."

I agreed saying, "Yes, I know. I really do know this. I do thank Alejandro for He is trying to get me "there", for both of us, more for those who need to know Him, and perhaps I can benefit too."

"What you have is a magnificent relationship with the Universe Diane in that it is rallying to assist you in accomplishing your destiny and at the same time, doing so will benefit millions of souls once the materials are available for others to read. You must not stop moving towards this goal or all of this work will be lost. Keep moving forward towards accomplishing the goal of publishing this material. The next step is to find a publisher. This you must do by beginning to contact publishers with your work. Find those publishers who have an interest in the ethereal and send them a copy of your bio, the selected chapters, and your marketing ideas for the book.

You already have these materials prepared. Make a dozen copies of them this week and send them out to publishers. Get your business plan developed too and once these things are done the Universe can work with you to get the book published. Work with the Universe to help you by setting things in motion. You can't just wait for it to happen."

"I realize that I cannot just wait for it to happen. But it is confusing to try and do these things all at once. Confusing. I cannot seem to stay focused with so many tasks to be done at once and my husband is home recovering. I have many interruptions. I have had many things happening all at once since January and all I can say, is that it is overwhelming."

"I can see that it is overwhelming and that you are attempting to stay grounded by exercising, but you must choose the time to work and establish it as sacred time in order to propel yourself forward to success. Make certain that your husband respects that in order for you to get published, you must work on getting the materials out to publishers and you must spend time with Him to stay centered on priorities and to get His direction for your work."

"Yes, and I have six people now lined up for Thursday night clearings too. I would like to know if they can all be done at once. Is there a faster way to accomplish this? Also, they need to be the last that I must do without compensation as I have work to do that is my own and a life to live."

Arthur offered that he would suggest to Alejandro that perhaps I could be freed now from assisting people in the future for free and "that you may begin to receive this compensation for this work as promised. Now you must confirm a time certain when you will meet with Him to set in motion that which has been given to you so that it can be accomplished for you and for His name."

"I would like to get up by 6:30 a.m. to meet with Him and spend one hour with Him for this purpose. And, if we need more time together, I will make it 6:00 a.m. Is this acceptable to Him?

Alejandro, is this acceptable to you? I need to start my day with this interaction with Alejandro!"

"I am certain that He is agreeable Diane. Wait upon His confirmation to you. It will come.

In the meantime, make plans to be there for Him to speak with you. You have much to do and your life is busy yes, but this is your destiny being set in motion. Move ahead and watch it begin to take place."

"Thank you, Arthur", I said. "I will begin to take the steps to copy my bio, letter of intro, and the chapters for sending copies out to publishers. I also need to get the publishers selected who will receive my book without an agent. Perhaps Alejandro can assist me with this search.

We have just had a time change to mess me up even further."

"Look at life as a challenge to overcome, each and every day accomplishing something towards that destiny which awaits your completion of it. Move ahead. Don't wait for another day to do something towards achieving it. Do today what you can and tomorrow accomplish something else. Move forward each day with another task towards achieving it. Step by step."

"I will," I told Arthur, "But this week has obstacles to that end. I have to drive my husband to the desert. This is going to take two days. Then I have to visit my doctor and I need time to prepare my house for an appraisal too this week. When do I do all of this copying and searching for publishers?"

"Set your day in order. Choose when you will do the proposals and just do them. Choose Wednesday and do not allow anyone to steal the time from you. Choose Wednesday for the proposals and tell everyone else they must wait for you have a book to be published and it must be distributed to publishers in order to be reviewed for publishing."

"There is one glitch Arthur. My husband is planning to be in the desert on Tuesday night, and I must drive him due to his recent surgery, and I will be home later on Wednesday."

Relentless is this one. Arthur merely said, "Work when you get here. Do nothing else until you have copies ready for the publishers."

"I will do it," I answered. "Wednesday I will do it. Alejandro help me to do what needs to be done and in the right manner so that the proposal is received by the right publisher and accepted."

Arthur told me then that I would have the help that I needed when I began the work as I always do. He said, "You know this by now don't you?"

"Probably."

"Which means that you do," Arthur stated. "You do not want to leave this world with unfinished work to do. Get it done and you can rest in eternity. Get it done."

I said that I would get it done with Alejandro to help me for His name's sake."

"That's the spirit. I will be on my way then Diane. Read my books. You will learn something that you do not already know. Thank you for sharing your energy with me. I will be returning home now. Take care of yourself but do not be afraid of a little work."

"Adieu Arthur. Thank you for your assistance. I will look for Alejandro in the morning. My beloved Father in Heaven."

Christopher Columbus

Born in Genoa, Italy – Died May 20, 1506

This was a fun exercise I must say because this soul today would be someone that I knew something about and I credit that to my early school teachers for introducing this explorer to me as a child during history class. I had imagined what it might have been like to cross an ocean in a ship such as this person would have sailed in and it did not sound like fun at all. It isn't as though you would have had access to five star meals and clean showers and Hollywood entertainers. It would have been a rough going indeed. Let me introduce you then to this explorer.

"Good day, I am here. How may I assist you? Tell me your name please and we can begin."

"My name is Christopher Columbus."

"Really?"

"Indeed, Christopher Columbus. I sailed for Spain to the Americas to lay claim to the land for the Queen. I have come to petition for my freedom from the Great God of Heaven. Will you assist me?"

"Of course, it will be my pleasure to assist you Christopher. Tell me your story if you will."

"I was an explorer but I was other things as well. I was patriotic about my own country but one thing that I was good at is following directions. I could read a map well and I could sail. I was selected by the Queen of Spain to sail to find the yet undiscovered land of the Americas to claim it for Spain. Thus, I set off on my journey with three sailing ships; the Nina, the Pinta, and the Santa Maria. You know those names Diane I see that it was easy for you to pull the energy through."

I told Christopher that as a child in school they had a rhyme for us to learn the names of the ships on his voyage. It went something like, "In 1492, Columbus sailed the ocean blue".

Then they had us memorize the names of your ships. The rhyme helped us remember the date."

"Clever indeed. I planned the voyage, gathered my supplies and men to assist, and we took a few others who were interested in going on such a voyage of exploration. The voyage was not easy by any standard. We had difficult weather, sickness and it took much longer than we anticipated to get where we were headed. Supplies began to run low and we became a bit despondent.. Eventually, however, we did discover land. But it was not unoccupied as we were to discover. It had inhabitants in the land. Now how does one country arbitrarily lay claim to a land when it is already occupied by another? This is not the way of the world. We would have to return to Spain only to reveal to the Queen that the land which she desired was already occupied by another kind of people. I was not looking forward to the return trip particularly carrying the news that I had for the Queen."

Nonetheless, off we went with some new supplies from the lands we visited, and we were successful in our return home. I was relieved to get there but less enthusiastic about meeting the Queen. Of course, I could do nothing about the facts of the matter. People already lived there and this would be the truth. The land could not be claimed for Spain. Unfortunately, the Queen did not see it that way. What we described to her were savages, tribal people, not sophisticated governed people. "What claim did they have to the land," she would say? Who was I to argue with the Queen? She wanted us to stake a claim for the new land so stake it we did."

This is the dilemma as I see it. The land was inhabited when we arrived therefore the land was not ours for the taking. This creates an imbalance in the land between the people. The people will have discord when an injustice is done one to the other. This is how I see it from here and this is why there is continued unhappiness between the Indians and the white race of the world.

The Indians occupied the land and it should have been to them to give the land to the white race as they saw fit, sharing it as they liked, with compensation to them given as agreed upon. This unreconciled dispute must be rectified to bring peace in the land. Now, what can be done at this later time to reconcile with the Indian culture? It is not an easy solution but they must not be confined as a reservations. The nature of this act segregates this people from the rest of society and makes them feel like outcasts. They must be free to integrate into the rest of the society and to be received as equals in the land. How can this be achieved?"

"This must be considered together with the tribes which remain in the Indian nation today. talks must begin to reconcile he tribes with the rest of the people so that peace may come to the land. Do you now see how old this problem is to date? It is 519 years old. It is time to put this energy imbalance to rest Diane."

"How do we do it," I asked? "What needs to be done and who needs to be the representative to achieve this peaceful negotiation?"

Your husband is the one to do it for he is known by the Indian people. He is a good, respectful and honorable man and he is the one to resolve this imbalance."

I then asked, "Is Alejandro going to instruct him in this matter?"

"'Indeed he will instruct your husband. But there is the matter of prayer on this subject.

It must be bathed in prayer in order to achieve it."

"What recommendations are there to this end?"

"We will post this information on your new website. We will tell the world that the world is in turmoil due to the treatment of people in their own lands by those who wish to acquire the land or its natural resources against the will of the inhabitants of the land. This creates great imbalances of energy in the world and it is enough to destroy it. What must happen now is that the world's people must come together in repentance before the Father of Heaven for the sins of the fathers who have taken that which was not theirs against the will of the people who live in the lands in which such resources or land was taken. Repentance must take place around the globe for this turmoil to end."

"When do I speak about this?"

"You must get your website up and running. Let's make the site an informational site at the moment giving the truth about what the Father of Heaven says about the conflict in the world and what is causing it, and what it will take to resolve it."

"We must get the site up as soon as possible before the world is completely out of balance."

"I see," I responded. "Am I to share this story as it happened?"

"Yes and no. We will tell the story another way. Would you like to record it now."

"Yes, I will."

"Alejandro would have you say this in your first blog on your site."

"This truth is being brought to you from the heavens as it were, coming to me vibrationally from those who do not share a body at this time but who do witness all that is done here.

It is this voice from the heavens which shares our love for this world and her people enough to wish to assist us in our life dilemmas. It is certain that without this assistance now, we will destroy what is good and right for all of us. It is apparent, from the civil unrest around the globe, the world is in peril. If you are interested in knowing why, the conversation must begin and it must begin now. There is a remedy, but it is necessary to implement it quickly if hope is to be restored that peace can again exist in the world.

Now those of you who are convinced the world is ending. You are not helping the situation with that kind of thinking, in fact, you are inhibiting the growth of new ideas, new remedies, and a resolution of the matter. You must return to the Father of Heaven and ask, "what is the solution of the matter?, and begin to do what you hear to do. To hear and to act is to be change agents who love the world, who love the Father of Heaven, and who are willing to do what is given to them to do to bring about resolution of the conflicts in the world between nations today.

Understand this, what you are seeing now in your world is due to an age old problem of covetousness. Now this may be too simplistic for your minds however this is because you do not understand the power which enters in when people do not obey the guidance given to them by the Supreme Being which is how to live in the land at peace with one another. There are some standards of conduct which were handed down to mankind and though they are attributed to only one religion, they apply to all religions, for without them, you have exactly what exists today, chaos."

In order to restore order in the world today, all people must return to these standards of conduct, all people. Not just some while others continue as they do behind the scenes, stealing from everyone else, taking what they want from government collected funds to run their own businesses and families, but all must begin to obey these standards of conduct. If there are those who continue to take what is not theirs, whether it is land, oil, natural resources, or even woman and children for their own pleasure, the land will not heal."

"You may say that it is impossible that such behavior is responsible for all of the world's troubles at this time, but you would be wrong. All are inter connected for you are all energy, as such is the land, the inhabitants in the land, and that which you use for life, etc. It is all energy.

One contributes to the state of the other."

"So let me open the discussion here and now. What must happen to restore the earth to its pristine condition if the problem is that mankind has discarded the rules of play if you will, for life here on earth? What steps must be taken by her people? If the nations are throwing out their leaders, what then? Who will lead them to behave in accordance with the rules of conduct as established by the One who created the experience in the first place. There must be order, for without order there is only one other choice . . . chaos. Are the people on the planet now willing to submit to the Creator of the planet experience to have peace?

"If so, keep listening in. You will receive additional guidance as to what you must do to get there and then, spread the word. Engage in the discussion about how to bring it about around the globe. It is necessary and the sooner the better from the looks of things globally."

"You may leave your comments here. If it contributes to the greater good, your comments will remain for all to see. If your comments are ridiculing, and improper, they will be removed. Finally, come back for the ongoing conversation. See what there is to be done and how you too can contribute to a better world. Do your part. That is what we are here to do each one of us doing our part to make the world a better place. So be it."

"I got it. Thank you, Christopher. Where are we now?"

"That looks very good Diane. Post that on your website and let the people create the solution.

This is what we are allowing them to do. Meditate and create. We are also encouraging them to return individually to the Father of Heaven rather than simply steering them to a church, we are telling them to return to Him in their own behaviors for they are accountable to Him directly.

They will not face the church when they return to Heaven, but Him."

"Excellent point, Christopher. Well thank you again. Are you free to go home now?

Or were you already there?"

"No, I was here, where I still am until I leave, and with your light, and allowing me to do this work, I can leave having contributed something back to the world other than conquering a land which was not mine to conquer. Now I am free to go. Thank you Diane for sharing your love with the world and the truth.. Without it, the world will perish in its present state. The energy will not return to its former glory and it will be tumultuous like other planets you see "out there". The energy brought to those planets became so tumultuous that life became impossible. Let's do what we can to undo the conflict here so that doesn't happen on earth."

"I will do what I can by telling the truth. Then the people need to do their parts and return to Alejandro. Blessings to my Father in heaven.

Peace to the earth and blessings to those who help to create a solution for this undoing of love."

"Adieu Diane. Nice to see you," said Christopher Columbus.

"And you Christopher. Love to you too."

Isaac Asimov

January 2, 1920 – April 6, 1992

Today is March 26, 2011 and though it is a few weeks since my last documented transition testimony, I have been helping many others between recorded dates. Some were to be included and others not. Today it was Isaac Asimov who came through, another person who I did not know very much about but here he was nonetheless. Apparently, Isaac was an accomplished writer and as a Professor had taught biochemistry at Boston University. He was popular as a writer of science fiction with some of his book titles being I, Robot, The Human Body and he even wrote a book entitled Asimov's Guide to the Bible. Interesting!

I asked Asimov where he was currently to which he replied, "I am definitely free, not in the body, not in darkness, free . . . amazing grace. Isaac is my first name. I am here to educate you about space, are you ready?"

"Yes, I am ready Isaac."

"Okay, let's begin," he said. Space and time exist simultaneously thus it is possible to get published in one day."

I asked Isaac to show me."

"First, you need your contract with the publisher. Then we will attach all of the energies of "COMPLETION" to the contract. We will add the energy of "RUSH JOB" and "24 HOURS to COMPLETION."

I asked Isaac if there were any other energies to attach.

"Yes, "INTEGRITY OF THE DOCUMENT" will be added – "NO EDITS TO MATERIAL", only initial caps, typos and punctuation and such, as you deem necessary. Nothing else."

"Alright then, anything else Isaac?"

Isaac said, "SECURITY" – the energy of guaranteeing security of the company who publishes you, and your family. Add the energy of "PUBLICATION DATE" to the contract. Alejandro will choose the publication date."

Then I heard Alejandro Himself say, "May 11, 2011. I am taking back the number 11.

Secure this date to the contract. When you get the contract print it, lay your hands on it, attaching these energies for all time and eternity, all in Alejandro's name.

5-11-2011 add up to the number 11. PLATFORM PLAN: Add the energies of 'PROPULSION FORWARD TO IMPLEMENTATION' and 'FRUITION' –

'BRING THE PLAN TO FRUITION, 'CAPITAL – CAPITAL TO IMPLEMENT THE PLAN', 'TIMING IS NOW', 'FULFILLMENT', 'RELEASE OF AGENT TO ASSIST DIANE NOW!'.

This was the end of the transmission.

Ricardo Gonzalo Pedro Montalban y Merino

November 25, 1920 – January 14, 2009

The soul who would come to me on March 26, 2011 was one whom I had seen in movies and who had a distinctive accent. He was unique and different from most actors that I saw in television programs as a kid. Ricardo was Spanish having been born in Mexico City he came to the United States as an actor and was well cast as a Spanish gentleman. Having been quite handsome he often had the part of the leading man in his films. Ricardo Montalban gave me some insight about these things when he came through to me on this day.

"Tell me your name please," I asked as I felt the next soul's presence today.

"I am here young lady awaiting a time to speak to you. My name is Ricardo Montalban.

I was an actor for many years in Hollywood. I was an advocate for my homeland country as well, Mexico. It was my dream to see the two countries merging their ideals and their people to be as one, in love for all. I am not talking about a loss of sovereignty of the United States of America, but rather an acceptance of one another as equals in life. There are many Mexican people who are hardworking, good, kind, family loving people. But there are also many talented, professional and intelligent Mexican people. My hope was to build a good relationship between both peoples but I was shunned by Hollywood elite who did not wish to have me do such a thing. They were not interested in building bridges, quite the contrary. But for the token Mexican actor, they were not depicted in the film industry as heroes, seldom shown at all."

Ricardo continued, "This bias was typical throughout the industry. My organization which I established to demonstrate appreciation for those who were Hispanic in the industry, Nosotros, was ignored for the most part, but for the notice that they gave me by blackmailing me from parts for my establishment of such an organization in Hollywood. They were not interested in supporting it. They were not interested in me making a big deal out of their selectiveness when it came to those of Mexican descent."

"Now I know that they have acknowledged this person or that person occasionally, giving a nod just to keep the critics at bay, but honestly, they are not who you think they are. They are self-interested, self-motivated, and selfish men and women who run Hollywood. They are not in the business for the purpose of uplifting America or its citizens. They do not care about this at all. In fact it is just the opposite. They are only interested in what makes them rich.

"Again, you can find a person here or there who has stood the test of time against them only to make a few films with a wholesome message, but those films are rare these days. See for yourself. Go to the movies for 10 straight weeks and rate the movies yourself as to whether or not they are uplifting to the moral code of America. I dare say that you will not find five movies of such quality in 10 weeks' time of movie releases."

"My point is that Hollywood no longer exists to benefit the people of the country. They exist to make money. Pure and simple. Anything else is just not the truth. They are pushing agendas now, not just entertaining, which is why you see so much of certain behavior being advocated in films, sitcoms, and popular television shows."

"Why are they doing this," you ask? "This is a question for them to answer. Ask Hollywood producers why they only select certain films, demanding certain acts be added to "spice it up", and certain language too. Ask them why they do not produce the spirited and uplifting movie which would teach morale certainty and courageous behavior? Ask them. But you will have to press them for the answers as they shy away from being exposed as to who they really are."

It was my turn to ask a question. "Mr. Ricardo, before you continue, I must ask, "Where are you? Are you in eternity already? Have you been asked to come to speak with me?

If so, is this message for my book, or is the book of The Trilogy of complete?

What does Alejandro say about that?"

"I am happy to answer your question Diane. I am here, in the darkness but as we speak, my light is coming up. How did I get here? By not standing up against the flood of evil which overwhelmed my industry and as a result, the people of the country. I supported the industry by working in it therefore I am guilty of what they do to the country's moral condition so say those who lord it over all who are in the darkness. They do have a point however, for I did not serve the God of Heaven. I served myself and my desire to do good in the world. Quite different than doing that which He would have me do in the world. Upon my death, I was met with those who knew the truth and they used it to entrap me here eternally. But for you, and your willingness to help others understand that the God of Heaven does not judge His own, I would most likely have spent eternity here just like the rest of them here."

"I am here because Alejandro is allowing me to speak with you now for it is important to understand the nature of the people in Hollywood. They turned from doing what is good and right and to make a profit, began to depict that which is not good. They did it for no other reason than to make more money. This puts them in a difficult spot with the Almighty, for it is not His will that His own would use their talents, influence and opportunity to denigrate the society in which His people live.. So it is that I am here to tell you that unless Hollywood does soon repent, it will begin to see what

Alejandro can do to bring it about. They may soon find themselves out of business for it is upon the heavens to bring about healing on the planet, and Hollywood is one of the worst offenders of teaching immorality to the people in the land."

"Now here is the distinction between choosing for yourself to try a thing in the world, and a wealthy, organization as such promoting evil, programming the world's people with repeated acts of evil as though it was normal, and acceptable for all in the world and rewarding people who portray evil with accolades from the community of actors and actresses and giving their winners statues. One is in itself innocent at fist. Evil exists in the world. To examine evil is one thing. To participate in evil is quite another and seen differently by the Creator of Heaven, for He has shown us what is good and right as an example to us. We are to choose accordingly, and it is within each of us to know what is right. When we choose evil against our nature, our very soul testifies against us. This is what is happening to those who are with me here in the darkness. Our very souls testify against us as to our choices in the world."

"Now you may say what evil did I do, "Ricardo lamented? I do I had other gods before Him. I chose to work for a community which was promoting that which was anti-god and anti-family, anti-marriage, and in favor of promiscuity, broken family units, violence and murder in films, rampant drug use, and immorality, and that is just to name a few. They do not have a moral compass any longer in Hollywood and I chose to work there all of my adult days."

"Needless to say, upon my death, my soul had a few choice words for me and I could not refute them. How could I? My soul was right. I knew not the God of Heaven."

"Hold on Ricardo. Alejandro is here to speak with you. Alejandro, welcome to our conversation. I bless you with love and respect. Thank you for joining us."

"Ricardo is telling you the truth Diane. He did work in Hollywood regardless of what he saw that they were doing. Though he attempted to do some good for his people there, it was not allowed and it cost him some work as a result. I am aware that he was a man who had a belief structure, however, when he had an opportunity to make a difference in the midst of Hollywood, he feared to do anything. He missed his destiny as a result. I cannot use a man who fears other men more than Me and I am not one to fear if you are close to Me. I will protect you and bless your life and assist you in accomplishing your destinies. I cannot work with those who do not seek Me however and, I do not. My hope was that Ricardo would step up and be counted for righteousness' sake in Hollywood, making a difference, but he caved preferring to get his livelihood from them than from Me."

"Do you see the problem, asked Alejandro?" Men choose other gods before Me out of fear of loss of livelihood. They would rather continue even though it is against their nature to do a thing, than to stand up against the tide of mediocrity and make a difference. This is unacceptable to Me. They allow a piece of paper, a contract, to determine their future out of fear of retribution against them by an industry which is supposed to be about entertainment, not threats and bullying against the very people who assist them in making their money. I see all and know all and nothing is hidden from Me. They have long gotten away with intimidation of those who seek to work in their industry but I moving My hand now to put a stop to this kind of treatment in the world today by any "employer", if you will. I will no longer allow My people to be bullied and abused for the sake of work. I will no longer allow My people to be used as slaves for some other agenda which is not even known to them by those who take their souls as payment for the jobs they are given. This is no longer acceptable to Me and I will be the one to stop it from happening any further."

Test Me in this and you will find that I am quite capable of doing that which I promise to do. the times they are a changing now. My people have invited Me back into their lives, and I am back. Now you will see how mighty I am to do that which I promise to do on behalf of those that I call My own.."

"Blessings be to the Father of Heaven, and may the love of His people be His reward for assisting us in the earth to be protected from those who do evil. May it be done for His name's sake in all the earth. Alejandro!"

Ricardo had been listening and now spoke. "I am in awe Diane. I have never before heard the voice of the Almighty, and I am in awe. I must now speak to Him if He will hear me.

Father of Life, I do beseech you to hear my petition before you. I do humbly beseech you and to hear my petition before you. I do humbly beseech you and ask for forgiveness for I did not serve you in my life in the body. I did not lift up your name in the place where I worked where so much was done to undo civilization, making it much less civilized in many ways.. I humbly beseech you for forgiveness for all that I did that was against You and for all that I did not do that would have been for you. Please forgive Me Alejandro and allow Me to come home."

"I have heard your petition," said Alejandro, and now I will speak."

"Many do come to me in death to ask for forgiveness and I am accommodating however, I do not do so without a quid pro quo. Now you will serve Me, Ricardo, and you will do so in this way. When you arrive in Heaven, you are to begin to send energy to the people in Hollywood to receive My daughter Diane, for she has the truth to tell them about what their business is doing to their own upon their deaths, causing them to become trapped and unable to go home. You must send energy to the Hollywood empire opening the doors for her to speak there, to redirect them in their work back to what is good and right. If you will do this, I will allow your return. Speak and I will listen to your answer."

"This is more than acceptable to me," Ricardo answered, "that I might serve you now."

"I agree to send energy of cooperation to Hollywood, that they would entertain listening to what Diane Freeman has to say to them. I will serve You in this way for as long as it is required."

"Now you may return home," replied Alejandro. "I will see to it that you comply with this agreement for all eternity"

I spoke at that time to Ricardo whom I sensed was still near.

"Yes, Diane. I was asked to wait for you to return because I need to tell you what I will do for you when I return to the heavens. It is upon me to assist you in some way and so I am promising you right now that I will work towards Hollywood agents receiving you for the purposes of getting your letters to Michael Jackson's mother, Priscilla Presley, and then also Heath Ledger's wife, Michelle. You must get your letters off to the particular agents and tell them whether they notice their clients or not, the book will be published. Tell them that you have attempted to reach them and are denied access. You are leaving this in the hands of their agents and if you do not hear from them giving you an opportunity to speak with their clients, you will move ahead without their input. This is permissible by Alejandro. So, this week Diane, send out another letter to each of these people's agents and the rest is up to them. I will clear the way for them to receive the letters. That is all. Thank you for assisting me to get home. Bless you and yours. Adieu. Also, thank you for loving my home of Mexico.

I see that you and your husband do love visiting her. Thank you for treating her people with respect and honor. They are good people. Til then."

"It is our pleasure. We only pray that Mexico will stabilize and that her people will have an awakening that they too must return to Him who can change the nation bringing peace to the people. They must rise up against the tide of evil. They must fight the good fight. If we don't fight the good fight, joining with Alejandro for success, we lose."

"I do agree Ricardo. I will pray for them as well. Bye for now."

Benjamin Franklin

January 17, 1706 – April 17, 1790

What do we really know about the men who have served as our Presidents in the United States of America? Is it possible that we really know very little due to the destruction of the truth by those who wish to erase history as we know it and make it something else entirely?

How are we to learn from past mistakes if the public record of the history of our leaders in the land is erased? Where are the history books written by the men of this time concerning the workings of government for their age? It is surely something to think about for the past may be rewritten before we can do anything to stop it.

Alejandro, our true Commander-in-Chief if you will, reached out to me on March 27, 2011, and He requested that I let a particular soul pass who had come presenting its energy to me.

"They have been waiting all day Diane. Please assist them and then I will bless your time at your gym."

Alright then, I asked, "Who do we have with us?" I thought I heard Benjamin Franklin.

"Benjamin Franklin is the correct name Diane. I was a Statesman, President, but also an inventor. I have something to say to you about what you and Dick are embarking on."

I remarked, "It remains to be seen if Alejandro does do what is necessary for such a lofty idea to come into being. It takes a lot of money to even campaign for this position any more, sadly."

"Yes, well let me tell you a few things about the process. First, he will have to submit his name for Alejandro to create the means by which

he could win. He must submit his name. This will create quite a stir
for none of the others know his name and those who control the others
don't know him either. Do not worry about the controlling factions to
out there. You are not a member of their elitist membership and you
do not intend to become one so don't engage in discussions with them
either. Leave everything to Alejandro. Submit your name Richard. In
order to raise the capital necessary to support you, your name must
be heard by those who hear Alejandro. Then He can move His hand
upon them to submit to Him in supporting you. It is not upon you
to raise the money by yourself for you are connected to the God of
Heaven and He is mighty to persuade His own to do His will. Watch
it happen once you submit your name.

The money will come. The donations will come. The heavens are
moving ahead with His plans to promote you to serve Him but there
are a few steps left for you to do. If you are now asking "when should
I submit my name?", this is a good question. Review the submission
process for the Presidency and find out when the last date possible
is for submission of a candidate. That is when you will submit.
This is the power of the heavens to create that which is Alejandro's
will. We do not want to give the opposition time to create a defense
against you.

They cannot find anything to oppose you and it will frustrate the hell
out of them. This is good.

We can keep them occupied looking for something wrong with you
while time passes them by towards the election. We will raise support
for you not just monetarily but in moral and electoral votes for you.
The people want a change now for it is certain that they do not want
to lose their country. They will want to find out who you are and we
will be ready for them."

"Take some time now and write a few words about why it is that you
would want to be President of the United States of America. Begin

to think about it. Why should you be better for the country than Barack Obama? What is it that is happening to this nation that you are opposed to in the leadership in the land? What can you do better than they are doing?

What is your background in leadership? What do you know about domestic and foreign affairs that would make you a good leader? These questions will come forth and more.

They do not have the right to pry into your private affairs, but they will try. You are not required to answer any private questions about your family business, your children particularly, or your wife. They must focus on you and who you are and why you are running for President."

"You are being asked to consider these questions now prayerfully and Alejandro will guide you in appropriate answers to each of them. It is time to consider these things as this election will soon be upon the nation and We, those of Us in Heaven, are not about to let you lose, for if you do, We lose the nation to the usurpers. This cannot happen."

"Know that the power of Alejandro is with you to succeed. That is all you need and to obey Him in a few areas such that the process can commence. Do not worry. Do not fret. You are not the one who is to make this happen.. You are the one who is chosen to act when it does happen on your behalf. That is enough Again, Alejandro will do the rest."

"That is it for now Diane. Stay tuned for more as time goes by. Take care of your husband. The Black Cherry syrup is an excellent expectorant and will serve him well. Three tablespoons every 3 hours, particularly if he awakens in the night.. Take it. It cannot hurt him. It may serve you to take it as well but just 2 tablespoons every 4 hours for one day only. That should take care of your cough. Avoid cheese as much as you can. We know that it is a challenge when you are vegetarian. Adieu."

"Thank you for this information. Blessings to you and to all who are with you. Love to Alejandro."

Dr. Albert Schweitzer

January 14, 1875 – September 4, 1965

Dr. Schweitzer was born in Alsace, Germany, a small town. His father was a Lutheran pastor.

I mention this because many of us have had some exposure to some truth about heaven as a child. He was no different. He became a Doctorate of Philosophy and then went on to serve on the pastoral staff in a church in Strasbourg, Germany and earned an advanced degree in theology.

He authored books on theology and was quite successful. But I believe he had an epiphany which led him to study medicine with the plan to go to Africa and to practice "the religion of love" as he put it. This was noble but would not make him popular today with the Elitists who want nothing to do with love being promulgated in the world. Allow me to share a bit of what Dr. Schweitzer had to say to me from beyond.

The date was March 27, 2011. Albert Schweitzer began by saying, "I was a scientist of the highest order of life on earth and yet, I dare say I missed much of the truth."

I asked Albert if his story was for posting elsewhere or was it for my book here along with the others.

"Alejandro says I am to tell you the truth about science. There are those who control the curing of diseases, the information concerning greater health and the remedies to avoid illness. Yes, you can find some who are promoting wellness but it is not your government."

"Your government plans to control not only who is well but who gets treated of the sick among you. Don't think for a minute that they do *not* have an agenda to do this. They do and before long facial recognition programs will be securely in place to stop you should you attempt to get treated by changing your names and of course those who lord it over you in your electorate will be exempt from compliance for they will cite examples of the need for immediate treatment of those who serve the government."

"The Illuminati have turned the tables on those of you who worked hard to excel, becoming educated at your own expense and working half of your days to finance Elitist families who do not work. Why should they? You do, that is enough for they see themselves as gods upon the planet usurping authority from the One, true God and His people draining your energy and life force to oppose them. They have decided they have no more need for the peons on the planet."

"Therefore they are inciting civil unrest around the globe and when they finish there, they will bring it here to America. S.E.I.U. is only one of their organizations. They have many, many of their created groups round the globe. Why do you think they needed all of your money? to finance it. All of the training, the programming, and the weapons cost money. Why do you think they want to sell arms across the border? If you think it is merely for the drug lords, you are mistaken. It is much, much more. They have made agreements with these men too. Sell our weapons and you can sell your drugs."

"The same thing is going on around the world. Quid pro quo. Evil for evil. Greed leading to destruction. It is the same old story and do you ever wonder why? Your President has been usurping your power since his inauguration, breaking the laws, and writing his own.

Now he is publicly overriding the Constitution in an attempt to incite Americans.

"I tell you the truth, the minute any of those who oppose him take to the streets, he will stage a terrorist threat and start arresting you all."

"So do not protest. This is ineffective at best. Rather repent and pray for Divine intervention.:"

This was the end of this transmission.

Alexander Haig

December 2, 1924 – February 20, 2010

"Tell me your name." It is April, 2011, this must be the year for souls to transition and this day too would prove interesting and enlightening to me. I asked the soul present to exert its' energy so that I could hear them. I thought I heard a name. "Alexander Haig?"

I looked his name up before continuing and learned that he had been Secretary of State under Ronald Reagan and White House Chief of Staff to both Richard Nixon and Gerald Ford.

This just could be fascinating.

"Yes, for I was the one who served Richard Nixon. I am here to tell you something about the Reptilian race. They are definitely here and we have no way of sending them back to where they came from. In fact they like it here. The atmosphere above the ground is not so suitable to them and so you see the suit they wore in the 50's whenever they came above ground. They have perfected this suit now."

"Yes, I know."

"Well, it seems that you are troubled by their presence."

"Weren't you Alexander?"

"Yes, but in a situation where you can do nothing about those who live on the planet with you, you do the best you can. You certainly cannot kill them all."

I asked Alexander how many of these other beings were there who are of the original warring nature.

144

He answered then, "About 5 million."

"Where are they", I wanted to know?

"Underground," he said.

"How far underground," I asked?

Surprisingly he answered, "That is classified but as President and First Lady you would soon know. They manipulate world governments for one with their ability to create media. The television and the computer. They are technologically advanced."

"Do we stay here or move them? Or do we create a new world for ourselves?"

Alexander then offered, "It is a difficult problem, one that is being worked on as we speak, the solution."

"How long do we wait. They pollute our water, our food and eat children and rape people to steal their energy. I have a difficult time with these things."

"Believe me, I know Diane. But you can appeal to Alejandro now and ask that he do something. To love all is one thing but to allow some to take full advantage of another allowing them to fully suffer is another."

"The people have to turn back to Him and He will help them," I told him.

"You must press on with your book. It will awaken many but do not speak of the Reptilians."

"Anything else Alexander," I asked.

"Know that we are working on the problem. Do not worry or concern yourself daily with it.

It takes time to awaken the people and then to implement the solutions. Stay connected as you have and know He will handle all things."

"So be it."

Elizabeth Taylor

February 27 1932 – March 23, 2011

This next soul would be someone whom I had some interest in watching during their life. She was rich, beautiful, troubled, yet admired and followed by many. When I asked the soul that was present to identify themselves I heard the following.

"Elizabeth, Diane. Elizabeth Taylor. Now we can talk."

"Yes," I said. "It was difficult to listen to you while I was walking around and then driving. Is everything alright with you?"

"Not yet," she answered, "but I am hoping that it will be very soon. Though we never met Diane, I have heard many things about you in a very short time. Those who have been waiting to speak with you are many and there is talk here that you have assisted souls already in transitioning from here to heaven. Is this true?"

"Yes, it is true," I told her.

"Then it is my honor to meet you for I did not know that many people who were either not in Hollywood or otherwise connected in some manner and I fear that this was unfortunate.

Of course, I did marry Larry Fortensky and he was considered an "outsider", but that did not last long and I was back to my old connections. It is a pleasure to meet you my dear.

It is sad that it has to be in this manner where we cannot see each other "eye to eye" as it were. I came to see you at the request of Alejandro, for I was needed to assist you in directing you towards Valentino. I was chosen for my taste in women's attire. I don't know if you knew anything about me but I did have a taste for the good stuff when it came to clothing. I had much experience with trying the many different designers and I thought that the one that would suit you best would be Valentino."

"Thank you Elizabeth," I replied. "I loved what I saw and now I love my new suit. I have never purchased anything to wear that cost that much money, ever! Not even my wedding dress cost that much money." Now what I was referring to here is related to a very small inheritance that I received from my mother which allowed me to follow Alejandro's guidance in choosing something for myself that did not come from TJ Maxx or some other discount store where I was a regular shopper. I wanted nice designer things but felt guilty to even go to the store where things were much more expensive. I could justify buying things that were nice enough and costing me less however so that is what I had a habit of doing. After Alejandro told me to find a designer that I liked and to go and buy a dress that I loved, I did it and that is what I shared with Elizabeth Taylor here.

"I saw how much it pained you to hand over so much money for the clothing but Diane, you will have more money that you can spend as soon as your message gets out. I believe that there is talk that it will need to be made into a movie so that many will see it worldwide."

"I asked her if I should allow a particular publisher named Tate to publish it?"

Elizabeth stated, "This I will need to ask. I do not know. What do you think?"

"I need to send them the full manuscript and they did do right by Cliff Graham who wrote, *Call of Duty*. I need some assurances from them and I don't want to pay them $4,000 because I need my money right now."

"I can see that you do. We will have to get funds to you as soon as possible so that you have money with which to promote your book and website."

"How may I assist you Elizabeth," I asked.

"Good question. I am here aren't I? My, that sounds terrible. I hope that you will heal quickly from that Diane. I certainly had my health issues in the body. Anyway, I would like to move on and go home but I feel tired, I don't have much energy. I also feel remorse for I did not do anything to serve Alejandro in my life. I feel regret for not having lifted up the name of God in my career, or in my personal life to my children, or in any way really. I regret not doing anything in particular . . ."

Something occurred just now and I lost the connection with Elizabeth until the morning.

"I have been here all night waiting for you Diane. Do not worry. Where can I go?"

"Let me apologize to you please. My daughter came in last night from a date and we began to chat. It was quite late as it was already late when you and I were talking so I needed to move on too."

"Can we finish now," Elizabeth asked?

"Of course," I answered, "and to that I am here. You were saying that you had regrets. You regretted not serving Alejandro in your life. You regretted not lifting up His name or sharing Him with your children.

"Yes, Diane. That was me acknowledging you. Amazing isn't it? That we can communicate and I no longer have a body."

"Yes, it is fascinating. So few believe still but it is coming and then we can evolve again into a greater understanding of our nature."

"I began to tell you of my regrets", Elizabeth offered. There are so many as you can see. I also regret not having assisted Michael Jackson more in his life. He gravitated towards me for some reason and also Brooke Shields early on who he adored. He was insecure in many ways. I suppose that I could have helped him more but in what way? I did not have the connection to Alejandro which you have and that is really what he needed to encourage him in a world which is not only filled with those who are greedy and manipulative but there is danger here too.

Some do not allow you your freedom any longer once you are in their hands for success, if you know what I mean."

I answered that indeed, I did know what she meant.

"I was a victim to that and I lost a part of myself when I gave myself over to that scene. I was glorified for all of the wrong reasons. Beauty is not a characteristic of a noble person Diane. It just is. I was worshipped for my beauty so as I aged, what did I have? There needs to be something more in a woman's life aside from her beauty due to the nature of life and the aging process. Beauty escapes you and without a way to explore other aspects of your character, you end up with very little at the end of your life. So make certain that you do follow the suggestions given to you for developing your entire nature. Take some art lessons at some point. Learn to sing. Play the piano. This is the greater nature of who you are."

"Thank you Elizabeth. You are lovely, inside and out. I will explore those things. Perhaps you can see however at the moment, someone keeps me so busy to do much even in my house to keep things tidy."

"Yes, I see that you are very busy right now attempting to be published. This will happen and you will have much to do but in the time that is given to you to rest, spend it on yourself a bit.

Your husband will need to develop the other parts of his self as well. He is not merely a golfer, but he too is a writer. He should begin to write."

This is good news and I was curious as to what might be his topic of interest asking Elizabeth if she knew.

"Ask him", she answered. "He knows a lot of things but he is particularly interested in world politics. He knows the law which he has practiced for years and could write something anecdotal or he might write something about the game of golf as a lawyer sees it. Both of you need to expand yourselves so that as you age, you have activities that interest you besides going to the gym, and having coffee."

"Indeed, you are correct. Elizabeth, let me say this. Are you beginning to see that Alejandro does not judge us for our experiences in the world? We are here to experience different aspects of ourselves as we interact with emotions from other people, as we handle different challenges of the nature of the world, to determine if we can evolve to something even better than what we are now and all of it is determined during the experience here. When we die, if not before, we send the emotional energy back to its origin, light, and move on. Alejandro will welcome us back. Although He wants to participate in the experience of life with us, and we can achieve our perfect destinies by remaining in Him, seeking Him and receiving guidance from Him; we are able to return if we ask and know that we are forgiven for all things."

"This is comforting Diane, I cannot tell you. I wish to have my own children understand these things. Will you promise me one thing?

Try to contact my daughter and give her a copy of your book from me. Tell her that I did indeed ask you to give it to her in memory of me for I want her to know that I found my way home and that you were the one to help me to get there.

All is well with my soul. Tell her Diane. Then she can tell my sons."

"I can do that. I will wait until I am published because it is difficult at best to get in touch with these people who are celebrity status."

"Okay, Diane. I trust that you will then. I can feel your energy is pure and you are trying to do whatever you can to be published. This may give you a bit of access which you do not have now. Keep trying. I see that your book will be published by a famous book publisher and you will gain much notoriety in Hollywood for the things revealed in your book. Some will like it. Others will not. It is the nature of who they are that will judge it. Remain true to yourself. You are not judged by man but by Alejandro."

"This I do know. Hard to keep in mind sometimes but I will remember what you have said to me. Are you comfortable with the knowledge of who you are Elizabeth? Are you feeling better about going home?"

"Yes, Diane, and I am looking forward to it. This is no place for a soul to be. It is empty here and I can see that others are very unhappy here, trapped, not knowing anything about why they are here or how to escape the madness of being lost."

I responded that the book has to be published and read by many so that others can assist all of these souls in going home. There are too many for one person to assist. I must get the book out, maybe it becomes a movie?"

"I see that too Diane. Your book will be made into a movie. There would be many stars Who would participate playing the parts of departed actors and actresses, telling their stories in brief vignettes each. The other side could be represented as you see it, with the orbs floating in the darkness in the great vastness that is this dimension, but with colors within those orbs that are new, fading as times goes by, to being just a blip of light instead of a vibrant being. The light that is left by visiting souls is like a tracer of light. It fades over time but is renewed as you interact with the souls here giving hope again to those who are here. They find it and wait and then they grab onto it hoping to be released by you and Alejandro."

"Is there anything else you can tell me Elizabeth please?"

"There is a darkness here of another kind. It is a darkness that is not of Alejandro.

It is something else. It is not embodied but it is pure evil. It speaks evil to those who are here causing them much sorrow and anguish about their lives on earth and what they did, or did not do."

"Elizabeth, is that evil you speak of capable of manifesting on earth to people here?"

"I think so. It is what is called the shadow people by many who have seen them. Their intent is for evil. They wish to steer men to do evil. I hear them saying murder them, hate them, and destroy life."

"Are these eternal beings," I asked?

"Apparently so," she answered. "They have been here since the beginning of time."

"I feel for these poor souls who are trapped there enduring such torment," I answered.

Elizabeth then said to me, "You must help those who wish to make a movie about all of this understand that these beings are what they are for no understandable reason. They just are.

They are not human nor were they ever human. They do not exist in the world because of Alejandro for why would He choose such a thing for His people? They exist because they do.

The power of His people have is to remain in Him and He can keep you from them. This is His admonition to His people, remain in Me, and I will remain in you. Apart from Me, I can do nothing."

My thoughts were, "So the Universe and our world is filled with many things but our experience here can be had and we can take all of the good of it with us when we leave, but to leave, we have to remain in Him so that we are not trapped by those who know how to grab our minds, and enslave us?"

"Yes, this is true. The shadowy beings know how to cause much anguish to those who do not know who they are and they spend all of eternity there doing it to those who become trapped.

They are also eternal."

"What you are saying is that there is no particular reason for why they are doing this. They are just what they are and it is best that we do not get trapped in that dimension when we die or we will experience mind manipulation and torture of our being eternally."

"Correct.", Elizabeth continued. "Alejandro has attempted to make it very clear to His people that they are to remain connected to Him while having this body experience and yet His people feel that this staying connected is only to control them and to take away their freedoms. This is not the truth. The exact opposite is true. Without remaining in Him, you will lose your way dimensionally and be pulled into that dark dimension as your light diminishes with death. They can't wait for you to get there."

"It sounds ominous if you ask me. Not fun. I don't want to see that place."

"Not a worry for you Diane or your family. You are protected for you have given much to the cause of helping His people find their way home and thus He can use us to bring new energy to the earth and wake even more of His own. This is how it should be. We help each other have the experience and keep each other safe while having the experience."

"I love this. Wow." I said.

"Quite challenging for some to embrace but it is the truth. The dark side exists and it is like hell to be here for there is no place for your soul to go. You can roam in the darkness but you are apt to meet the dark lords and torture awaits you, demeaning, degrading, deliberate torture of the mind. They know no decorum of behavior. They are just evil."

"Elizabeth, and these are the shadowy figures which have been seen on particular video cameras when these unprepared men or women go into "haunted" spaces and capture a shadowy figure on camera who can manipulate the energy of a man and cause him to go "blank" as it were?"

"Yes, but they are limited in what they can do here. They only come when summoned."

"What," I asked. "What does that mean?"

"If you summon forth the darkness it will come and it then has been given permission to be here.

It will stay as long as it is given access by the one who summoned it."

"Are there those in positions of authority in the land who are summoning forth these evil beings to do evil to others on the planet?"

Elizabeth hesitated and said, "Probably, but I am forbidden to talk about these things Diane.

Just know that they are evil and should not be summoned by anyone. If they are, that person is in jeopardy of losing their soul to the darkness, and their life too at that moment that they summon forth evil."

"Not good then."

"Not good," Elizabeth agreed. "Let's move on Diane. I want to tell you that I will go to heaven and open the doors to your having a relationship with Valentino such that you are able to give input to how you would like your attire to be for purposes of representing Alejandro. If you are spending lots of money with a particular designer, they are willing to do some favors for you in creating individual designs just for you. This will make you even more unique. So I ask that a door be opened unto you for this purpose. I see that you are unable to find earrings to wear that are not pierced. I will also ask that you are able to find a designer to work with who can make gold earrings for you that are not pierced for gold is the lightest of the metals and the easiest to carry on the ear lobes."

"Yes, I agree, I need this as earrings can be stunning particularly with long hair."

"Good. I am happy to be able to assist you in this way Diane. Your light has empowered me enough to make my journey home and home I will go soon. Let me add this. I will also ask that your agent reaches out to you within the next week. The next week, so prepare yourself. Watch your diet. You want to look your best. Do stay away from milk products. What the public does not know is just how many hormones and stabilizers are added to milk to keep the product fresh longer and this interferes with cellular activity. Once you are cleared of this, you will do well. Watch the sugar too. Sugar as you know makes the cells bloat, thus weight gain. Don't eat it. Lose weight. It is simple."

"Thank you Elizabeth. It has been a pleasure visiting with you. I send you love and best wishes for a lovely eternity. Love to Alejandro and to all who are with Him there."

"It seems it is time to go Diane. If Alejandro sends me again, I will look forward to another discussion with you. I wish you well. You will do well. Have faith and don't give up.

Push through with your quest to get an agent. They are there and they will represent you well. Find them today. Til then. Adieu."

"Adieu to you Elizabeth. Much love to you."

Lewis Meriwether

August 18, 1774 – October 11, 1809

"What is your name please?

"Meriwether, Lewis," "Yes, you found me there. I saw my photograph."

"Great, I will post it here and you can see it while we talk. I asked him to wait just a moment and when I put up his picture he did see it.

I commented, "How about that? It has your signature too?"

Lewis replied, "I like it. I haven't seen anything such as this since my death and the computer is marvelous."

I replied to him that it was wonderful to meet him, and of course I knew who Lewis & Clark were for it was impossible to grow up in Virginia and study history in my schools and not learn about the early explorers in the Americas who explored and mapped the western territories. Their names are all over the land in the Louisiana Purchase territories for they discovered many different species of plants, animals and apparently a few other entities as well which is not so much known or talked about by those who do know.

So I began asking, "How may I assist you, sir?"

"Diane, I am invited here at Alejandro's request as it is my turn, you might say, to speak to you and to receive my forgiveness. As you can see from your notes, I was Governor of the Louisiana Purchase at one time in my life. I was overseeing the work of exploring the new lands out west. This was a daunting task for there was much land to cover and not as many explorers as you might think who were willing to travel into unknown parts without any idea of where they would end up or what they would encounter out there. Nonetheless, it was exciting a and I loved it. The only problem was sometimes we found things that were not like ourselves and understanding what we did find was a challenge to the most provocative mind."

"I did not have a scientific panel to take my findings to when discovering the unexplainable but I can definitely tell you that we found things not of this world, and plenty of it. Not all things are as you imagine indeed. We are not alone in this world Diane but we share it with a number of other beings, not like ourselves. The difficulty is that you as humans do not perceive them yet.

Your people are able to find remnants of their being but not the being itself. A dilemma at best I would say, and yet these beings see you perfectly and in fact intermingle with your people daily."

"Great, just super," I said.

Lewis continued, "I dare say it is a problem for you due to their particular nature. They are not like humans descending from the One, true God of heaven. They are of another kind. They descent from other parts unknown to you as yet and they followed the footprint of creative energy which was creating the environment you call Earth in coming here Let's just say, it is like the light in the darkness which the souls have followed to find you. You left an imprint. So did the Creator when He created the Earth in all His glory. It was inevitable that others would see it and be curious about it. Unfortunately, they are a warring kind of being. It is in their nature to be at odds with other beings. They desire to dominate."

At this time, I felt the energy of the Lord, Alejandro. I sent Him blessings and welcomed Him to our conversation.

"Thank you Diane," Alejandro spoke. "I want to express something here to Lewis. Lewis, I would like to know why you and others who were with you never called out to Me in your wanderings of the unknown. Why when you encountered the "unknown" did you simply move on, not considering the higher truths of what you saw? Were you not drawn to the Higher Power who created some of what you saw?"

"I humble myself before You, Alejandro for I have not known You as such. I do beg your mercy upon me for not asking You or desiring to know You. I have no real excuse for my behavior but to say that all I knew was before me and I did take it all in not considering the how or why of it as much as the excellence of it all. I do pray now for forgiveness for not honoring You for the experience of life which I did have in the body."

Alejandro spoken again, "I must speak to My daughter a moment. Diane, you must consider going without sugar or mile products for a season. Allow your body to adjust to the new energy without introducing confounding substances into the mix. That sounds painful and I do not wish to see you in pain."

"I will heed your guidance," I responded. "No milk products and no sugar. Thank you."

"Back to Lewis," said Alejandro. "I have heard your request for forgiveness and of course I do grant you forgiveness, but still I do not understand how it is that you of all people, who explored much of the wilderness, could see it in its majesty and not wonder how it came to be.

I will listen to your answer."

Lewis attempted to explain but said, "I cannot explain it. Perhaps it is that it was more my duty to do this exploring rather than it was my destiny. Perhaps that is it. It really was not my destiny to do this work, but something else."

Alejandro liked this response and said to Lewis, "Now we are getting somewhere. This is what I wanted you to discover on your own. You did not achieve your destiny. Now what do you suppose your destiny in fact was that you did not achieve?"

To this Lewis responded, "Perhaps I was an explorer of another kind but I did not even understand myself at the time. Perhaps I was to discover the truth of who did create all that there was to enjoy in life and instead I went about exploring the created rather than the Creator Himself."

"There you have it now don't you? Your desire was to come to the planet at a time when exploration of new land was commencing in order to make certain that those exploring would not forget Me as they went forth. This was in fact to be a protection to them for what they would encounter on their quests. They would see things not seen before and they would encounter things not encountered before. It was important for them to not go forth alone, without Me, and yet you and others did just that."

Lewis was apologetic. "For this I do apologize and I do ask for forgiveness. We did not take news of You into the new lands. We fell short in our behaviors in the west as well towards the Indian people I am afraid. I see that there are still problems due to the lack of courtesy to them in many ways. How sad. What can I do now to make a difference Alejandro? Is it too late for me to achieve a destiny?"

"It is almost never too late for time and space exist simultaneously. Here is what I will offer to you Lewis, and we will see what you think of it. I will allow you to come home to the heavens with this one caveat. I will require you to send to this new nation I am creating, the remembrance of Me in its leadership. I will require that the energy of emergence of the truth of Alejandro to the nation that is to be called by My name, "America", for I did choose this name before even the creation of the earth itself. I wish to have tribute given to My name again and that it would once again have a place of honor in the world as before. Do you agree to My terms?"

Lewis was excited and responded, "It is with great appreciation for this opportunity to assist in lifting up your name and the nation which I loved that I accept Alejandro. I will return home and I will then send energy of the truth of your name to this nation, and to surrounding nations, that it would circumvent the earth. I accept wholeheartedly."

"So be it. Consider it done. You have your repentance and I have My will to be done on Earth. You are to be received in the heavens in My name Lewis. Welcome home."

"Oh joy above all joys Diane," Lewis exclaimed. "This is a glorious moment. Thank you for helping me to see my destiny."

"That was Alejandro Himself, Lewis who helped you to see your destiny," I replied.

"Forgive me but without your light, I could have seen nothing. I was in total and complete darkness. You have no idea how dark. I do thank you, both. I give thanks to Alejandro of course first and foremost, I do. Now it is upon me to serve you in some manner Diane.

I would like to offer you the following in return for my release. I would like to go to heaven and ask that a door be opened for you to have your letters accepted by both publishers that you would receive an offer from both Tate and Strategic for your own records. Then you can decide which one will serve you best in the interest of Alejandro's name."

I thanked Lewis for this blessing telling him that I could certainly use a blessing on those letters. I am sending the second one when we finish here.

"Consider it done," Lewis exclaimed. "I will open the door for them to be given special consideration and endorsement of your book The Race to Eternity and even for the republishing of Freedom Come under the new publisher's name, where it will receive the benefit of adequate marketing. We will push for a contract by mid-April shall we?"

"Yes, of course, and let's see who has the best deal for me and who can have the book ready the soonest."

As I write these words now, I know how urgent it is to get the message from these souls out who have engaged the darkness and the dark lords there to those in particular who have taken on the prospect of delivering people and their homes from these entities and others. They must learn more about who they are dealing with and who it is that they must have at their side when they encounter these dark, cold hearted entities, for without Alejandro, individuals run the risk of endangering their own souls while trying to release the oppressed. Did He not say, "Apart from Me, you can do nothing"?

"Do you realize that your book will sell millions of copies Diane? It will. I can see the power of its vibration and the energy coming to it will push it exponentially towards success."

"I do realize that," I answered. "I believe that. Thank you."

"Don't thank me. I can also see the time and energy you have put into attempting to tell the world the truth and it has been at times frustrating and overwhelming. No recognition. No income from your efforts. No appreciation or recognition. All of these words are a thing of the past. The new words coming to you are of a higher vibration. They are success, fame, intelligent recognition, understanding, fortune, appreciation, beauty and demand for you to speak about these things in your book. These things are coming to you too, and soon."

"Soon is best. I will prepare my voice, my body, and other things. I just need to know I am doing it with purpose."

"No need to concern yourself with that either. It is coming your way. You will have your contract, your book will be published and available to the public. Your website will be finished. You will create two new videos to capture the attention of the world and you are on your way."

"Lewis, thank you for the confirmation that all of this will be seen by those who can benefit from its truth. What does Alejandro want me to do with this record of our conversation?"

"This is for Alejandro to tell you. Keep it with your other stories."

I thought to ask Lewis something after having read a few things about him when he contacted me. "Lewis, why didn't you marry?"

"I never found the love of my life that is why," he said. It is difficult to meet a beautiful lady when you are out in the wilderness but then, later I was consumed with politics and did not find time to meet her then either."

"Thank you. I just wondered. Okay then. I must get to work. Blessings to you in the light and to all who are with you. I will catch up on your many other truths and stories sometime in the future."

"Wait one moment, Lewis. Alejandro is here once again to speak to you."

"Diane, it was not Lewis's destiny to marry this time. It was his destiny to share Me with the expanding colonies. He will have an opportunity to do that now in Me. Let Me say this, Lewis did pave the way for many to make their way west and for this, I thank him. He was a good man, but to be good is not enough. To make a difference in this world, one must remain in Me for I know the ways of the world, and I can help men to achieve their destinies."

"Thank you Alejandro," I replied and then added, "Adieu Lewis. Blessings."

"Adieu Diane. Thank you once again my fair lady."

Mark Antony

January 14, 83 BC – August 1, 30 BC

Most of us who are baby boomers know something about Mark Antony for he was a famous Roman, born to rule in ancient Rome according to him. He knew no other destiny but to serve his family and Rome and as such served as a General in Rome and a politician turning Rome from a Republic into an autocratic Empire. He was not kind to God's people showing them no respect or mercy for that matter for they were considered as ignorant, having no power and knowing nothing. Let's see what he says when coming face to face with the Almighty. It is his only way out of darkness after all.

"My name is Mark Antony."

"Is this you? Tell me about yourself."

"I was a politician in ancient Rome. My family was all about ruling Rome. This was my destiny from the time that I was born, to rule in the country. I knew it. I accepted it. I was determined to perform my duties to my highest level of perfection. I wanted to be remembered as the best leader of Rome ever known."

"Really," I asked. "Did you achieve it?"

"Sadly, no" Mark remarked" "I wasn't remembered in the way that I had hoped due to sanctions that were against me and who rose up against me, challenging my leadership. A battle ensured and I lost it."

"Let me ask you, who did you serve?"

"My family honor of course, and then Rome. I served my calling and my family name, and then I served my country of origin. This is as it should be."

"Forgive me sir, but what about the God of heaven, and His name. Do you even know it sir?"

"I daresay that I do. The God of heaven is God. What do you mean?"

"I would have to tell you that you are incorrect. His name is not "God", it is Alejandro. Did you ever seek to know Him, His name or to serve Him?"

"By virtue of the fact that I served Rome, I served God, did I not?"

This was an easy answer for me. "You did not. I must tell you the truth. They are not one and the same. One is political and other is . spiritual. The God of Heaven is capable of guiding us to our true destinies if we abide in Him, seek, listen to Him, and obey Him in His directions to us. He can lead us to our destinies thus achieving much in this world and He is protecting us in the process as well. Which of these things did you do?"

"I dare say that I did none of those things. I was serving my country, not the God of the world."

"Did you achieve your destiny?" (I had to exit for a moment for an important call and came right back to hear Mark's answer.)

"Hello Diane. I have been thinking about what you did ask me in your absence. I do not think that I did achieve my destiny. I thought that I had but when you asked me if I had served the God of Heaven, if I had known Him, and whether I did seek Him, and I knew that I had not, then how could I know whether or not I had achieved my destiny? I believe my destiny must have been tied to knowing my own Creator. If I never knew Him, how could I possibly have known my destiny in the world? This is very disturbing to me."

"Mark, were are you? Do you know where you are?"

"I am in a place not fit for beggars. It is not fit for any soul and here I am. If you know anything at all about me Diane, then you know that I have been here for a very long time."

"Why do you think that you are there Mark?"

"I presume at this point that it must be connected to my lack of reverence to my deity. I did not choose Him so He did not choose me. Seems fair I suppose."

"Really? You think that you are there because you did not serve Him? What have been your thoughts all of this time there Mark?"

"Thoughts are not allowed here but I suppose that I have engaged in thinking. There is hardly anything else to do with my mind. So, I have done some thinking."

I asked Mark what he had been thinking about.

"I have done some thinking about what I did with my life. I have thought perhaps that I could have done some things differently for instance. Perhaps I could have been a better man, father, husband, these kinds of things. One develops a conscious down here and in this situation. As I said, I had time to think about myself."

"Do you say then that your soul testified against you as to how you may have lived your life apart from the God of Heaven or merely that you may have lived a better life as a man?"

Mark responded, "Both I suppose, though I did tend to push out the thoughts that would cause me to feel badly for not seeking to know God, whomever He is."

"Why do you suppose that you do not have a love for Him in your heart? Do you know that He loves you? Do you know that the only reason we are speaking now is that He loves you and sent you to me?

You have not sought Him, nor loved Him, nor served Him and yet even after all of this time, He still loves you and wishes you to come home. How does this make you feel?"

"Pathetic, honestly, for I fear that you speak the truth Diane. I dare say that I know that you speak the truth for I can see it in your energy field. There is no guile in you at all. You do not wish to do me harm nor do you wish to tell me what is wrong or that which misrepresents God."

"Before we continue, let me set you straight on one thing and this is not meant to appear judgmental. His name is Alejandro. Alejandro!! His name was hidden from the Jewish people during their captivity in Babylon and at other times so they would forget Him. This siege against the world and her people began during ancient times, perhaps even before. If the people do not know Him, they do not know themselves. If the people do not know Him, they have no power against evil. Do you realize this?"

"Alejandro, Alejandro," Mark declared! That is a marvelous name Diane. This name makes sense to me. It is the word of praise and it makes sense to me. Now what am I to do for I am guilty of not lifting up His name in my time on Earth. I am guilty of not serving Him or seeking Him and I dare say that I ridiculed those who did. I was a Roman after all."

"What you can do is repent before Him, acknowledge your lack of love and faith in higher beings. Acknowledge that you did not serve Him and ask for forgiveness for He is gentle and kind and loving towards His own. He will forgive you but you must repent of your own doing."

"I shall do it! Right now! Heavenly father, whose name I did not know, but it is brought before me now, I do hereby humble myself before thee and beg thy forgiveness for I never knew you, nor did I seek you in my life. I fear then that I have missed my destiny in life however I would like to ask for forgiveness for Diane is telling me of your love for me, and I do believe her. I would like to receive this love for myself. I would like to know You.

Is it possible to be forgiven so long after my death or am I restrained to be here for all eternity?

I beseech You then and ask for my freedom if I may."

"Mark, I will wait upon His reply. Stay near." (Some time did go by without a response from Alejandro. I have learned to just wait for He has said that he does get busy with other things.)

I called to Mark again to give him an update.

"Mark, are you with me now? I apologize for not coming right back but there was no response from Alejandro. I cannot speak for Him in these matters. But He has come and said to me that He will answer you now. Are you there?"

"I am here Diane. I am here. I wondered what happened to you quite frankly and I was concerned that you might not come back to help me. I do not wish to remain here, not under these circumstances. Again, I have stated my repentance unto Alejandro and I do wait for His replay. Did He speak to you on my behalf?"

"Not yet, Mark," I answered. "But He did say that He would speak to you I am again waiting for His answer."

"Patient one you are I must say. I do not have that kind of patience. If I want to know a thing, I want to know it now. Why wait?"

"Why indeed, that is the question? It is not for us to hurry up the God of Heaven. He is multitasking as it is you know. The world is a big place."

"My apologies, I can see that you are tired. I am aware of the Earth's shifting energy patterns Diane and this must be hard on the body to adjust. But adjust you will and then you will see the amazing changes to the body. The new and improved you."

"This is excellent news, Mark! I embrace it now. Alejandro, Mark Anthony and I are here now, and we await your presence to speak to Mark's repentance unto You. I humble myself before You and ask if You would please come and speak to us now."

While waiting I asked Mark, "Mark, what about repentance for the number of lives you did take for I believe it is necessary to acknowledge that you did take the lives of people and they were not your lives to take. This is an important factor in repentance asking for forgiveness for these things."

"I understand Diane," he replied. "I suppose that I ought to admit the wrongs that I did before Him, and ask that He pardon me for my wrongdoing against humanity."

"I will remain quiet Mark while you speak to Him regarding this and I will record it."

"Almighty One, Alejandro, as it were, I am h ere again, Mark Anthony, and Diane has instructed me yet again to consider the things which I did while in the world. I have therefore considered my acts against humanity as not being worthy of a son of Alejandro. I do hereby repent for my deeds against humanity, against life on earth, and ask for forgiveness for such things that I did while a man. I did not know You nor did I have others who told me of your love for me. I was without your love in the world to guide me. I misjudged others just as I misjudged my own character and destiny. I served man and not the God of Heaven. For this too I repent. Can you find it in your heart to forgive me and to take me under your wing and teach me now what I did not learn then?"

We waited and again, did not hear from Alejandro at first. I did feel a soul and asked, "Who is this?"

"This is Mark, Diane. I have been waiting once again but to no avail. It is disconcerting to me that there is no answer from Alejandro as yet."

"I am in a quandary myself Mark.. I did not hear from Him about you yet. I am having difficult today feeling well and I must admit that I have not been as attentive as usual, however I do not think that He has summoned me to speak with me. Let us wait here again, and we will try something. Is there something else that you would like to add to what you have already said to Him, or to me?"

"There is . . . I am sorry. I am sorry that I did not seek You, Alejandro. I apologize for not demonstrating any love for you in my life, whatsoever. I am sorry that I did not consider the heavenly things for myself, or for my family. As I wait here in the darkness for Alejandro, that whom I never did know, I realize that I have missed so much in not knowing Him. I did not know His love, His guidance, His reasons for creating life, and me. I did not grow to understand the greater picture nor did I realize it, ever! It was all about me, and what I was doing, period.

I am ashamed for this reason. I am genuinely ashamed. Why should He wish to speak with me?

I did not seek Him until I was bound in inequity here in this wasteland. Why would He desire to help me now? I was a fool."

"Mark, what did you think during all of this time that you were there after death? Did you not consider the things of heaven even then? If not, why not?"

"It is forbidden to do so and punishable if discovered by the dark ones."

"Alright, but I am curious about this. How do the "dark ones" punish someone who has no body?"

"They torture your mind. They come at you endlessly to destroy your belief system, your ability to remember life as good, your love for anything and they tell you that you are worthless, unlovable, not worthy of God's grace, etc. They are relentless to destroy your mind if it is discovered that you are engaging in the "thinking" process."

"We need to move those dark ones on to another place and help those who are Alejandro's to repent and to go home. But in order to go home, Alejandro must know your heart is true. How can He be sure that your heart is true unto repentance and love for Him? Why should He believe you now in your desperate situation?"

"I suppose a man sometimes does not humble himself before God or anyone else for that matter unless he is reduced to having nothing. Am I so different from other men that I should not submit to Him having found my own depravity through these circumstances? I know that I am capable of much good for I did attempt to serve Rome, and my family to the best of my ability. My allegiance was well intentioned and towards doing good, but I was mislead in believing that this is all that there was for me, family and duty to Rome."

What I wanted to know was, "Where were the people of faith then Mark? Did you ever hear them out? Where were the enlightened people? Did you ever see them? Did you ever hear of miracles being done in the name of the God of Heaven? What was it like then as far as belief in a Higher Being?"

"I dare say that it was similar to what you are experiencing now Diane only much, much worse. Those who believed in such things were outcasts. They were not welcomed in the political circles of intelligencia for we were far too sophisticated for such nonsense. *We* were ruling the country, and those people were ruling nothing. Their presence in the land was considered more of a nuisance, and in some cases, a threat to our rule for when they stirred up the people, we of course were the ones they were not happy with any longer. This was stopped form time to time as you know through intimidation. Of course, if they did have any power, wouldn't they have stopped us?"

"Indeed. That is precisely what I am hoping for . . . now. That the righteous who love life, and love the Almighty, will return to Him and in doing so, He will demonstrate through us, the power we have who come in His name on behalf of the people and the land for there is no power mightier than His to heal us, to heal the land, to do whatever is necessary to return the land to a peaceful place for all life. It is His hand that saved my husband's life you know."

"How so," asked Mark?

"Do you wish to have a taste of the miraculous?"

"I welcome anything at this point," he offered.

"Let me tell you what faith in a Higher Being did for me one night. My husband and I were walking in the evening having dropped our son off in college that very day. We left our house on a walk together, and were on the return part of the walk home coming up a steep hill when he fell backwards to the ground and hit his head. I went to him when I realized he was not next to me and he did not utter a word. I watched as he breathed his last breath in fact. I was praying and telling God that He had told me that He had a plan and a purpose for my husband's life and my husband was surely dying without achieving his purpose.

I said that if He was not a man that He should lie then He would have to get my husband up and save his life. I continued praying, and praying in the Spirit which was not of my understanding, but the Spirit prays for you. I kept asking for God to please do something when I noticed that my husband was being picked up and held underneath his arms by an unseen force. He moved through the air, and was brought in front of me. He began slowly to be set downwards and I knelt to capture him from behind so he would not hurt himself.

I continued to tell Mark what happened.

"I prayed continuously as my husband was not breathing. I said that I needed to know what to do that only God knew what to do. It was then that I felt energy come down through me and it went from my heart chakra through my husband's back which was in front of me and to his heart apparently for he blasted forward out of my clenched hands. He hit his forehead this time on the curb and I heard him say, "I think I can walk now." I insisted that no, he could not walk as he did not realize what had occurred. He insisted and got up and at 6'4" and 210 pounds walked unassisted up the remainder of the steep hill. I found two men at the top of the hill at the golf course who called an ambulance, for medical assistance. In the hospital, the heart surgeon came to me and demanded to know how did my husband's heart get started?"

"I told the doctor but he said, no, you do not understand. He said, "I have had four men die of this exact thing in the last two weeks and yet your husband is sitting up in there talking and I haven't done anything yet.""

"There you go, I told him it was God, it was the Lord, the Spirit but it had not been me or the ambulatory assistants for when they came he was already breathing alright and I did not know CPR. The doctor insisted on showing me the ultrasound and all of the blockages and continued to say that "It is impossible.""

"Mark, Alejandro is here. Are you ready to hear Him now?"

"Please, I must," Mark answered.

"I have come to speak to Mark, Myself, Diane. Tell him this. Mark, your name has come up to the heavens for review for it has been some time since your death of many years ago. I chose you for this time due to your allegiance to the government rather than to me as an example for others to see what happens when men serve the law and not Me. I know that it has not been pleasant for you there and I do accept your repentance unto Me. However, this will not be quite enough for though I believe that you are indeed sincere, there is a price to pay for those who oppose Me openly and who chastise and punish My own people."

"I will require that upon arriving in the heavens that you spend the rest of eternity serving Me by sending anti-government energy upon the earth such that the people will return to Me, opposing the ruling of men over their entire lives. A world in which men are governed by other men will never be equitable for the nature of man is filled with the potential for much hatred, jealousy, and the like. Men can only be ruled by a Higher nature than their own. I offer this to My own, if they will humble themselves before Me, I will assist them in their lives, to achieve their destinies. I guide them towards that which is good and right while still allowing them to choose for themselves which way to go. If they choose badly, there is forgiveness and they may return to Me for further guidance. I do not turn My back on My own, ever!

I also am a kind and gentle God in that those who wish to serve Me, I will hear and if I find that their hearts are sincere and they are not attempting merely to manipulate Me along with the rest of the world, I will honor their request before Me. Therefore, Mark Anthony, I do forgive you and you will be freed to serve Me for all eternity. Is this acceptable to you?"

"I am in awe of your majesty and power and authority Alejandro. I am honored to have you speak to me. Certainly I am the lowest of the lowest and yet you do love me as Diane said that you do forgive and will allow me to reach my destiny."

"But you will and for this you shall have your freedom. Serve Me for the purposes of freeing the people from government which destroys their ability to have liberty and freedom. We shall have a new form of rule under Me. I will enthrone Myself over the people and they shall know Me as I am. This is coming soon. Now Mark, do not think that I can be deceived. I cannot.

Those who think that they can deceive Me will remember the day they tried to do so. I accept your repentance, now you are free to come home."

"What a glorious day this is Diane. I am free from this monotomy. I am free from this accursed place. I cannot thank you enough or Alejandro enough for assisting me in my understanding and in His ways. I have learned much from spending time in your light Diane. There were none like you in my days I can assure you. I will go to heaven and I will learn what I must do and I will do it for the glory of Alejandro that His name may again be lifted up in all the land and the people may again be free from oppressive government rule. What a wonderful day!"

"Blessings of love to you, Mark Anthony, now you shall have the joy of doing something for the Kingdom of Heaven. Now you shall have the love you have never known and it is immeasurable, immutable, and beyond belief. I send you in love for your soul, for Alejandro, and love for all who have gone before you as well."

"I will remember this day eternally Diane, the day of my release, of my freedom. Thanks be to Alejandro and to you, again. Some day we will meet and we will celebrate the release of mankind from government. Adieu Diane. Be well."

"Goodbye Mark Antony. Adieu."

Ronald Reagan

February 6, 1911 – June 5, 2004

I had my eyes opened again today when this soul came through to me for I thought that I knew something about this man or enough to think that he was good and if he was good, wouldn't he at least have gone to heaven? Are the men who are seemingly good who we choose to rule good to a point and then overruled by those who really control the workings of the government? What else don't we know that these people find out once they are permitted to serve as Presidents in our country? Are the Elitists working with an unseen enemy of man towards their own goals of gaining world power, dominance and money?

I didn't ask for this truth to come to me but come it did and it just keeps on coming because the Almighty did say that everything hidden would be revealed.

I felt two souls this time while was getting a walk in outside. I asked them to please tell me their names, one at a time. "I am willing to listen and I have about ten minutes. Tell me your name please."

"My name is Ronald Reagan."

To confirm I asked, "Is your name Ronald Reagan?"

"Yes, it is Diane. I was President of the United States of America for a season, a movie actor, and other things but mostly remembered . . ."

"Whoops. I lost the connection momentarily. Where were we Mr. Reagan?"

"Diane, I was the 40th President of the United States and served from 1981 until 1989. I believe that we did indeed meet once in the

Presidential Library in Los Angeles for I do see this in your energy signature. It is upon me to speak to you and so I have come."

"I am so surprised Ronald, but it is my pleasure to speak to you once again. I wondered about you and if you had gone to the other side of life."

"Unfortunately, I went, but not where I would have liked to have gone. There were many things about me that the general public did not know and unfortunately I could not state in public. I was a member of the Masonic order not by choice so much as by recruitment by those who oversee our government. I served as Governor under their watch and then they chose to make me President. Sadly, it is not the public who chooses such things these days. it is their organization for they have the power, influence and money to do whatever it is they choose."

"What am I to do with what you tell me here?" I inquired.

"You are to tell your husband for should he be selected by Alejandro to serve in the land he must understand something about how those who call themselves The Elite operate. They operate in secret but now that I am no longer under their jurisdiction, it is upon me to do my duty and reveal the truth so that the country may again come under Divine leadership. As I said, I attempted to bring forth my own ideas as I saw fit and up to a certain point, it was permitted.

After that, it was no longer my choice or my will and they made that perfectly clear when they allowed me to be shot by a man whom they had manipulated into doing their dirty deeds. Now you know that mankind can be hypnotized by the reptilian race and all that the Illuminati types need to do is get them in front of the shape shifters and the deed is done The person will do whatever it is that they are programmed to do and remember nothing of having done it. This is how a random act of violence takes place against political figures who have not fully cooperated with their wishes. Do not worry however because in each of these instances where it has occurred, the person did not have Divine protection.."

"Excuse me, what about Martin Luther King? He was a preacher and a threat to the Illuminati. Why didn't he have the protection of the heavens?"

"There is a difference in serving what you know about Him, and actually serving Him, Diane. Remember, Martin did follow the tenets of faith of religion. He was not actually speaking forth what he heard Alejandro say. I tell you this now as I relate all of this to you, all things are known to me for this very purpose that you would know the truth. In return, I will be freed to go home by your sharing of your energy with me."

"Thank you Mr. Reagan."

"Please call me Ron. Not that it much matters any more for that identity is now gone as I transition to go home."

"Alright then, I understand."

"What I am to tell you and your husband is this. The Illuminati is worldwide and they consider themselves gods over the rest of you because they have access to the reptilian's race intellect and technological advances. They use whatever advances they get from the reptilians to manipulate world opinion to their advancement in their particular governments and families.

They do not care if others benefit from what they do. They cannot for they themselves are compromised in their nature too. You cannot align yourselves with evil and come out smelling like a rose. Your only hope is full repentance and deliverance from evil by Alejandro. Few escape this connection to evil without Alejandro. He helps whom He will upon an evaluation of the heart. Now if you are going to serve as leaders in this country you must know the players now and who they are. They are all of the Bush family and those who have served them are like them, particularly George Bush, Sr., for he has certain tastes for life that are not acceptable to the rest of the world. Of course his nature is no longer his own for he has submitted to the hypnotic energy of the reptilian nature and it does lust after the women of the earth. I know that this disgusts you Diane but it is what it is. There are men who will do anything for power and when they are not as persuasive with women as some others, they will do what they can to have what they want. Let's move on as I know that this is uncomfortable for you"

"What I am about to convey to Dick is that if he does in fact serve as a leader in this country, he must avoid these people at all costs. He does not need what they have to offer to effectively do his job. He need only seek wisdom from Alejandro to make the hard decisions and otherwise, whomever Dick does select to be his advisors and I advise him to exercise caution in whom he selects. The Illuminati will want to infiltrate the leadership with spies and known informants who will tell them what is being outlined or planned. Now this is the way that the game is played As long as Dick does not enter into any agreement with the Illuminati or their people, they cannot touch him or interfere in his decision making. This will not stop them from trying to spy on him or manipulate him. That is their nature to do so. But Dick need not worry about his life or his family members. We are here to protect him, and I say "we" for I speak of the Kingdom of Heaven for Diane's work has provided much in the way of allegiance to her and your family and this is what will protect you. I did not have this for myself and as such, I was injured by them for purposes of controlling me for they had their agenda for war and for control of America and its resources."

"Moving on, so Dick is protected heavenly and is able to effectively push forth a heavenly agenda from his position of leadership. Again, as long as he does not align with those whose desire it is to control the world, he is protected. No secret meeting with people he does not know. No speaking at their functions. Do not go there. The minute you show up at one of their functions, they will bring out their secret weapon, the shape shifters with the ability to hypnotize a human in order to compromise you making it impossible for you to serve in the capacity as President in the way that Alejandro would have you serve. They will record everything and hold it over your life permanently."

"This they have done to many Presidents and men of influence both in the Senate and in the House. They are capable of falsifying documents to indict whomever they please in order to get rid of them. Again, they can do this to whoever is not protected by the Almighty. This is not you and your family are afforded much protection from the heavens due to Diane's service to souls, many souls and we all are part of that heavenly rank who will protect you and yours while you bring divine guidance to the country. Knowing this you ought to feel more comfortable throwing your name in the hat. Others have not had this opportunity given to them to serve while being divinely protected and their sphere of influence was genuinely compromised and what The Elite could not control, they eliminated, case in point J. F. Kennedy and Abraham Lincoln."

"Martin Luther King had to go because he was capable of stirring up the public to follow his religious ideology and bringing people to an awareness of a belief in a higher power again.

This was not acceptable to The Elite., But, Martin had not yet connected to the Almighty as Diane has and therefore his life was not submitted in the same way. Here is why. Martin saw himself more as a crusader for his own kind, and Alejandro works only for the greater good, even though those He does protect. As long as you are working for the greater good, He will bless your life richly too but the work must benefit all, not just some. Martin was not there yet.

You do not see many people of other persuasions supporting Martin Luther King Day because he did not serve all, but some."

Ron continued, "Now I am willing to be an advisory help to you and to Dick as you step up to serve in the country and I will come as directed by Alejandro to speak to you. This is not unusual for Diane has spoken to many people who have served in the country who are now giving her advice for herself and the family. This is a blessing afforded by Alejandro in reward for serving His people. We are permitted to assist you in return in your life on earth. Call us angels if you like but we are not. We are just like you only no longer embodied. All you need to do is speak my name and wait. I will make my presence known to you in the same manner that I made myself known to Diane. That is, I will latch onto your energy in the following manner. It, will initially feel like a pinch, or a cramp, in your foot. When you feel this, you need only ask who is there. This is our energy, which is a different quality than your own, attaching to yours. Ask who it is and who needs to speak to you. Then listen.

Try hard to make out the name. Ask the soul to speak louder if necessary to spell their name. It will come. Be patient. You will need this Divine guidance as it will come down through many of us whom Diane has assisted in crossing over to glory for your ability to know things that you cannot know without us. We can see everything from our side. There will be no other leader like you who has been able to connect to the God of Heaven in this way and you will serve the country to bring up the vibration and it will again prosper."

"You need not worry about the connection or when or how it will manifest, it just does. As you see Diane experiencing this, it will happen to you for the benefit of all. You don't need a doctor if you stop and listen. The pain goes away after you listen to the soul who is there to help you."

"Now you already have been told by General McArthur that he will assist you in knowing what to do in military matters. Next you will have me, former President Ronald Regan and I will assist you in diplomacy matters for that is one area where I soared. I was good in front of the camera too. I can guide you. Speak as if you are talking to a friend, who is not as well informed as you are, and they will listen. Speak as though they need to know what you have to say because they are hurting out there and you wish to help them. Be sincere. Do not talk down to the people as Obama does. People do not like to be treated as anything less than equals. I can also guide you to become an even more eloquent speaker in your choice of words. Much of what I said, I wrote. I felt passionately about America and until I lost the ability to speak well, I spoke from the heart. I regret ever submitting to the plans of "the enemy" of America, but as I said, I was not protected as you certainly will be. Think of it this way. You live and you die.

The only thing that matters is what you do to serve the God of Heaven during that time. If this is true, than most men do not achieve their destinies. If you accept this leadership challenge, you will achieve your destiny and you will be protected due to your family's connection to the heavens."

"Again, I will be available and all you have to do is sit and ask to speak to me. Ask what I did in certain situations I will tell you. Ask me for guidance and I will give it if I can. Of course, it is not as though I am the God of Heaven. I can only speak form my experience as a man who served in the position of President but I can tell you what Alejandro is impressing on me to tell you and this I will do for you."

"Finally, do not worry about your health. I was a lot older than you when I served and I managed just fine. If I had merely served Alejandro instead of men, and I would have not suffered a gunshot wound and been under their control Your health will take care of itself and you should take care of the body. Eat more nutritious foods and more living foods. More fruits and vegetables and less meat. Allow Diane to do some healing energy work over your body.

Perhaps we can bring up the metabolic processes for you to endure the cold more than you have been able to so far. You are in good hands there Dick. Let her help you out as she has helped many of us get to heaven. She knows what she is doing and can assist you too.

"Last, but not least, inform your children too that they must not join any of these Elitist groups, particularly Brian, Dick you must caution him as he will be sought after by these men who wish to have access to his intelligence and his light. They will attempt to recruit him promising him prestige and money but he will not need it if his dad is President. You can assist him in getting any position he wants and in fact, the heavens have plans for him too to serve.

Protect him. No secret meetings. No secret handshakes. No promises of riches and glory. It is a set up, a lie to lure him in and hypnotize him so that the dirty deeds can take place and shame him into compliance. I have seen it done hundreds of times in my life sadly but I could do nothing to stop it. I kid you not. It happens all of the time. They know no shame."

"I hate this stuff."

"I apologize for having to tell Dick this through you Diane but it must be done if he is to be protected and his family too. You too Diane, do not go to their Eastern Star meetings. No cults for you. Stay close to Alejandro and He will direct you to those groups that are safe to attend.

All will be well with all of you if you abide in Him, Diane. He will show you the way."

"Thank you Ron."

"That is it Diane, for now. I will be off and thank you for sharing your light and energy with me. Now I can remove myself from here and go home. I am delighted. Say hello to Nancy for me. She believes in this stuff you know. In fact give her this note from me will you?"

"I will do what I can. Proceed."

"Dearest Nancy:

This is your beloved Ron speaking to you through Diane Freeman for she has a unique gift that is tied to the heavens which allows her to hear those who have departed the earth. In my case Nancy, I had not served the Almighty as you know, and this did cause me some shame and guilt upon my death. I was unable to move on due to those who participle in harassing recently departed souls keeping their minds locked you might say, unable to go home due to the feelings of shame and guilt for not seeking to know the God of Heaven in order to achieve their destinies. I know that now. I was to assist in lifting up the God of Heaven's name and to that purpose I came. I lost my way and I do not want you to lose your way Nancy. I want to encourage you to seek the God of Heaven and ask what it is that you might do for His name's sake before your days have ended upon this earth so that when you do pass, you will pass right into glory escaping that which awaits men who do not know God. He waits to hear from you so that He can guide you to leave a legacy greater than that of just serving those who control this nation as I did. I want to see you leave something beautiful to this country. Think about that and what it might be for I am with you always my love.

Yours,

Ronnie"

"She always called me Ronnie you know Diane. She will like that. Tell her that I told you that she used to phone up Jeanne Dixon from time to tie to ask her what we ought to do with certain tasks before us. Jeanne had good ideas but she did not have the total access that you do Diane. Tell Nancy that she was the "apple of my eye" and that I loved her so."

"When should I send this to her, Ron", I asked him.

"Wait until you publish your book. Then send her a copy of it when it is published. I will see that she gets it. Don't send it to the library but send it to our home in Santa Barbara. She is there now. I will accompany it and send my note in the book to her. She will like that too."

"Okay, my child I am on my way. Share this with Dick. He is a fine man as I once was and his integrity is still intact. He can keep it that way if he avoids the bad guys. Be strong. You don't need them, they need you. Best to you Diane. I will be here if you need me, just call.

Adieu."

STEVE MCQUEEN

March 24, 1930 – November 7, 1980

Despite a rough beginning as a child, being the son of a divorced family twice and having to be raised by his grandparents for periods of time, "The King of Cool", actor Steven McQueen became one of Hollywood's most beloved actors. He had been understandably rebellious against those in the world especially abusive stepfathers who were controlling and harsh towards him and he found life difficult moving back and forth from his mother's home to grandparents to even being on the street at only 9 years old to escape an abusive stepfather. Later he bounced from one mediocre job to another. It is apparent that he did struggle to find himself.

Not only was he handsome and excellent as an actor but he was kind and generous giving back to one of the boys institutions where he had spent time during his youth. He was admired by many of Hollywood's finest actors and actresses as well as by the public in America. What you will learn about him here comes directly from him before he did depart and go to the heavens. It is enlightening indeed and he speaks to his peers giving them sound advice for their careers and life choices in general. Worth your time and, for those of you in Hollywood today, Steve McQueen wanted to leave a legacy of truth for you and it is contained herein.

Today is Sunday, February 13, 2011 and I am trying to hear the soul who has contacted me.

I believe I heard the name Steve McQueen. I asked whether I had his name correct?

"Yes, I was a race car driver, an actor and I was married though none were greatly successful."

188

"Steve, how did you come to me."

"You said it earlier When you said my name I heard it. I had to connect with you Diane. I do not belong here for though I did not serve God, I was not opposed to God. I should have lifted him up in Hollywood for it is certainly a Godless business. There are many "I should haves" that I can think of. I should have raised a big family who had the knowledge and love of God so the world would be a better place today but I failed at this sadly. I have left behind some western films and a few others which did not add anything worth being represented in the world.

I lived for myself and by myself without God in my life."

"Steve, we all have forgotten God at some point or another but we do have regrets. Just a moment. Alejandro is requesting to speak to you."

Alejandro presented this question. "Ask Steve what message he would give to Hollywood now from where he is? What advice does he have for those who are actors and actresses?"

"I would say to live your lives with only yourself in mind is a disaster to your soul. To spend your lives to see only your name lifted up so you receive all the glory is to leave you in guilt and shame at the end of your days for you leave behind no legacy for the generations which follow you. This is regrettable to me and will be for those of you who follow suit."

Steve continued, "Life is too short to live it only for yourself. Time will show you that the best lives are those lived for the soul purpose of making life better for others. How can you improve Hollywood so that you begin enriching the lives of others? Currently, films are made which glorify the worst choices in life. What about representing the goodness of life overcoming adversities, reaching your dreams in spite of hardships, staying in marriages and demonstrating to your children what is possible when love is given despite challenges in a person's life."

"There are so many films to make about love touching the souls of men to make them better men. Where are the films about the love of a man and a woman which go beyond mere sex?

Where are the films demonstrating the love parents have for family, their child who has physical challenges or mental difficulties who overcome these challenges to find success? The world has seen enough devastation, murder, suicide, child abuse, and drug use, rape and pillage. As one of your former actors, I am holding Hollywood accountable for the social degradation you have brought about in God's nation."

"I will go to heaven and ask that for a new creation of films depicting the overcoming of adversity, hardships and tragedies in spite of difficulties with faith, hope and the love of God so people will again learn something about how to navigate life from that which they see and hear from the world's actors and actresses."

"So again, I ask God that a door be open to truth in acting godliness of characters who demonstrate attributes that men, women and children might emulate to make the world a better place."

"God bless you in this Steve. Your point is a good one and one I make *all* of the time. I agree with you and join you in submitting this to the heavens. May God hear it, bless it and create a new entity for the performing arts which lifts up godliness. What might it be called? Sunrise Productions—a new day in entertainment. So be it created. Bless you with love Steve, forgiveness and hope. Godspeed in your journeys. Send us love."

"Diane, you are a beautiful woman inside and out. You can demonstrate to the women of America grace, beauty, charm, and strength of character. Teach them how to overcome adversity with love. Teach them how to be women not succumbing to every whim of a man and in the process losing their dignity. Not all things are permissible and if a woman objects, she needs to be honored accordingly. Hollywood is being irresponsible and degrading of women. From a position of leadership, show women how they can have the respect they deserve and need by remaining firm in their desires to be loved and honored by their men.

It is needed. You will do well. I will ask God to open the door for you to lead women back to loving their femininity."

"Thank you, Steve. Thank you very much. I send you love. I thought you were very manly and handsome and I looked for someone like you."

"Thank you, Diane. This is a nice compliment. If I led one woman to look for masculinity and a good man, my life was worth it."

"You did! Both you and Robert Redford."

"I see that!"

I then said, "Happy Valentine's Day then too." and I added a heart at the end of that on the page and Steve could see it.

"Thank you for the heart Diane."

"I am sending you light and love to transition home Peace be with you. Love to all who are there and to the God of Heaven. Thank him for me for the open doors."

"You have my word Diane."

Karl Marx

May 5, 1818 – March 14, 1883)

Today it is Alejandro who is speaking with me and he asked me how I enjoyed my spin class. "I did," I answered. "Good. Now let's get some work done shall we? First, help this soul Diane. They need to speak with you now. Holding on for them is not always easy if they have not transitioned. Their energy is already depleted. Help them now. Call Me if you need Me."

"Will do and thank you Alejandro. To the soul who is standing by waiting for me, please tell me your name as I am here to listen to you."

"Karl Marx, yes, that is me."

"Alejandro, do I have this name correct please?" I asked Alejandro this because I knew who Karl Marx was and I was not too sure that I should have to deal with him. His contribution to the world was far, far less than positive and still resonates evil in the world in my opinion.

I had looked up Karl Marx on my computer and I "showed" if you will the soul and asked if this was a portrait of him.

"Yes, I even did a little Napoleon hand in my shirt pose. This is me Diane. I can see that you do not have a good reaction to me."

"Karl, why should I? You did much harm in the world to control people, to manipulate people and the working class. Your teachings have stuck around and they are still manipulating people. I prefer that you did not have the power still to manipulate minds and shape them into a controlling class over others."

"Some of what you say is true about me. I did not intentionally attempt to bring harm to the world however. I was bringing forth what came to me to bring forth and it was to others to decide if it was for them or not. Isn't this what you are trying to do? You bring forth an idea and if others agree with you, the idea flourishes"

"I suppose that if the idea is an idea that is for the greater good, than I could support the idea.

But if the idea is for a controlling class over others that treats those who do not grasp their ideas as well like slaves, then I cannot support this idea. Nor can I support an idea that threatens the freedoms or liberties of any man. This is against the nature of the creative force of Alejandro. We have our own destinies. We do not need to have them controlled by one group versus another but we ought to be free to explore the possibilities of our nature and to propel our way through life to accomplish the goals of achieving our own destinies."

"The goal should not be to exploit the ignorant so that you can make more money for yourself and your friends, or so that you can have more power for either of those. What do you think of what I have said?"

Karl had this radical thing to say. "Indeed, you have a point that men ought to be free to explore their destinies but I did not honor that premise of life. I found that men needed guidance and direction and often did not know how to achieve anything at all, and so having a controlling elite was beneficial to them. They could work for those whose grasp on life was greater than their own, and then they too would accomplish something contributing to the whole."

"Wrong. Your ideas use men. Your ideas control the minds and liberties of men. Men ought to be free to seek divine guidance to reconnect to their Divine destinies. You are not Alejandro, who is the God of Heaven, who oversees the Earth. You are not sir. You are somewhat arrogant in your thinking that it is your right to order men to do a thing for you do not know the destiny of each man. To control them in life is to keep them from their individual destinies and you are not the One who has created life as it exists here nor are you the One who knows the destinies of each man. So how can you assume to order their lives in any manner?"

"I see your point however that does not change the fact that I too had a destiny," Karl retorted.

"How do you know that you achieved it? Did you connect to the God of Heaven while living? Did you know Alejandro? If not, then I suggest to you that perhaps another one not Him ordered your steps and you went in the wrong direction indeed. Did you know or serve the God of Heaven?"

Karl answered quite quickly, "No, I did not."

"Then where did the wisdom you had come from? Who did you seek for guidance? Where did it come from?"

"My wisdom came from searching for how to control others for The Elite. The Elite were seeking ways to gain control over the working classes. I became engaged in the process of assisting them in creating a way to move the working classes toward accomplishing the goals of The Elite."

"How so," I asked Karl. "How did you become engaged in the process?"

"Let's just say that I was recruited by them. Those with a leaning towards radicalism are sought out by The Elite in the rank and file of the school systems, the military or wherever they can be found. Once it is known that an individual is known for his stance against the status quo, against individualism, and against freedom of the individual, then they are fodder for The Elite. They can work with that let's just say."

"And where did they find you?"

"They found me on the streets where I lived. I was not quiet about my own beliefs. I wouldn't say that I was dangerous but I was not quiet. People knew who I was by the way in which I presented ideas."

"Where did you get those ideas do you think?"

"I honestly don't know. I suppose that there may have been an incident, or maybe two, when I dabbled in some dark arts, and perhaps I opened a door there. I suppose that is it Diane. I hadn't really considered the origin of the thoughts that permeated my being. It was just there after a certain point in my life."

"Okay, I want you to think back to when you first began to have these notions of the need to rob men of their freedoms by controlling them. When was it? What age were you when you first noticed it? What may have precipitated it?"

"I am thinking Diane. I think it may be a book that I read on satanism. I believe that this was it. It was in my teens or early 20's. I discovered a book on satanism and read it. That must have been the door. Once opened, the information just kept coming in. I didn't know the God of Heaven."

"Can you remember what happened, Karl? Was there a feeling associated with this? Did you resonate with any of the books teachings? What exactly happened? Did you feel a change? Think."

"I am remembering now Diane. I was reading the text of the book and it seemed to pull me, like a force into it. It had an energy to it, a power. I didn't necessarily agree with it as much as I was drawn to it, inescapable drawn into it."

"Do you know about how old you were when this happened?"

"Yes, I would have to guess I was around 21 years old. Yes, around 21. I was an inquisitive youth and interested in many things. I thought I would check it out and see what all the fuss was about."

Now we were getting somewhere. I asked Karl, "What changed after you read the book?"

"Everything changed, particularly me. I became very outspoken about the things I believed and I was beginning to believe in a bit of a different philosophy. I lost any interest in the individual and became enthralled with destroying the individual's right to choose his own life. I was a different person inside and I could feel it."

"Did you feel unhappy about that? What did it feel like to the person who was *you* before you read the book?"

Karl thought for a moment then said, "It felt like I was no longer myself but someone else was controlling me. I was not Karl anymore, but some dark thing was manipulating my thoughts and actions."

"Karl is that darkness still with you there?"

"No, it had better things to do now that I was trapped here. It left me when I died. Moved on to someone else I suppose."

"Do you realize the impact of the nature of the works that you left on earth? Do you realize the movement that is afoot on the earth to destroy personal liberties and to destroy the destinies of men? Do you realize that The Elite which you supported is moving to destroy nations?

Livelihoods? They want all of the money, all of the land, all of the resources, and all of the people to serve them! This was not good energy which you left on the planet Karl and it has affected many young and impressionable people negatively and now you know where it came from because it left you when your life was no longer worth anything to it for the purposes of destroying life."

"This saddens me," Karl responded as he realized the weight of the matter. "What can I do?

I am no longer in a body and I am in a dismal existence here. I can do nothing."

"What is certain is that you can do nothing apart from Alejandro, who is the God of Heaven, in case you do not already know this from my energy field's history. I must tell you that you may repent if you are willing to do so before Him. Ask Him for forgiveness and ask what it is that you might do to make amends if that is possible. I do not know for the world is upside down at the moment and many need to pray if we are to attempt to get Alejandro to help us, to protect us, to somehow restore the land and its people. It is a mess. Planes are dropping toxins on the people around the world and who is behind the wheel? Those men who serve The Elite either through mind control or otherwise willingly are flying the planes. Poisons are added to the drinking water of the common people who work hard to have success only to have to surrender much of what they earn to those who do not work or lord it over the rest of us through manipulation and lies. Is this what you wanted to leave the world with as your legacy? Do you now that some of the leaders know quote you when they rant? They love you. Do you see what this means? They love the satanic being which worked through you while you lived with this evil energy manipulating you?"

"I see. I see now how that worked Diane. I see it and I am remorseful for having read the book on satanism. Remorseful. My poor mother for she never knew what caused me to go in the direction that I went. She never knew. I never told anyone that I can remember. They just thought that this was of me, these words of power and manipulation

of men. I am fraught with the notion of what to do now for I have
caused much harm to the peace of the planet. I was a voice for evil
and not for good. This is tragic for me Diane. I don't know if I can
live with that, and yet, I have no escape from it. None."

"Your only escape is to repent before Alejandro and allow Him to
help you in letting go of all of the harm that you did to the world,
its' people and its' history. You have no other alternative for He is
the One to clear you, heal you and forgive you. His love is for all
of humanity but He does give admonitions to us to remain in Him
during this experience on earth so that we do not fall into the hands
of this darkness that is always near too. It waits for us to desire it
and not Alejandro. I could say that it is a shame that you were caught
up into this but why did you not think to ask the God of Heaven for
help? Did your family ever have faith in Him? Did you not have any
religious upbringing to fall back on?"

"No, I had nothing, Diane. No one spoke about these things in my
family and certainly not in church. No one spoke about the dangers
of reading books on satanism. I cannot even tell you where that book
came from and yet, it was there. My mother never knew so she could
not offer any assistance even if she was a religious person and she
was not. I tell you the truth, I did not know what I was getting into,
or rather, what would get into me should I read that book. It forever
changed my life. I lost my life to whatever came into me when I read
that book."

"Are you willing to speak now to the God of Heaven Karl and to ask
for His forgiveness?

Alejandro will give it to you for He is kind and gentle and forgiving
and He is also not willing that any would perish. You will perish
there if you do not go home Karl. Would you like to say something
to Alejandro? If you say it to me, He can hear you."

"Yes, yes. I do wish to speak to Alejandro and this is what I want to say. I want to ask for my forgiveness for I did not know what I was doing when I opened that door into darkness. I did not know what I would do to myself and to my future or to the future of the planet. I do ask Alejandro if He could look at me now and see that I am telling the truth. I did not know what would happen to me. I entered in on my own will yes, but I did not know that I would perish there on that very day. Can you forgive me for the sadness and oppression which I have brought to the world by bringing these teachings into form there? I repent for doing so. I repent for having sided with the enemy of the God of Heaven. I repent for not having sought you for guidance in my life and for not seeking you to find my destiny when I was lost not knowing what to do with my life. May I be forgiven, is it even possible?"

"Karl, though the world is indeed in a mess, I am by way of my own energy submitting your request to Alejandro. Then we must wait upon His response for He is loving and it will come.

Now brace yourself, for though He is loving, He may require something of you to give back for your freedom. Are you prepared to give back to the world for your freedom?"

"I will do whatever He asks of me if I may be forgiven."

"This touches me greatly because I feel that too many young people are misled today and can be easily pulled into the same darkness due to the lack of love for them in the world. Without Alejandro, they do not have the love they need to survive this mess and it is heartbreaking . . . truly."

"I feel your pain for the young people Diane. I feel it. I know that it is real and that you do love the lost. I trust you."

"We must wait on Alejandro. The decision is His to make. As soon as He comes, I will come back to you Karl. Think what you will say to Him while we wait. I will do a few things until I hear His call but I will return.. You have my word."

"Okay, Diane.. As I said, I trust you. you are kind and gentle and good to help me for I know that your heart was not in it to do it when you heard my name. I will wait for you to return.."

It is now 10:13 p.m. I felt something and asked "what was that?"

"It is me Diane, Karl Marx. (When he said this I felt the pinching on my arm again.)

"I just wanted to make certain that you knew that I was here. It is me. Not another soul. I have been waiting for you and for Alejandro to speak with me, to answer, my request for forgiveness."

Sometimes this does happen. Alejandro is ruling the world and busy doing the things that he does. I have to wait for my energy contact to reach Him and for Him to have the opportunity to respond. Even if my request reaches Him immediately, perhaps He is waiting for more from those I am assisting before He makes His decision known to them.

"I have been waiting for this hour for Alejandro did ask me to come back now to help you. What have you been thinking about since I last spoke with you? Any new considerations of your life and what you did do with your life?"

"Yes, Diane. I have had a million thoughts already in this time since we spoke. I do not have an excuse for what did happen to me in my life for it was my choice to read that book but had someone said to me, "if you read that book, you will certainly be changed by a dark, negative force", do you think that I would have read it? I don't think so. I was young but I was not stupid. If it had been emphasized to me that this book had a negative quality to it that could change the course of my life, I would have burned it to keep my freedom. Who knows what I might have done with my life had I been let free to choose."

"Well Karl, I cannot answer that question for you. I don't know what the course for your life was, I only know what course you did take as history has documented it. Odd that historians seem to want to keep a record of what does happen in the world that was evil and not keep a record of the things which happened for good. History books are edited frequently by the people who believe in what you wrote, and act upon it. Teachers are teaching these radical views as though they are meant for all people and they intend on forcing these views on others who do not believe in them. The radical, socialistic agenda has gained momentum in our country and around the globe. This is not a good thing, I might add, for they are anti-God and they are anti those who love Him. No one can blame one person for this agenda but there is a case for having brought these energies into the world and not ridding the world of them later. They are here.

How do we get rid of them so that men can remember that they are able to know Alejandro, to choose Him, and be guided and protected by Him, so that they can achieve their Divine destinies, not the destiny carved out for them by something that is anti-God."

"I am mortified at what you have told me and that the world is in such turmoil. I can see the record of these things in your light. Diane, I am ready to do whatever is asked of me in order to bring some positive change to the world for the wrong that I have done to turn His people away from Him and towards destruction. Is He here?"

"Let me see. I will pray and invite Him to speak to us here. Wait. In this time while you are waiting, let go of all negative thoughts, and send them back to creation, to the light. All shame, guilt, hatred, anxiety, regret, all thoughts such as these, send them to the light.

Begin sending them while I invite Alejandro to come."

Before I could begin Karl interrupted me. "Diane, I want to say something else before Alejandro does arrive to speak with us. I want to say that I did not do what I do with malice towards anyone for I did not have that in my heart. What I had was a burning desire to see those who were oppressed in control in the world, and this desire seemed to come from being a part of an underclass and perhaps this is what the darkness used to their advantage I felt like I was part of an underclass. Then in reading about the darkness, the force of evil behind Satanism, I allowed it in through the one weak spot I had in my need for revenge against the upper class, If it were not for the fact that my dad was Jewish, we could have stayed in our original home. I would not have been uprooted. He was denied respect and work because he was Jewish. I felt this shame that he felt too. It did not leave me. So when I read the satanic book, the evil found its way in me through this undercurrent of hatred for others who had mistreated my family. As I waited for you here, it came to me."

"Remarkable Karl, I can see how the enemy has used man's inhumanity towards man in the world today to cause one uprising after another, and it stirs in the hearts of those of different races around the globe for they have not surrendered their hatred of others because they have suffered for no other reason but for their differences of race, creed, or color or choice of religion in their lives."

"I wanted to tell you Diane, that the wars that were fought on this earth have primarily occurred between different people groups, one attempting to control the other. It is not merely to own the other's land, or to rob the till. It is always more than that. It is for the mere differences that exist between people themselves which are not controllable by the people who exhibit the differences for they are inherent in that particular race."

This was fascinating to me. It is new revelation that comes forth as souls are transitioning so they can go home. The light is wisdom. Souls who are trapped in darkness for some time have very little wisdom left but as they are exposed to new light they are quickly caught up to speed and go beyond what even we know at this time in the body.

At this time my body felt an energy surge and it was identifiable as Alejandro. I have much practice in identifying who it is that wishes to speak with me and so I knew that it was Him.

He confirmed it and that He had come to speak to Karl.

"Karl, I have good news. Alejandro has come to speak with us. Blessings to you Alejandro.

I welcome you here with love."

Alejandro spoke. "Good evening my daughter. I have come to speak to Karl, and you of course, for the purposes of addressing his comments to Me about his life, and his repentance.

Karl, I have heard your words to me and I will speak to them here. It is not to me to judge you for having read the book of satanism. What is mine to judge is your turning your back on Me to serve that which is of satanism, the darkness therein. If you had called out to Me, I would have saved you then. If you had asked for Me to intervene on your behalf when you felt the darkness moving upon you, I would have saved you, but you did not. As a consequence, you did sacrifice your destiny to serve that which is not of Me and the earth has suffered since then for that which you allowed to come through you into the earth. This energy is not of Me. Your words are not of Me, they come from a dark source, which is combative and wars against Me to this day. I had hoped that you would awaken and repent during your lifetime, but it was not to be. Now your works still resonate in the land causing many to miss their destinies and even worse, they stir more men to evil against others, warring and planning much evil in an effort to take that which does not belong to them but that which was created through the hard work of others who work towards their own destinies. This I will not tolerate any longer. If I am to consider your act of repentance in forgiveness of your sins against Me, I will require something of you. Are you read to hear what it is that I will require of you in return for your freedom Karl Marx?"

"I am ready to hear whatever it is that you wish to say Alejandro. I am humbled by your presence and that you would speak to me."

Alejandro did speak again to Karl, "I have a good relationship with my daughter Diane and it is because of her that I am able to assist you now Karl. You can thank her as well but first let Me tell you what it is that I will require of you. First, I will accept your repentance unto Me but I will require that when you return to the heavens that you serve Me in eternity in this manner.

You will send the energy of repentance for serving the enemy through satanism throughout the world and you will do it for eternity. Do we understand each other? You will send upon the earth the energy of repentance unto Me for the sacrifice of innocence unto this "religion" against Me. Are you with Me, or against Me, Karl? What shall be your answer?"

"I am speechless . . . for your request makes me feel the enormity of what I have done in bringing forth the teachings that I did in the world. I will serve you in this Alejandro, just as you have asked. I will do it gladly and with love for humanity for my heart was not to do evil, but to serve the greater good by emphasizing those who were the less fortunate."

His answer. "It is a twisted logic and does not compute with My teachings. Men are to be free for I created them to be free. No governing body of men is necessary over My people for I am the One to lead them and they need no other, not men of religion, and not men of government.

I am not in need of another to teach them for I am the same today as yesterday. I have not lost My voice and I have not lost My passion to be with My own. I will teach them again and they shall again know that I am He. Now you will serve Me, Karl, and you shall know Me as I am.

Do we have an agreement then? Speak for I am listening."

Karl was indeed humbled by these words and it was reflected in his response to Alejandro.

"I am in awe of your majesty and power Alejandro. I give you my solemn word that I will serve you as you have requested all of eternity with my soul. I will send the energy of repentance upon the earth for men to feel it and to repent for practicing Satanism in all of the earth. Men and women will feel this energy and know that it is from You, Alejandro, and they will repent unto You, for You alone are the God of Heaven, and there is none besides You."

"Now you do speak the truth. Would that you had done so when you were living. I do hereby accept your repentance and you shall have your freedom today, April 12, 2011, in the year of the Aquarian calendar. So be it."

Alejandro did wish to speak to me now.

"Now Diane, this word is to you my daughter. Do not speak to others of this exchange yet.

It is not for others to hear it yet. It will be given at the right time and then it will make quite a stir. Wait upon My word Diane. You have done well to assist Karl. It was the right time and for the right reasons.

We must clear this energy of satanic worship off the planet once and for all eternity. Well done."

Yes!! So good to hear His compliments to me.

"Thank you lover of my soul. Thank you. Love be with you and to all in the heavens.

Wait please, Alejandro. Should I keep looking for an agent? A different publisher? Will you tell me that now?"

He was quick to answer and put me at ease.

"Not yet Diane. Finish with Karl. He has something to say to you my dear. Come to me in the morning. You can skip spin. (I was an avid spin cyclist at the time.) Just drink those two bottles of water near you and you will do fine without the exercise of spin. Drink. You have spent much time in front of this computer today. Your body wants water. Good night Diane.

Again, well done."

"Good night. J"

Unfortunately, Karl was a bit unsettled from hearing Alejandro. He still wanted to communicate with me.

"Karl, are you still there?"

"I am weeping Diane for the enormity of what I have done and what Alejandro is giving to me nonetheless for this will allow me to heal. That I can serve Him now, even now, will allow my soul to heal and I have waited a long time for this opportunity to come to me, never believing that it ever would come but what choice did I have but to hope for it? I knew that I was not where I should be and yet I could not fathom ever being allowed to go home. I cannot thank you enough and I cannot do anything for you that would measure the enormity of what you have done for me Diane. Nothing compares to this, nothing. And yet, I must ask, how may I serve you upon arriving in the heavens? What do you need that is not done for you yet?"

"Well," I thought, "I have been looking to find the right publisher and/ or agent to assist me in finding a publisher. I don't know which one is the right one. I don't know if I have to keep looking or did I already make the initial contact already and I must wait for a response?

I don't know. What if you asked that a door be opened for the right agent or publisher to contact me within this week who is to publish my book? I also must make the distinction as to whether the book is to be published by an self-publishing company or an traditional publisher who does not require payment from me. Finally, I must have my monies returned to me by a company whose name I won't mention here for they have defrauded other authors.

I have asked for a cancellation of my agreement and for my money back. Can you ask on my behalf? I apologize for the long answer, but can you please ask?"

"If someone is defrauding you now, I am certain that Alejandro will make the way clear for you to receive the return of your money. But I will ask that it be done for you. I will also ask that the name of the agent of Alejandro's choice get in touch with you. But prepare yourself Diane.

Study your book's content well enough so you can answer questions when they do contact you for they will ask specific questions about your vision for the book. Study the platform, your business plan, etc. Tell them it will someday be a movie, you feel it. Again, thank you Diane.

Your heart is golden and you are beloved of Alejandro. I felt it when He did come to you."

"He has said it to me Himself, Karl, He loves everyone, not just me."

"Diane, do not take His love lightly when He says that He does love you, for He does love all of humanity but not many are those who seek Him as you do to serve Him with their whole heart. Not many. I can attest to that from what I have seen in my life. So I will bid you adieu Diane. I will never forget you. I will speak highly of you in the heavens you can be sure. My best to you and to your success. Karl."

"I am pleased to have been of some help to you Karl at Alejandro's request. Adieu."

Dr. Thomas Walker

January 25, 1715 – November 9, 1794

Today is April 13, 2011, and another soul is reaching out to me. The name that I thought I was hearing was Thomas Walker. He said, "Diane, this is Thomas Walker." Honestly, I did not know who he was. I looked him up on the internet and then asked if he was the Thomas Walker, the explorer born January 25, 1715 and then who dies November 9, 1794.

He was also a physician from Virginia who led an expedition into the area in and beyond the Allegheny Mountains. He is known to have explored Kentucky long before Daniel Boone.

So when I asked if he was born on January 25, 1715, he quickly answered, "Indeed, I was. I was an explorer from your home state of Virginia." Interesting, how the souls do know who we are once they begin reading the truth contained in our energy fields.

"Well, I said, "Well, you explored this situation out didn't you? Who sent you?"

Thomas tells me then, "I was sent by Alejandro for I have been given a chance to plead my case before Him through you Diane. I apologize for the pain which I caused you in your foot. I can only imagine what that feels like for I never knew such things were possible, and yet, here I am."

I asked Thomas if he wished to tell me what his situation was a the moment."

"I suppose that is what I am to do," he answered. "I am here, in this place of darkness because I did not know where else I was to go or how to get there. That about says it all. I was not connected to the God of Heaven and so instructions were not given to me before or at

209

my death as to what to expect. Oh, people always say that you will go to heaven but why do they say that?

If you have no relationship with the Father of Heaven, why would you go there? And how does one go there after all? Isn't there a way to prepare one's self for what is to come at the time of death? There ought to be for I for one did not know what to expect and I assure you that neither did my wife or children. It is a sad tragedy that this was the reality of our lives. Where were the leaders who would have otherwise shown us the way home? There was no one to shine the light in the road so to speak. We were on our own. Church was very predictable. No miracles there.

Just singing and reading from the scriptures. No real direction. Just obey the commandments and you will go to heaven. I am here to tell you that it is much more complicated than that Diane. I can testify to that for you if you want. Tell the people that Thomas Walker was a good man but he says that he did not go to heaven and he wants to know why no one told him how to get there.

(At this time I had an interruption which does sometimes happen due to the frequency in which these souls were coming to me. I needed to tell Thomas that I was going to have to complete our session a bit later.)

"Thomas, I do wish to speak to you but I must go with my husband to get some food for our dinner. I promise you that I will return when we are finished. Do not leave please. I will call your name and we will finish this conversation."

I returned at 9:45 p.m.. and asked to speak with Thomas Walker asking if he was there.

"Is that you there now Thomas?"

"I am here Diane. Thank you for coming back for me."

"Of course Thomas, I apologize but I do have to maintain some semblance of routine here in the world with family and there are many who do wish to go home who are trapped as you are."

"You are too kind Diane. I see that you did a little research on me. Yes, I was the father of 12 children. It was one of my greatest works having those children. My wife and I were very happy with them too. We may have had to struggle a bit here and there and were challenged when it came time to send them to the schools of their choices, but you know what that was like don't you? I do see that you come from a large family too. A man can only do so much in a day despite the number of children born to him to make enough money for all of them. If I had to do it over again, I would make my children work earlier to help with the expenses of running a household. It wouldn't have killed them to work a bit and contribute some of their earnings to the things that they each wanted out of life. I suppose that is what parents do, in hindsight everything looks differently. We think of things the way we did them and wish we had done them differently."

"That is for sure. You don't have to die to think that way either. It happens to us long before we die that we start thinking that we wish we could have done a few things differently. But no regrets! Live and learn and don't sweat the small stuff. Let me ask you Thomas, what was the best part of your life? What do you remember most distinctly and what will you always cherish about your life on earth?"

"I loved exploring but I also loved my family life. There was so much to learn from each of my children that I wish I had spent more time getting to know each of them separately.. But time goes by so quickly. I was exploring and setting new areas of land for the government and every time I would come home, there was so much to hear from everyone."

"And I see that you were married to Mildred Thornton, Thomas, is that true?"

"Yes, she was my first wife and we had 12 children together. Her husband left her quite an estate and we lived well but no matter. There was always a need for more with a family of that size you can be certain."

"Thomas, why did Alejandro send you to me today."

"Well, as you can imagine I do wish to get out of here. There is nothing here for anyone and I have been here quite some time without a hope or a prayer of going anywhere until I heard about you. 'The light in the darkness people were saying. Find it. Cling to it.' That is what I heard and so as an explorer it didn't take me too long to find you."

"Tell me what has been on your mind during this time of no existence in the body, and no existence in the spirit either. What has it been like for you?"

"I can only say that I wish that someone had spoken to me about faith in God the way that you do speak to those you have helped in crossing to go home. I wish that someone had taken the time to tell me that I needed to remain in Him so He could show me why I came to earth in the first place. I did not know my purpose other than to go about life doing whatever pleased me.

My life would have been different but in a good way. Knowing the God of Heaven loved me and desired to show me my destiny would have altered the course of my life and maybe the lives of others. it is unfortunate that there was no one in my life who could present the truth to me Diane the way that you present it to people."

"It is unfortunate indeed Thomas for you but to tell you the truth, I tell people what I hear from the God of Heaven and they look at me funny as though I am not quite right. Not everyone wants to hear from Him. Some want to know, "where is the proof of this truth from Him?"

But they need to choose to be open to listen and then they have to choose to listen to Him. They also have to believe that He wishes to be heard by them. He is not deaf or mute. He hears us and He speaks to us, we just don't see Him and we choose not to listen when He does speak through someone who does hear Him. But I don't want to leave out the most important thing of all . . . love of Him. He wants us to love Him for indeed He does love us."

"This is the most beautiful thing that I have ever heard. I can only imagine now how my life would have been different had I chosen differently."

"Thomas, what you need to do is to let go of all negative thoughts and emotions and send them back to creative light, releasing them forever for they are part of the earth experience and meant to teach you something about yourself. Emotions exist here in this world and are felt by the highly sensitive abilities within the body and energy field and interpreted by the brain to teach us something about the interaction between ourselves and others. Are we making a difference for good or evil when we interact with others? How does what we do make other people feel?

Unfortunately, there are those who are tampering with the systems of men by poisoning our food, water and air. This makes it tough for us to be who we are here to be. We can't function the same while we are undergoing a hidden onslaught by a hidden enemy against God and mankind. The world is not a better place to be at the moment. Count the blessings that you have from the experiences of being in pristine nature and having the adoration of 12 children."

"You have a way of stating things to give me a much better perspective on life. I will cherish my life that I lived on earth. I learned many things about my own ability to survive in the wild against many odds. I learned that to be a father is a wonderful thing and a great responsibility. I learned what love truly is through the love of a woman. I learned that the love of country is a wonderful thing too but part of that is the shared freedom that we do have in a country that is established as a free nation, for all of its people need to wake up and remember freedom doesn't come easy to the people on earth for you are engaged in a war against an unseen enemy at this time and most of the people do not even know it. You cannot fight this battle alone for it must be fought at another level vibrationally. The people alone cannot stand against this enemy of God. You must realign yourselves with Alejandro if you are to win this battle for the nations."

"I am going to give you a few ideas as to what to do to awaken the people to pray Diane. First, finish up your website Take10topray. This site can be a place where Alejandro can give you a daily prayer to post for the nation and you can just send it to everyone you know and ask them to pass it on to 10 other people. Tell them that their God will move His hand when He hears the prayers of one million souls. That should get their attention. Next, consider getting some bumper stickers that say "Take10toPray.com . . . our nation needs you, Or "Take10toPray while you still can. Try something like that. You need a winning statement to make them go there.

On the website simply do a new prayer posting every day. Ask Kyle if he can help you with it and what would it cost. Find out tomorrow."

"Good idea. Thank you for that. I have been trying to figure out what to do with that .com and how to circulate the call to pray."

"Diane, you don't need an expensive site for now. it is more important just to get the people praying."

"Thank you Thomas. I will work on this tomorrow too. Many things happening all at once and I don't know if I have completed the task of sending my manuscripts or queries to enough publishers/agents yet to be expecting one to call and want to work with me. Anyway enough of me, is there more that you wish to say?

"Yes, I want to say that I want you to use my name on that website and say that Thomas Walker from Virginia has asked that all men and women should pray and ask the God of heaven to move His hand so that all of humanity may know Him and how to seek Him for their lives so that they may each achieve their destinies."

"Well said, Thomas. I will agree with you then Thomas Walker."

"Excellent! I, Thomas Walker, no longer of the body, do hereby make an agreement with the living, Diane Freeman, that all men and women of the earth shall again know Him, Alejandro, as the Creator of all things, that they may know His love for humanity and His will for their lives that they may each reach their Divine destinies."

"Here, here. I agree."

"And it is so. Well done Diane. We have already made history have we not?"

"I should like to think it is so, Thomas."

It was getting late as I often was asked to help these individuals in the early evening and it could take several hours to converse back and forth with both the heavens and those bound in the darkness. Thomas noticed my tiredness.

"I can see that you are feeling tired. Let me say this to Alejandro and I will be leaving.

Alejandro, this is Thomas Walker, your son, and I do wish to express my deepest regrets for never having sought you for my life, for family, or even in exploring the land in America. I regret that I did not know you in my life. I apologize to you with the deepest remorse and beg your forgiveness for my soul's pardon.."

"Alejandro, on behalf of Thomas Walker, I come before you and present his petition of repentance for he does wish to have our forgiveness for he did not seek to know you in his life. For this, he is remorseful and feels both guilt and shame. Will you forgive him Sir?"

There was a bit of silence and then Thomas spoke to me. The way that this works is I speak to the souls who are locked in darkness but they hear Alejandro as He speaks to me.

"Diane, are you waiting on Alejandro?"

"Yes, sometimes it takes a bit. Interference gets in the way of our connecting with Him.

But He *will* speak to me about you. If we are patient, He always comes through. Thomas, while we wait, please consider those negative feelings which have been delivered to you while there in the darkness and release them forever to the light, sending these also home. Think about whatever negative feelings are still there, gilt, shame, regret, those kinds of feelings, and send them directly to the light, acknowledge them for what they have shown you about life, and set them free now."

For a moment or two, I didn't hear anything so I asked, "Thomas, are you doing it?"

"Yes, yes I am, and I feel marvelous. A burden of intense pressure is being lifted off of me."

"Thomas? Alejandro is here. Blessings to my Father in heaven of love. Thank you for coming to assist me here."

"Diane," Alejandro replied, "Good to see you."

"You as well Alejandro, though I am feeling quite hot."

"Apologies about that my love. Mr. Walker, this is Alejandro. I have heard your repentance unto Me. I do hereby release you from the bounds of darkness to return home upon this day.

You have nothing to fear any longer for I am releasing you now and you shall have your freedom again."

"What would I have done Diane if you had not come? What? I am so appreciative of your love for me that you would help me. I am amazed and dazed by your caring for humanity to do these things for others. Alejandro I am grateful that you have come and I do thank you with my whole being for my freedom. I shall honor you always and in any ways of your choosing.

Thank you."

Alejandro now spoke directly to Thomas. "I have something in mind for you Thomas Walker,",

I have chosen a new destiny for you did not achieve your earthly destiny before Me. I have chosen you to explore new ways for the people to be reminded of Me on earth. I shall ask that you send to Diane ideas of how to reach the people with her new book her blogs, her newsletters and her new website Take10topray. We must reach as many people with the truth as possible if I am to stop the war against My people in all of the nations. Your will serve Me to eternity and you will send energy to direct Diane in how to reach My people so she is successful in all her endeavors to do so. Then many more people will know Me and My nature and My ways which are not their ways. They will understand the nature of life and how to reconnect with Me.

Do you accept this calling, Thomas?"

"I am honored Alejandro, and I do accept with humility. Thank you Alejandro for giving me a new destiny. I look forward to this work. When do I start?"

Alejandro answered Thomas immediately, "Right now. Begin to send the energy of vitality to her work. Send the energy of loss of wait so she can move about with ease to accomplish all that I have shown her that must be done to have success with My book. Send these to her right away for she is already tired from illness and the poisons put in the air over her home and city.

Send the energy of rejuvenation of her beauty and vision for she must see well to be able to stand in front of others and speak well with notes. Send her the energy of knowing which affiliations to make with companies with high vibrational nutrients for both her and her husband and to promote on My website. I need these things now so send her the energy. Send her the energy to complete her website. Just do it. Send her the energy to finish it as much as possible this week. Now you are doing My will. So be it."

"I will gladly serve in this way and now I must go. I wish you much success in bringing forth the truth so many will not perish but rather they would have eternal life. Isn't that a true saying?"

"Yes Thomas, and I wish you love. Love to the heavens too, all of you. Alejandro is an awesome God!! Adieu, Thomas."

"Adieu, Diane."

Heinrich Luitpold Himmler

October 7, 1900 – May 23, 1945

Today is April 14, 2011.I was about to go and prepare some dinner for a hungry husband and myself when I felt the presence of a soul. I decided to take a moment and find out who this was so I could schedule the plan to assist them later that day. So the question is, "Tell me your name please?"

Here is what I heard and you will most likely be as shocked as I was when I heard it.

"My name is Himmler. I was a Nazi in Germany."

Nooooooooo. I thought I was going to be helping *good* people get to heaven who otherwise lost their way. I looked up his name on my computer and confirmed what I already knew.

He was not a good person in the choices that he made while serving Hitler. I asked him if the information on my screen was about him. I said, "If so, it is not a glowing report. Not something I would want my mother to read about her son."

"Yes, this is who I was unfortunately. I was a ruthless man. I was a godless man. I was despicable in every way. I know that now and I have been sequestered here due to my horror as a person. I deserve nothing better I know."

"How in the world did you become this person?"

"This is a very good question. As I look back at my childhood I do not recall exactly being an evil child. So, I did not entertain the idea of it as a child."

"When then Heinrich? When did you contemplate doing such horrible things to others? When did you give yourself over to such horrible ideas and thoughts?"

"I suppose that it was when I came to know Hitler. I surrendered to all of his ideas for he was a powerful figure. He was authoritative and very demonstrable. I could see myself serving him for these reasons. I thought that he would help me to be like him if I served him. I gave myself to the whole idea of Hitler. Completely."

"We will continue this conversation shortly. I will come back and call you. I must do other things for the time being."

"I am ashamed for I know that I did do much harm in the world. I did more evil than anyone could possibly do in one lifetime. I ordered it of others ruining their lives and I participated in much of it myself. How could so much evil generate from one man? I was saying that I did not see myself evil as a child and it is true that my father did ask me to spy on my peers when in school for he was taskmaster and a disciplinarian and at times, I did loathe him for what he made me do.

Perhaps it was this hatred of what my father made me do that allowed me to move into even deeper hatred of men for reasons I could not understand. I gave my allegiance to Hitler and in doing so, I sold my soul to whatever it was that was controlling his destiny. That same darkness now controlled my own. I merely served it by obeying every command to murder given to me.

I was not my own. I felt the nature within me to do evil. I felt it. I could not escape it even if I had wanted to do so. It was so powerful. It was wicked. I cannot say the day or the hour when it entered me, but enter me it did and I became its pawn to do evil to men."

"Alright then Henrich. Next question. What feelings about this being right or wrong have you had since your death as a man?"

"There is no question Diane that since my death I have considered the enormity of my sins.

Once I died, that which was evil left me to find another like me who would succumb to its demands to harm men. I was dead. What good was I anymore to do its will? Men are living and it is best to use one who is living to oppress the living. Though I have seen that they do try to oppress the living by other means, it is not nearly as effective and they do not enjoy it as much for it is less of a personal involvement for them. For when they can impose their nature on a human, they are engaging in the evil themselves. They see it as kind of a mirror image of the holy spirit coming upon a man only it is an evil spirit imposing itself on a man who has engaged an evil thought, imaging it for themselves. So they seek the living who are disengaged from the God of Heaven and who are disillusioned with Him in the hopes of finding one who will do their bidding. It is a game of sorts for them. They keep trying until they find a willing soul to do evil and there I was . . . angry with my father. Hating what I was made to do as it left me without friends and I was mocked by my peers for being a snitch. My father did not respect me more for assisting him in knowing what was going on in the school. He merely sued me, just like Hitler used me to do his dirty work. Was this my destiny? I do not think so but it is too late for me now I suppose. I am here and I deserve to be here. If I were the God of Heaven, I would not release me for I killed more of His people than anyone since the beginning of time and I did it with pleasure for that was the nature that was upon me at the time. Evil. Murder. Hatred. They were all there. It was a hollow existence for it was not "me" who ruled in my body at all. It was them."

"Possession is what we are talking about here. You were possessed by the spirits of murder and hatred, Henrich."

"There were others as well. They mocked me constantly saying that I did not deserve forgiveness when I died. They reminded me of the evil that I had done and they were relentless to tell me that I had murdered thousands upon thousands of innocent people. They only leave me to torment others when someone new comes to them. I am tired, exhausted in my mind from thinking of what I have done. I do not wish to live and yet I cannot die. I realize the truth of what I have done, they are right and yet I exist to relive it over and over again. No escape."

"It is my duty Henrich to tell you that despite the evil that you have done, there is forgiveness even for you. I know that this sounds ridiculous but you do not know the God of Heaven.

His name is Alejandro, his name was hidden so very long ago from the people and so it is difficult to know something that has been hidden from the consciousness of our being. There are those who have worked hard to keep us from knowing Him, from serving Him, and from being taught the truth about Him through the ages . . . particularly from knowing His true name.

These men work with evil to keep us in the dark, to harm us, to poison us and to kill us. Their desire is to keep us from our heavenly destinies. These men did exist before your life began Henrich. Did what they do contribute to the evil that was there to tempt you? Very possibly, but you did make the choice yourself to do evil, to submit to evil and to do its bidding. When your father asked you to spy on others, to judge them and "turn them in", you agreed did you not?"

"I admit," Henrich responded, "but he was the authority over me. He was the one to teach me what was right and good and if I did not do what he said, I was punished."

"Yes, but we are judged by what we choose to do. All of us are judged by what we do that is contrary to the nature of our God in Heaven. Now it is not He who judges us, but it is our soul who testifies against us, and the nature of that which exists as evil in the world. Again, is that evil here because we created it, "we" meaning mankind with our thoughts from the beginning of time, choosing to do that which is evil rather than that which is good? Those are good questions for Alejandro."

"Do you know that you were loved by Alejandro. That he still loves you Henrich and wishes that you would repent for what you did do on earth? Do you know that you can be forgiven? Are you capable of loving Him in return? Do you know that all can be forgiven? Even you?"

"Is this true? It is not what I have heard from those here. I have heard just the opposite. There are some sins that are just too monumental to be forgiven such as what I did while serving Hitler."

"Who would you choose to serve today Henrich if given the chance, Alejandro or Hitler?"

"I would most certainly choose to serve Alejandrro. I have had enough of serving evil. I have had enough of those burdensome thoughts to do harm to others. I do not wish to entertain them anymore and I wish to be free of them. Is that possible? Can I experience freedom Diane?"

"We will have to see what Alejandro does want to say to you. He is the one to determine what is to become of your soul. He must determine if you are telling the truth about whom you will serve for you did not choose wisely before. Are you willing to repent for the things that you did to so many? If so, present your case to Alejandro and he will hear it. Do you know that planes have been flying overhead in my city poisoning the skies? Toxic fumes coming from planes just to poison people with potentially a toxic nano-organism which can be breathed into the lungs of innocent men, women and children in this town, and in others throughout the world. We are being attacked by an evil which has grown steadily since you participated in creating such a huge energy of evil in the world. You must repent and you must ask Alejandro to remove this evil from the earth, forever now. Our freedoms, liberties, and our very lives are at stake around the globe. Evil has grown far surpassing the ability of men to seek God for these evil men poison our water, our air and our food keeping us tired, complacent and out of energy unable to lift our heads enough to fight back the evil or even to remember to ask Him for help. It is tragic. Tragic!!"

"Is it true? Is it true that I am responsible for creating this evil that is still on the earth and growing?"

"What do you think, Henrich? Why don't you ask Alejandro? Why don't you speak your peace to Alejandro? It is your time to speak to Him."

"But how can I face one so great, so good, so loving with the shame of what I have done upon me? The guilt . . . . the remorse. How can I face Him now? I cannot stand in His presence with such evil upon me?"

"You can begin by preparing your mind. Begin to let go of the thoughts of remorse, regret, shame, guilt, etc. and send all negative thoughts to the light and all thoughts of murder, torture, and those kinds of thoughts, send them back to creative light so that they can be absorbed, and perhaps used for good next time, and not for evil. Do this. I will wait for you.

"Diane, I have acknowledged these evil thoughts and asked that they go to the light. I have done this and I am experiencing a rejuvenation. I am experiencing a regeneration of my being. Your light has shown me the truth of who I truly was and I was covered by an enormity of evil, so much so that I lost myself in it, no longer recognizing my soul, my being, and my God. I was lost."

"I wish to speak to Alejandro now please, Diane. Alejandro, this is Henrich Himmler I come before you having released the evil of my ways and the evil thoughts of my being to the light, and I am asking to be washed clean of all this evil energy and its nature for all eternity. I do repent for the unkind, and murderous things that I did against your people, and against the whole of humanity for Diane tells me that this evil has grown in the earth and still does harm to mankind despite my death. This is appalling to me and I do wish to see it end for all eternity.

I ask that you would forgive me, and cleanse my soul. I do repent for my lack of love for You, and for not serving You in my life. I choose this day to serve Alejandro and I submit myself unto you this hour. I know that I am the worst of the worst but Diane tells me that you are a God of love and that you do not condemn your own. Am I yours too? Can you forgive me please Alejandro? What can I do to serve you and be saved? I humble myself before you."

This was incredible to listen to as the go between and I was welling up with tears.

"Diane, do not cry for this one. I will handle it. Henrich, you are correct in saying that your deeds were the worst in the history of man, for I have seen many come and go who did harm to men, but I have never seen the likes of you on earth. What your father did to you is nothing compared to what you did do to others under Hitler's regime.. I know.. I saw it all and I wondered at how one man could have so much hatred for others. So much hatred. You never did ask Me at any time during all of that time with Hitler to stop you from yourself. You did not cry out to me to stop you. Why? Why did you forge ahead with this evil knowing that it was not of you?"

"I don't know," Himmler sheepishly replied, "I don't know that I knew how to break free. I did not know You or how to cry out to you, and why would you listen to such a wretched man as me? I had already done so much that was against You. I had too much shame and too much guilt to face you, even now, I feel it."

It was Alejandro's turn to reply to Himmler and it would be forceful.

"I will remove the guilt and shame if I do indeed have your word that you did not know how to seek Me and you were compelled not of yourself, but of evil, to participate in it and to do evil against man.. I do know this nature, and it is not of Me. But I do know it for it seeks to devour My own. I will accept your repentance unto Me now though I will grant your freedom Henrich, it is not without a caveat for Me. You will serve Me forever in eternity to repay your debt to society by sending the energy of repentance upon the earth for siding with evil to do harm to mankind against Me, and against My nature. You will send the energy of release of the captives for I will no longer allow My people to be controlled by a religious or legalistic energy which keeps them from hearing Me. You are the one to free them this time Henrich for you are the one who enslaved them with this evil. You are the one who enslaved them for when you perpetuated such an evil upon My people, they no longer believed that I spoke to them and they no longer believed that I could hear them, for what kind of God would allow such an evil to come upon them? This is what they cried out when their lives were stolen from them, their destinies, their children, and wives. What kind of God they said, 'would allow us to be killed in this way?' And yet, it was not Me who did this to them, it was you. Therefore, you will serve Me forever in eternity to repair this damage done to My people until they are all free and then you will serve Me to prevent it ever from happening again. Understood?"

"I understand and I accept this proposal to serve you Alejandro. You have my word to do as you ask and I humbly accept your terms. I am humbled by your mercy for me. Thank you Alejandro. I will also praise your name in the heavens as a merciful God."

Alejandro though merciful is no fool and speaks with authority back to Henrich Himmler.

"You will serve Me as I have called you. I have others to offer praise unto Me. So be it Diane. You are free to go and relax. Henrich is My matter now. You again have done well to lesson the burden on the world for people will begin to see the error of their ways, repenting unto Me for the energy of war, torture, poisoning and killing shall be lifted and then men will see who they have given themselves over to be, and they will feel the guilt and shame of who they are, and they will repent. This is a good thing and the whole world will rejoice as the evil abates.

You will see. A new day is coming Diane. Celebrate for you have done well once more. I adore you. There are none like you. Not one who could love another enough to set the wicked free from their transgressions to free the world. Who would think it?"

"You would think it and thus I can. ☺ For you are me, isn't that what you did say? Now please enough poison for one week. PLEASE . . . no more poison in our skies. No more planes tonight, please! I beg of you. Make them go home. Please clear our skies of this poison. Haven't I done something tonight to be granted this request for the people in the land here?"

I know that this appeal sounds ridiculous perhaps particularly to those who do not even "see" the planes in the skies dumping all kinds of chemicals on the heads of the populations worldwide to damage our lungs, cells, and immune systems but I see, and I have been outraged from the first plane I saw doing this in our State. Outraged! Particularly when the local weather man on television claims that the day will be clear, blue skies and beautiful without having ever mentioned the presence of strange, obscuring white fumes almost like bug spray across the atmosphere.

"I will see what I can do," Alejandro said to me. "You have earned it. I will see what I can do. Well done Diane. Rest well. Tomorrow is a new day. Truly! A new day in the earth has come.".

I immediately felt the presence of a soul's energy as Alejandro signed off. He said this to me.

"This is Henrich, Diane. I must thank you for assisting me in finding my freedom and for showing me the love of Alejandro. You have given me a reason for being by reconnecting me to Alejandro and I must thank you. I would like to do something for you upon reaching the heavens. May I offer something to you?" (I asked Henrich what he had in mind.)

"I would like to ask that a door be opened for you to find your agent this week still. It is time for you to get your book published properly. I want to send you your agent. Keep your eyes and ears opened. You will not need to self-publish. Do not go with Bow press or the others. Your agent is going to call you. I will see to it. Look for it to happen. It is Friday tomorrow. Not much left of this week is there? This is my gift to you. It will happen. Adieu then Diane. Thank you. I know that this was hard for you but I was not an evil man. I was overcome by it in the world. I was not evil."

"I believe it Henrich Himmler because I trust Alejandro. Adieu to you Henrich. Love to all in the heavens. Show them who you can be . . . love."

"Just one more thing. Tell the world that Henrich Himmler has repented of his sins against humanity. Tell them that I was not evil as a child but that I opened a door to doing that which was evil, instead of choosing that which was good, and this is when evil entered my heart. I was not evil. I apologize to the world and her people for the harm which I did do while living in it.

I have repented to the God of Heaven, and I highly recommend that those who followed me or did as I did, repent, and forgiveness will be given unto you. Repent, and turn around, for there is no future in having followed evil. Your destiny is not there. Your destiny remains in Alejandro. Follow Him and you may still achieve yours. Adieu."

Franklin Roosevelt

January 30, 1882 – April 12, 1945

FDR was born into the prominent and privileged Roosevelt family and was the only child of James Roosevelt and Sara Ann Delano Roosevelt. He was educated at the best schools and later in life assumed the position of the Presidency of the United States of America and served during the Great Depression and also during the second World War. He sadly endured some long personal battles in his life with illness, when at the young age of 39, he contracted polio. He established the March of Dimes to assist others who suffered with polio and I believe the contributions were to provide funds for those with polio. I personally considered that perhaps a plot was involved with how he contracted polio to serve an Elitist agenda for pushing vaccines? FDR did not like the vaccine programs and he also hated war and did not want America to participate in World War II, and yet, war is a huge money maker for some. Different countries have different resources some of which can make those who extract those resources rich. When FDR married, he married his fifth cousin. Is that legal? I was also surprised to learn that he was the only President who served 4 terms in the Presidency. These are just a few trivial facts and a thought of my own thrown in before I begin this President's transition home to the heavens.

"This is Franklin Roosevelt. I was President of the United States. FDR they called me."

"Hello sir. How may I assist you?"

"By showing me the way home for it is certain that I am not there. Perhaps it is due to all of the compromise I made as a leader of the United States of America.

"Tell me more about that Franklin?" I asked.

230

"Well, if you must know, I sold out to money, fame success and power."

Not good so I asked the question which was so obvious. "To whom did you sell out Franklin?"

"The Elite for who else is there with their kind of power," he said.

This one was easy for me to answer. He asked that as a question and I had the answer.

"Certainly I know One, the Almighty, Alejandro!"

"Ok, point taken but I honestly did not know Him. I only knew myself and the men who promised me everything."

I had to ask him then, "In exchange for what Franklin?"

"Compliance with whatever agenda they were pushing at the time. Whether it was taxation, declarations of war, moving soldiers about to protect their own common interests and the promotion of vaccines too I was against it but who was I compared to them. Their power was and certainly is far reaching Diane."

"How is it that their power is far reaching?"

"Well, they are in every nation and in all leadership whether it be government, government entities, the private sector for they have purchased many companies and they control all of the higher learning in the country and most of the lower schools but for the few they did not fund with government money. Certainly you've seen this scenario played out. They will teach the children their ways; compliance with government, submission to their will and way of thinking. Now you know firsthand what captivity looks like."

"Yes, I do know Franklin, and I do despise it."

Franklin responded immediately, "and well you should too for you are not one of them and so it is you desire freedom and liberty to achieve your destiny."

"So what do you have to tell me that is new Franklin. These things are known. My husband says all of the stories here are the same. I don't agree and each soul has their own story and lessons to share however it is true that these souls did not acknowledge Him or achieve their destinies consequently."

"Not all of these souls were President for one thing hence what they did was of no consequence to a whole nation."

"Not true. All negative energy leaves its mark on the earth and we are affected by it."

"I see your point, Diane. Let me address a few things from *my* perspective that only the President is aware when chemtrails are done. The President is aware when other beings are being placated on the earth. The President is aware that we are providing "food" to these beings. The President is aware of who attacked the U.S. on 9/11. It was not Al Qaida.

They would have to have access to a lot of airline schedules and the planes would have to run "on time" according to them to coordinate so precisely three planes hijacking all at once. It is the same blindness which exists as to the chemtrails. The people cannot imagine their government would participate in such a thing. They don't do it willingly. They are placated.

They are subjected to mind control manipulation while they sleep and they are hypnotized as are the pilots of those laying down chemtrails. This is precisely why Alejandro does not wish to harm them."

"Yes, I know, He has told me so also explaining why He cannot take action against them. He is love and long suffering for His own."

"So He wishes to reach all of His people in order that they would fulfill their destinies. The hope of the world is in those destinies you know?"

"I do believe this is true," I said.

"He is not willing that any would perish Diane. This is the story of your light and your life as you continue to assist souls in their understanding so they may live."

"What else does He want you to tell me for humanity to know?"

"This one is complicated a bit. Are you listening now, Diane?"

"Yes, sir."

"The reason Alejandro wants me to speak to you is specific to the mind control programs going on through the government It is not limited to service men and their wives and children who live on government bases. It is much wider spread than just this here. It exists in every country, in all television programming and often it is hidden in the speeches given by your political leaders.

Do you realize that the person elected by the people no longer exists? He exists only physically.

His mind is not his own. Taken from him then by those who have the ability to do so.

They need only to get these leaders into a compromising situation and then they sell their souls basically. It happened to me. Lots of women were brought to me secretly but alas they were filming me for extortion. They would show my family what they would show the citizens. What chance did I have? Not only this, they are capable of exploiting those they wish to control further. They do this through fabricating lies about those they wish to exploit. They are very good at it and they have every possibility available to them. They own the F.B.I. and the C.I.A. don't they? False documents are their forte."

"We should get that . . . Franklin."

"So, who do you imagine is behind 9/11?" Franklin asked me.

"Not going to guess. You tell me you can see everything now."

"It was *not* who you were told it was and yet so many of the people believe these lies," he said with some passion I must say.

"Why do they believe the lies?" I asked him.

"Programming!" Franklin exclaimed. "How many times did they *tell* you who did it?"

Doesn't anyone think it ludicrous that the President was sitting with school children on camera when it happened? That was awfully early in the morning for him to do story time.

Gullible is the word here. The people are gullible."

"I know this is true, Franklin. I thought it odd that the President was reading a book about a goat to children that morning when I have never seen him in a classroom before this day.

The people are blind and do not have "eyes" to see. So what is the answer? One person can do *very* little."

"Your underestimate your value Diane. You do much to make the world a better place."

"Perhaps, I do underestimate my value. Thank you, Franklin."

I was not quite finished with this conversation with FDR and so I returned here to reconnect and to see what it was we needed to do further.

"FDR, we left off with you saying that I was underestimating my contribution to humanity.

Perhaps so, but we need more voices, more people listening, more people praying. We need to have an awakening of the people."

"I promised you Diane, you will have your reward. It is coming. I see it. Do not lose hope in this. It is coming. Now, the people have been deceived for a long time. The Elite have been deceiving the people since the beginning of time when they collaborated with the enemy, they made agreements with the enemy against the rest of you. It is quid pro quo. They do certain things for those who are not like you, and in return, they are given advanced technological systems to use as they wish to make money, to control you, or simply to enjoy as they wish.

It works very nicely for them. Why should they give it up? In their minds they have earned it."

"How in the world do they figure that one," I asked Franklin.

"They, the Elite, have helped this kind live and so they are getting rewarded for doing so."

"But at what cost did they help "this kind" live, Franklin? What lives did they turn over to them for their use? To eat? For sex? For experiments? How many people have suffered and been sacrificed for this purpose?"

"Too many to count I am afraid Diane. Best not to think about that one."

"I am going to have to come back to this again. My family wants to go and get some food. Life first Franklin. I am sorry. Please hold to that thought and I will return.

"It is now 9 p.m. and I am back from dinner and family time Franklin and you did *not* leave by the feel of my poor foot."

"I am here now Diane. That was not me."

That was weird. Some interference. I was hearing some rather negative commentary about leadership.

FDR commented on it also stating, "Some interference I am afraid. It is much better now.

Thank you for clearing that interference. You will not hear me speak of who is being controlled by these beings because to do so is to incite much fear in many and this we do to want. We must maintain some degree of decorum while awakening many to the truth. So, if you do hear something different than this, it should be cleared and ignored."

"Thank you for that bit of information. I will keep that in mind. Better not to focus on who is compromised and just get the truth out."

"Exactly," said FDR. "It is the truth which will set men free. Despite the fact that that too is the truth, it will be rejected by all of those who are not cleared first and then you lose them."

"Got it!" I said.

"Now, what I am to tell you is that you must be careful who you speak to about what the government is doing Not everyone is on your side. If you speak to those who are not on your side, they will reveal it to those who are on the lookout for such as you. They do not wish to have their boat rocked. They are on a roll. They do not wish to have the truth come out and one loud voice is one loud voice too many to the."

"I don't like this game, Franklin."

At this time, I felt the energy of Alejandro and welcomed him to the conversation.

"Alejandro is here Franklin. I send you love Alejandro. I apologize for being cranky this morning. I really was bad. Forgive me, please."

"My daughter, you do not need to apologize. I have asked much of you and you are doing well to assist many. I do understand that it is overwhelming to manage to live in this world and another at the same time, and in fact, you are juggling three dimensions at once, do you realize that this is what you are doing at this very moment? FDR is in one dimension, you a second, and Me, a third."

"Nice!"

"I wish to speak to FDR. We will call him that for short if you like. Franklin, this is Alejandro.

Do you know who I am?"

"I do and I am in awe at this moment to hear Your voice."

Alejandro continued to speak to FDR, "I am here to tell you a thing or two about your service in my nation. First, you did not seek Me when those who wished to control you came for you.

You did not call out to Me. Why?"

"I did not know what to do. I did not know who to call. I had not called You before, and why would You listen to me then?"

"Many of My people do not call Me until they meet with some trouble or another. How did you expect to do such a job without My help? It was inevitable that trouble would find you there.

The greater the calling, the greater the challenge to do the job. Evil loves to tempt My own, testing you, challenging you, and attempting to control you. This is the nature of the game in which you are engaged in the world. Those who persevere gain the highest levels of honor in My kingdom. Those who give in to the ways of the evil one are not honored, and so it goes. I cannot help those who do not call. That is rule number one. Rule number two is similar. If My people do not seek Me, I am not to solve their problems for them. They must seek Me and so it is written. Ask and it shall be given. Very plainly stated and yet My people do not ask Me for much. All of this trouble in the world, and My people do not ask Me to help them. Why?

They don't understand the game. I will answer those who seek Me, and I will help those who ask Me. So why didn't you ask Me? I ask you once again?"

"I could not. They threatened me. I was not to call upon Your name they said. If I did, they would kill me. I feared death more than I trusted that You would answer me. I did not know You. Why would You answer me?"

"As I said, most of My people do not need Me until they run into trouble, and then they do call Me time and time after time. I hear them calling when they cannot solve their problems but not when the problems are involving the whole nation. I do not hear them calling Me now for instance. I should be hearing millions calling Me now and yet, where are My people?"

"I cannot speak to this situation.. But I am aware of something that happened under my watch. There were those whose intent was to infiltrate the churches with false doctrine. They would teach that

You no longer spoke to the people through your prophets. It was understood that if the people did not seek You, then they would not know what to do, and so it was a game plan to send out those who would teach Your people that You no longer spoke to Your people. The message would be that Your doctrine was closed, and only what was written was to be allowed. This way no new guidance could be received by the people for You no longer spoke."

"Sorry, but that is just crazy," I chimed in. "Why did the people believe this and what movement was that? Where did it start?"

"It started in government and was taken to the streets, and then moved into the churches, one church at a time. It was quite successful don't you think so Diane?

"Much too successful. Is there anything written to this effect that this was the game plan of government? To teach this lie to the people? And which part of government are we talking about?"

"The same side of government which exists secretly to control everything. You cannot know them Diane by name, just by their nature shall they be known to you. Those are the rules of the game. By their nature you shall know them."

"Let me repeat. I don't like this game. People murder in this game. People cheat in this game. People lie, murder, steal, maim, rape and destroy in this game. I don't like it."

The next sentence was spoken by an imposter but I heard them. They said, "It is all about which side will win. Good or evil. Alejandro is convinced that good will overcome evil."

"I would certainly like this game to be over and let's just play nice shall we?"

Again, the imposter spoke, "You would like to see the game end?"

"That isn't what I said. I would like the bad stuff to stop now. Enough is enough. Why can't we have peace for a while where such horrible things just don't happen anymore?"

This one who is in favor of evil keeps speaking into my conversation. This time it said,

"Don't you think that life would be boring?"

"I don't want to think like this right now. You are trying to tell me that all of this bad stuff is important in some twisted way and I don't like it."

It was then that FDR broke back through and asked me if I heard it. He said, "Diane, did you hear it?"

I responded to FDR, "Do you mean the defense of evil?"

"Yes, the defense of evil?"

"So FDR, what was the last thing you said?"

"I said, that by their nature they shall be known to you and they defended their right to be evil".

"So whose "name" should go in place of your initials FDR in my record here?"

"This is a good question, Diane. Why don't you ask Alejandro?"

"Asking right now. Alejandro, apparently a couple of energies of another kind did jump in and have their say while I was listening to FDR. Was this at your request? Is this why I sneezed, when they left? What should I call "them"?

I told FDR that I was waiting for The Great One to answer us. There was no immediate answer so I invited FDR to come back.

At that moment I did hear Alejandro. He said, "A little lesson for you there Diane."

"Yes, but how often does that happen? Does it happen when I am listening to these souls?"

Alejandro's answer was "Not usually, because I oversee these transitions but you must know that they are about and capable of interjecting themselves into other people's lives at will."

"Is that what happened to Catherine Zeta Jones? She has suffered some kind of "attack" in my estimation.

"Precisely," replied Alejandro. "She cannot kick them out the way that you can because she doesn't know how. Do you want to ask her husband if he wants some help?"

"I would Alejandro but none of these people respond to me. The only way to them is through an agent, and that door is slammed tightly closed without an agent to help me."

"Let's do this. Tomorrow contact Diana at Authorhouse. Tell her that you are interested in publishing your book with them. Tell her you already have the ebook in process. Ask her if they can adjust the cost of publishing to reflect that these two biggees are done and paid for, but you are interested in the Hollywood package, and getting an agent to assist you. What can they do for you? Find out. Tell her that the book is engaging, and involves a number of Hollywood personalities and you think that it would make quite a story for a movie. See what she says."

"Will do. Thank you. Please tell me about the sneezing."

"Well, you had it right. You perceived the difference between FDR and the other nature. And when you recognized them, they left at My direction."

I know that I am persistent and sometimes He won't tell me what I want to know but I must ask.

"And they are . . . ???"

"A little creation of Mine to make the game more interesting I challenge My own people to see whether or not they will be true to Me and to their own nature"

"I don't know about this because then they suffer if they succumb to your temptations of them.

Is this playing nice?"

"As I have said before, I have to find out who they are."

So I asked, "Who can they be? What are the possibilities for who they are?"

He called me on this saying, "Inquisitive one aren't you?"

"You made me that way." ☺

"Okay. You have asked the question so many times Diane without an answer. Do you really want to know?"

"Um hmmm. I do."

"Well then brace yourself. You know that there exists another kind of being on the planet, right? And you know that they are capable of mixing their seed with My own, right? (yes) Well, there you have it. I have to see which one is the stronger dna. Mine, or theirs. If theirs is the stronger, then I cannot bring them home for they will destroy My people in their home. Though they attempt to absorb that which is My own, they cannot. For your vibration is greater than their own. They have tried many things to make it so but they are not successful. So, I have devised a way to test those who are My own to make certain that those I love are not lost. They are a tricky race. They try to deceive Me in so many ways and yet I see it all, know all, and am not easily deceived. If I can connect to My people, We will overcome this trickery. This is My plan. Are you in?"

"Yes, of course Alejandro. But I can tell you right now. I do not want to go to any of their "parties". They creep me out."

"I will protect you Diane. Abide in Me and I will abide in you. We are one, remember?"

"I do. Is FDR still here?"

"Yes, but I will move him on. Tell him so and thank him for participating in the little ruse to get you to see the way of the enemy. He is capable of leading people to think they are crazy. Bipolar if you will."

"Do you mean enemy if this one is created by You, Alejandro?"

"I created this energy to be the enemy of man to test you otherwise how would I know my own?

This is why you are not to hate these energies when you send them back to Me. I created them therefore love and do not hate."

"You are amazing. Very creative. ☺ Very creative, Creator, you are!"

"Why thank you Diane. That is a nice compliment. I like to think so."

"Wow, you know that Your people really don't understand the words of the bible at all and what they mean don't you?"

"Yes," Alejandro replied, "but you do and you can tell them. Visit my churches some more.

I will find you some people to listen to what you have to say."

"Persistent, you are. I don't like the feeling in there . . . in those churches. They are just not free."

"It is good that you know the feeling of freedom, Diane. Now help some of My people to find it too. Go and visit some churches."

"I am going to go to bed right now Alejandro. I was abandoned today by my husband. I thought about going today but I do not want to go by myself. He needs to come with me. Protecting me from those who devour."

"They won't bite your head off unless you provoke them. Only speak to those I show you. You will do fine."

"Okay. After vacation. Next weekend is kind of my Mother's Day celebration. I will celebrate Christ consciousness and freedom through knowing that we are energy and not just a body, and I will celebrate that You gave us the ability to have children by being mothers."

"Thank you Diane. Okay then. You are free to go. We will catch this other soul that is here tomorrow."

"Blessings of love then Alejandro. No pain in the feet then. These souls have to let me sleep without hurting my feet. This is not good. I want to sleep without pain."

"I will set the standard Diane. You are to rest without pain. So be it."

"Thank you Alejandro once more. Love to you."

"To you too beloved."

Though Alejandro told me that he would send FDR on his way, FDR came back to tell me something.

"Diane, I have to tell you something else. When I get to heaven, Alejandro would have me do something for you as well. I would like to ask that a door be opened unto you for the purpose of losing the wait that has clung to you for so long. You have waited for success for years now and it is time to release the wait."

"Praise be to Alejandro. Although I think others said that they would also ask for this??? So now, I am sending "I am waiting" to the light. So be it. Go to the light."

"And I will confirm that it is done for you accordingly."

"Thank you FDR. Thank you."

"That will be all for me then Diane. Well done. It was my pleasure meeting with you. You have quite a spirit and a destiny still before you. Do not give up. Push forward to the end and it will be done for you. Stay strong."

"Thank you. I will look forward to see "I am waiting" gone."

"Consider it done for you. Adieu Diane."

"Adieu, FDR."

"One last thing before I go Diane. Please tell the world that FDR has repented before Alejandro and asked for forgiveness for not serving Him as President, rather than serving men who did not love Him. I repent and I do ask for His forgiveness. I will serve Him now in any way which He determines that I should serve Him."

Now Alejandro is back to speak to FDR.

"I do receive FDR's repentance unto Me. I will ask that He serve Me in the heavens and in this way shall he serve Me. FDR, I have heard your repentance unto Me. I shall forgive you for not lifting up My name and for making oaths unto others who were not gods, rather than unto Me.

Now you shall serve Me, and no other shall you serve. You shall serve Me in this way. You shall send the energy of repentance unto Me unto the land of the United States of America, and My people will repent for what they have done in ignoring Me, and My calls unto them. You will send the energy of repentance for all of your days in eternity and thus shall you achieve a new destiny and the nation shall again be called by My name. I shall give her a new name in that day. Wait and see. So be it."

"Thank you Alejandro. It shall be done for You as You ask. I am Yours! Thank you.

This is good news Diane. Now I shall leave you. I will remember you all of my days Diane..

I won't forget to open the door to remove the waiting."

"Looking forward to that one FDR. Thank you and adieu.

"Adieu then Diane.

Henry Brooks Adams

February 16, 1838 – March 27, 1918

It was late on April 20, 2011 and I approached this task with first mentioning the lateness of the hour. I asked the soul to please tell me their name so that I might go and rest. I asked for a confirmation of the name which I heard which was Henry Adams. I told him that I looked up his name and I then asked him if the picture and information I saw there was related to him.

"Do I have your name correct sir? Are you Henry Adams who attended Harvard?"

"Indeed, you do have my name correct. I am Henry Adams." Henry Adams was born in 1838 to one of the country's most prominent families. John Quincy Adams was his own father's grandfather. Henry was born to a family where members had been fortunate enough to become President, wealthy members of society, and even signers of the Constitution.

His father served under Abraham Lincoln as Ambassador to the United Kingdom and Henry went to London also where he continued his education into politics and leadership. He later on went to the U.S. becoming a journalist and writer. Much later in 1912, Henry Adams suffered a stroke. Interesting fact, he had purchased tickets for the return trip of the Titanic to Europe when it sank.

"And to what do I owe the honor," Henry?"

"Honor indeed. I believe it is I who owe you the honor for speaking with me while I am removed to a not so pleasant existence I might add. I am here because I did not give any glory in my life to the Almighty, and I have had plenty of time to consider why it is that this was my life. I presume that much is owed to what I did not know about Him, for those of higher education spent less and less time discussing the topic of enlightenment. Much time was spent discussing politics however and this is where I found myself engaged, in politics."

"I see, and?"

"Well, as you can now see from the article written about me, I was also a historian. I did find history fascinating and enjoyed writing about the history of the world. Much of what was written by me was done secretly, due to some of my allegiances, I could not write openly about what I believed or came to know as it was forbidden."

"What? What do you mean forbidden Henry? You lived in America did you not? Who forbid you to write about the truth of history?"

"Those who wished to rewrite history of course. They wished to rewrite it and change the course of history. I was perfectly aware of what they were capable of doing for I saw it with my own eyes. I was a Harvard man remember?"

"What is that supposed to mean," I asked?

"I think you know, or perhaps you don't exactly know do you?"

"No, I do not know what you mean. Do you wish to tell me? I dare say much can happen to you now."

"Harvard is one of those schools which is akin to The Elite. They recruit for The Elite from Harvard looking for the best of the brightest to serve The Elite. You are invited in not suspecting that once you join forces with them you will never quite be the same. You lose your freedom the minute you enter in their doors I am afraid Diane. I watched many a fine man destroyed by this allegiance. Once free to be whomever they chose to be in life, there were now pledged to be whomever The Elite would decide that they would be. Freedom lost and nothing gained unless you are happy with being told how to live your life, what to believe and what to write about and what not to write about. I lost the ability to tell things as I saw them when I joined their factions.

Consequently, I was not the man I might otherwise have been at the end of my days. I lost all hope and will to live when I saw what could happen to even the most successful men. They could lose their lives at any time at the direction of The Elite. You see, I was supposed to be on the Titanic. I was booked to go on that maiden voyage and decided otherwise. Had I been on the ship, they would have been rid of one more reporter of the truth, Henry Adams.

"So are you indicating that the sinking of the Titanic was deliberate," I asked Henry.

"Let's just say that when there are a number of millionaires rising up in the United States of America who cannot be influenced by The Elite, they must do something to control the situation. There are ways to get millionaires to submit to the hierarchy of control. They have their means. Watch how many of them suffer "consequences" in their lives, just for the pleasure of being rich. A fair number of them must "go to jail" for the pleasure of keeping their money, which they earned, but if they do not wish to join The Elite, well pressure can be brought to bear upon them to persuade them otherwise."

"Great. So how do you avoid joining if they send in the thugs to threaten, discredit, and ruin your reputation to destroy you unless you do as they say? How can you win in this world if these bad guys lie in wait to destroy anyone who by their sheer will and intelligence and perhaps even with the blessing of the Almighty and His guidance achieve something with their lives."

"Well, you see, I did not have the protection of the Almighty because I did not know Him. You do. Many I did see fall did not know Him either and certainly none of those serving The Elite know Him, serve Him, or even acknowledge Him, in fact, it is forbidden to do so."

"How odd. I believe that many people who joined the Masons thought that they were joining a "do-gooder" organization with "Christian" leanings. Not so?"

"Hardly. The only connection to Christianity is how they don't like them, at all, and they are consistent in this throughout the organization. Though you may be led to believe something like this at first, there is no question but that once you are indoctrinated all leanings towards a God in Heaven are removed. Your allegiance is to the clan you belong to and not to any God in Heaven. You owe your blood to the brotherhood. You give your money to the brotherhood and you serve the brotherhood and no one else. If needed, you serve. If called, you serve. If anyone in the organization needs you, you come. You see, you are bound to them by blood for in blood you do agree to serve them."

"I will ask this and if allowed, you may tell me. Are the Masons, or members of the Masons, The Elite?"

"That is one for Alejandro to tell you Diane in due time.. You see, though you may know some of their names already, most people do not believe you. They do not wish to hear that their former leaders are akin to The Elite, the Illuminati, or the Masonic Order. It troubles their sensibilities that they could be so deceived by the very people they voted for to serve them in offices of the Presidency, the House and the Senate, or as Governors, Judges, School Superintendents, and the like. This would only serve to make them feel vulnerable for then they would have to see that they do not know how to judge a man's nature. Indeed, they do not for apart from Alejandro they can do nothing to know a man."

"You are correct. They do not wish to hear it. They don't want to believe it and so, they shut their eyes and their ears to the truth and pretend that it isn't so."

"And so it was in my day. People did ignore what they knew to be the truth to protect themselves. If they did not know a thing, then they could distance themselves from it and any harm that came as a result of whatever it as. Now mind you, this does nothing for the condition of a man's integrity. It is difficult to continue to behave as a decent human being while you look the other way to the wrongdoings of your fellow man. Accountability goes by the wayside as all men do what is right in their own eyes. Easy to do as I say when no one is looking so to speak."

"I did my share of looking the other way," said Henry, "and today, I regret it." Today, I do not feel that I did the right thing for I did not stand up for what was right for my country.

I was a great journalist and a good writer and capable of recording the history of the world for academia and yet, I was discouraged by those who did not wish to keep an accurate record of history. Why is that do you suppose? What is wrong with telling the truth about history? I will tell you what is wrong with telling the truth about history. Man learns from his mistakes and in the telling of how wars were won, or victories won, lessons are learned. Mankind learns why it is best not to go to war with one's neighbors. Much is lost, not just lives, but the record of humanity is lost. Wars destroy the record of man which is often kept within the land. This is a threat to those who wish for man to repeat his mistakes over and over again, having learned nothing from the experience of life. No record, no understanding of what not to do. No history recorded, no understanding of what was learned in the past. There is no opportunity to study the history to gain wisdom for the future. This must be avoided at all costs.. It is part of "the plan" to reeducate the world. Rewrite the history and change the lessons learned. Teach humanity new ways of looking at the world from the perspective of a new world order. History has become a danger to their indoctrination of the youth. They must control what is learned from the earliest age so as not to allow room for understanding from past mistakes. And so it goes . . . repeat the same mistakes over and over again. The goal? Lost lives. Lost destinies. More control and power for them."

Henry continued, "This is what you are experiencing now as history is stolen from you and your children. You must seek to preserve the history of humanity for it teaches your children about life. It teaches them that there are consequences for certain kinds of choices, consequences to individuals, nations and even the world. A price will be paid for making the wrong choices in life and sometimes it is an entire nation that will pay a price for the choices of its leaders. You are seeing that now in the United States of America and yet it is not too late to take a stand for freedom and liberty if the right people will step up and lead."

"I am speechless. And, I am getting quite tired. Two choices, one, we finish up but I perhaps miss talking with you more about important matters; or, I return in the morning to hear the end of this from you Henry. What do you think?"

"I think that it is best if you return in the morning for I have a bit more to say. I will be here. As you know, I can go nowhere without your assistance. I have more to say."

"I promise you Henry that I will return around 11 a.m. for I am going to a class in the morning. Hold that thought. I appreciate your contribution to the school of thought. I perhaps will be posting this, in part, for others to see. However, I cannot possibly mention "names" that would attract trouble to myself or my loved ones."

"I don't blame you and now you see the problem that I did have being so close to them in Washington."

"Frustrating. I will return in the morning, Henry. Bless you."

"I will be here."

"Henry, I did not make it a 11 a.m. I apologize. I have too many things to do but I would never leave you at risk of remaining there. I send you love this evening. I am here to listen to what else do wish to tell me about yourself, about this experience, about what you wish to convey to Alejandro."

"I am here Diane. I am so relieved that you did come back again. I apologize too for I did pester you to speak with me but please understand that there is no one else doing what you are doing to release those of us bound here. In order to leave, we need to be released from negative energies. In order to leave, we need to feel better about ourselves and we must have our energy increased. There is no one else helping us to achieve this and so, we are coming to you."

"Honestly, it is okay but when I need to rest, eat or have so much work to do. It takes time to sit and listen and to record the words of the souls who wish to speak to me. I just have to balance my time well. I did feel that one. Ouch!"

"Apologies. Just getting a good grip for I am sincerely ready to leave now. I wanted to complete my conversation with you. We were discussing The Elite and how I suspected that there was some involvement with the sinking of the Titanic and I noticed that you were suspect of the possibility already. Let me just say this, I suspected it, I was not able to ever confirm it. Who else might want to get rid of some of the wealthiest men in the nation in one big calamity? No one to fight against their jockeying for positions of greater wealth. No one to compete with their desires for property, and women, for if they were gone, so was their influence. I knew many of these men and they were not the finest men in the world. Their desires were for things of the flesh. They were not regal that they set their sites on creating the finest nation in the world which was charitable to her people, loved the God of Heaven, and found comfort in helping others. These were not those kind of men. Their interests were primarily in themselves and their own families and what they could do that would increase their personal wealth, not the country's wealth"

"Henry, I shared your sentiments about The Elite's desire to control the truth by manipulating the facts of what has happened in the world historically and he agreed that what you said had merit. Eliminating the truth about history does keep humanity repeating the same mistakes over and over, and the cyclical nature of behavior goes on."

"Indeed, and man does not learn anything about his nature. He does not evolve Diane. This is key. If the experience of life is to learn about ourselves and our nature, the idea is to grow from the experience, evolving and sharing what we have learned with those who are not here at the time that we are here. We can all evolve from having had the shared experience of life on earth.

History recorded assists even the next generation to evolve and more quickly for the lessons are absorbed and then they move on to the next quest, learning the next lesson, evolving again. This is not what The Elite want. They cannot control an ever expanding, ever evolving consciousness of humanity. They must control it at all costs."

"They are about to lose big time Henry and they may have to live out some time elsewhere while the earth is healed by the higher beings, so that we can continue the experience here as it was intended, learning what is not love, but hoping that in the end, love wins; thus lessons are learned for all to benefit from them."

"Good point. What I would like to do is to open the door again in heaven for the recording of history for the benefit of generations to come. I will ask that I am permitted to send energy to the earth for those who would be inspired to record the truth of what is happening now so that the generations of the future do not make these same mistakes. What do you think?"

"I think that it is an excellent idea Henry. For there are many who are blinded to the truth and who think that I do not know what I am talking about. They are so blind as to not see The Elite and what they are doing saying that I and others are believers in conspiracy theories when in fact, I am a believer in the truth, and the truth is being shown to me that there are factions afoot who wish to destroy freedom and liberty. I see therefore I know that I am right."

"Unfortunately, these factions have mastered the ability to manipulate the mind through television, computer images, and programming, and through the manipulation of the electromagnetic frequencies being sent from their positions in Alaska in an effort to placate humanity. They know that they are outnumbered. They cannot risk the people having an awakening en masse. It threatens their very livelihood and existence. They must remain secret at all costs and remain in power over the rest of you."

"Not as long as Alejandro is still in power will they rule over me. Not as long as I have my breath will I submit to them."

"That is the spirit but also you must stay clear of them Diane. They have ways of manipulating the most strident resister if they can get you into their quarters. Many a man has lost his freedom under their watch. I mean that literally. They do watch as men are robbed of their freedom by those who know how to do it."

"So David Icke is right then? Has he correctly identified these manipulators in his books and in his lectures?"

"I am searching for the truth on this one. Yes, he is correct. Why do you think that he is so abused by the press, media, and those on the left? They cannot validate him for to do so is to admit that they are who he says that they are. They will never admit it openly however they may be exposed very soon and there will be nowhere to hide then."

"Thank you for that as I believe him and I have read some of his books on what he has discovered about some of these manipulators."

"Once again, you will not discover their history written anywhere where you can find it easily. Perhaps in the hidden halls they might have a record of their masteries and mysteries of appalling acts against humanity. You see, they must hide in order to continue their agenda against mankind. They cannot control an awakened people . . . period. They will continue to deny, mock, berate all of those who speak of their activities as being nonsense, ridiculous, and preposterous. Few will side with those who tell the truth or fear of being attacked by the very people perpetrating the crimes against humanity."

"I look to the day when the Order of Melchizedek is in place and that which is good and right is ordained from the throne on High."

"That is a noble desire to have Diane. Bring it in on your thoughts and prayers. Invite them to come and to rule and to reign in the land again. This you can do daily. Invite like minded individuals to begin to pray for this leadership to return to the earth. If you will pray, they will come, and don't stop until you see the kingdom descending upon the earth. I will pray too that it will come in your lifetimes."

"Wonderful news. I will pray for this too."

"Diane, it is time for me to return home and I couldn't be happier. I thank you with all of my heart. You are a gem. I bless you and yours with love and protection for the days ahead are a little murky yet before that which *you* want will manifest."

"What I want, Henry?" I quizzed.

"The Order of Melchizedek. The people must be humbled enough to ask for help. This is first. Then the leadership of Heaven will descend on earth," Henry commented.

"More humbling. Egads."

"Do not worry Diane. You are under His wings. You and yours are protected. No harm will come to you."

"It was a pleasure to speak with you, Henry. I wish that I could find one of your history books. I think that it would be interesting and well written too. I think that Alejandro is here now actually to speak with you."

"Yes, Diane, I am here. Good to see you my dear."

"Love to you Alejandro . . . always."

"Alejandro then added, "I am here to speak with Henry Adams. I would like to hear his reasons for wanting to come home. What lessons has he learned from his experience on earth and did he ever consider inviting me to participate with him in his life on earth? If not, why not? I will listen to his answers."

"I can hardly speak for I am in awe. I wish to apologize to Alejandro. My life was spent in search of the truth of history and somehow I neglected to include You, the Almighty, in the revelation of that historical record. I don't really understand why I did not search out the truth about You, other than that it was forbidden by those in Washington who were my peers. It was strongly discouraged. It was never discussed among us and I dare say that if I had been one to bring it up, there would have been a shakedown of sorts to shut me up."

"Henry, is that your full answer to Alejandro," I asked?

"I cannot bear to be here any longer apart from love, apart from any feeling of anything that is good. There is only loneliness and despair here, sadness and grief. I do wish to come home. I *was* lost but now I am found. I believe that I am a child of Heaven and I lost my way in the world. I do ask Alejandro for His forgiveness for it was not my intention to do harm to others while in the body. I wanted to preserve the truth of history for generations to come but those who surrounded me were against it. They lorded it over me that I was not longer my own. I was a Harvard man under their jurisdiction as it were, no longer free."

"What about your consideration of seeking Alejandro or serving Him? Did you ever consider it?"

"Perhaps when I was young I did but in the process of educating myself about the world, I lost touch with the heavens. I lost my connection to Him. I am pitiful. How could I do this? How could I come here to make a difference and then when I arrive, forget Him?"

"Fortunately, you are feeling sentiments of the world, these feelings of being pitiful, or regret, or shame and guilt. Just send these feelings to the light and let that which is good fill your being. Alejandro's love is greater than these lower vibrating emotions. His love is eternal. His love is never ending and covers a multitude of sins of our minds. He forgives you Henry."

"But I don't forgive myself. I must ask for forgiveness and see if He will forgive me."

"I encourage you to do so. Repentance before Him is a good thing Henry. Continue then."

"Almighty One, I know You, or to uphold Your name in the land. I do humbly ask for your forgiveness in return for my freedom. I am but one man but I do ask that you would see that I am not a man of malice. I will serve you in any way you may ask in return for my liberty."

"Henry, I await His answer to you. Continue as you will to share your heart with him. I will not record it here."

"I have something else to say to Alejandro for I have been thinking. I would like to ask in return for my freedom the right to open a door in heaven to release energy of truth to the earth again. I would like to open a door of revelation of the truth of His name, and His nature, and His connection to mankind for this history has been denied His people. I do ask Him if I may have this honor in Heaven in return for my freedom."

"Alejandro, Henry is asking for the privilege of honoring you in return for his freedom. He would ask that a door be opened in Heaven for a release of the historical record of truth about your name, your nature, and your connection to humanity. Will you agree?"

"Sorry, I need to tell you something Diane. Please tell Alejandro that I would also like to open a door for the release of your success Diane. That door is not open yet. Your success is still just ahead of you but the door must be opened. I will open it for you in return for your assistance in setting me free."

"Excellent. I do welcome Alejandro to receive your requests before Him."

Perfect! Alejandro is here now. ☺

"Yes, Diane. I am back for Henry's sake. I apologize for My delay. Time is different than space and I was elsewhere. I must tell Henry a few things. Henry, you are now called to the Heavens to serve Me as My historian of record. I will anoint you for this purpose. You may record the truth of My nature, My being, and My creation. Let it be said this day that I, Alejandro have appointed Henry Adams to serve as my official historian. Do you accept this appointment Henry?"

"I am too stunned to speak. I am incredulous and ecstatic, amazed beyond belief. What an absolute astonishing honor to serve You in this way, Alejandro. I will most certainly serve You as Your historian of record. Nothing would please me more than to spend eternity serving You. My destiny at last to record history and to serve You. Amazing!"

"Then consider it done. You are welcomed home now Henry. Waste no time in coming.

History is being made as we speak. So be it."

"Well done Diane. Henry is a fine historian and you might benefit from obtaining one of his books to read of his perceptions of the times. He will serve Me well. Thank you for assisting him. Now you serve both myself, the souls you assist and you in that I will reward you for assisting Me in sending those to Me who can also serve Me. It is win-win!"

"☺ Funny to hear you say "win-win"."

"Why not? My people say it all the time. Am I not the same as My people?"

"You are so much more I think. Much more and I love you for blessing Henry Adams. I think that he is happier than he ever was in life right now in this moment."

"I think you may be right. Well done Diane. Go and watch your show now. The decision is made who will go home. I hope you are not disappointed."

John Wayne

May 26, 1907 – June 11, 1979

Today's date is April 22, 2011. I was about to have an encounter with a Hollywood cowboy whom I had seen many times growing up in different movies. He was no different than the other souls in his contacting me for assistance but he had the intention of sharing some fascinating truth about Hollywood. I asked in the usual way to know who it was that wished to speak with me and was pleasantly surprised to hear his name.

"My name is John Wayne. This was my acting name. I played a cowboy in Hollywood.."

"John Wayne, do I have this name correct?"

"Yes, I have come at Alejandro's request for there is more you need to know about Hollywood."

Even stars are sworn to secrecy. Secrecy about the "rules" for celebrities. Secrecy about their contracts. Secrecy about their relationships and what is encouraged to facilitate their careers. What is happening here is a hidden agenda to influence behavior and choice. These people too have compromised their integrity, lost their true freedom to be who they are and they submit to it for one reason . . . fame and money but primarily money. Fame is like beauty. It is elusive.

It comes and it goes. Our intent is to expose the truth about Hollywood for the sole purpose of reminding the viewers of Hollywood performances that it is a "show". Those behind the material being presented are attempting to show you how to live. Let me leave my mark in history now by saying what they are showing is immoral, anti-God, indecent and murderous in most instances."

He continued, "Behind the façade is a deliberate attempt to demoralize the society by showing it to you as if it is the norm for all people. Is it? Really? How many people have you met who were murderers? It is not normal. It is abnormal for the children of Alejandro to commit murder. It is not within your nature. This change was brought into humanity by those whose nature *is* murderous. It is their nature you are watching depicted in many of your movies and television programming. They are without a conscious so what they do does not cause them to feel shame or guilt."

At this time I began to feel the presence of Alejandro. He wanted to speak into the situation.

"Yes, Diane, I want you to ask John how did they talk to the actors and actresses about how to act in their movies and in their lives. Ask him how those in charge worked to change them as people too – not just as actors."

I presented the questions to John Wayne.

"This is good Diane for in the process of directing us we were to act emotionless, tough, without a conscious merely acting *not* thinking. Our private lives were to be hidden from the public as much as possible so that the public will see us only as the tough, emotionless character we were playing. This way they would achieve their goal of showing some people as "normal" who were emotionless. This was done intentionally so they would then be able to hide their own among you and you would *not* question why some people were just not capable of demonstrating emotion. It is *not* an act that there are some here now who are not like you for they are incapable of feeling regret, sorrow, pain, guilt or any other emotion. This is how murders are committed without any feeling whatsoever. These are not the children of Alejandro yet they are in part. Unfortunately, to remove that part of these people which is anti-God and anti-humanity will require His participation."

"This information is given to you now for this process of His removing that which is evil is going to take place soon. You must understand that this must be done in order to make the world a better place. Those wishing to remain evil at any cost will be removed from the planet. This experience was designed for those who wish to make themselves better beings not worse."

"You have seen too much of the opposite of your nature and it is destroying your ability to ascend. The heavens are going to respond to your need to be free of evil – for evil exists here that does not exist where you are from."

"Are you understanding me? The world will be a better place but some will have to be removed for it to happen. In order to see who they are a conflict will occur. Those whose intentions are only to rid the earth of freedom and liberty even if it means they must take lives will come out to fight. When they do, the heavens will be ready. So if you're nature is love you are not to engage them. You are to remain in your homes and defend only yourselves and family. This is critical to your life. Do not mix yourself in with those who do evil."

"To do so may cost you your life for the heavens are shifting now to expose evil. Stay out of the way and let the heavens do their work and you will fair well."

"This is the message I was given to bring forth at this time. Heed it and you will win and still have time to run the race marked off for you – your destinies."

"A challenging message John, indeed I pray for the people to have ears to hear."

I had to ask if John was still there as I did not hear him for a few moments.

"John, are you there?"

"Of course, I am here, Diane. Where can I go? I must complete this portion of my repentance if I am to be released."

"John, there is one thing that is confusing to me still even now. If we are forgiven already, why do we need to repent?"

"It is due to our need to feel forgiven," he replied. If we are feeling shame and guilt then we can also feel the energy of being forgiven, and it is that need that is within our nature to feel forgiven for having engaged in certain activities of this world that are against our very nature that demands that we repent before our greater selves."

"This makes great sense. This discussion ought to become a video."

Thomas Paine

February 9, 1737 – June 8, 1809)

I heard the name Thomas Paine this day and it is familiar but I asked him nonetheless, "Who were you?"

He answered saying, "I was a conservative, a populist I dare say for you may think me a revolutionary, I was not but I knew some who were. I am here to find my freedom of course but more than this to make a difference in eternity for if the truth of my experience can benefit the whole than I must see to it that it happens."

"I am listening Thomas. Please tell me about your life."

"I was born in New England for although we'd hoped to escape the elitists they also came to the New World. They were desirous of making money off the land, whatever industry developed and they wanted control. Nothing new there. Theirs is an evil based society I might add for they do get their advancements in eavesdropping wire taping, monitoring devices and such things from that evil. Now I refer to them as evil for they had *not* demonstrated anything less for the innocents in the land. They would destroy every life in order to control the earth you know?"

"Not really. I hear bits and pieces of information but nothing concrete."

"Those who serve them have surrendered their souls to them. Hence they become dark lords for they have aligned themselves with evil to do harm to others."

"What about Hitler? He did this too didn't he and yet he was spared."

"Here is wisdom, Diane. Hitler was compelled by evil. He did not surrender his soul. There is a distinction."

"Spell it out for me. I need to be rid of confusion about all of this, Thomas."

"Here it is.. Those whose anger is far surpassing their capacity to love have signed a pact with evil and even entered into blood rituals with them ensuring the perpetuation of their bloodlines."

Still not satisfied I asked, "How? George Bush has only two girls."

Thomas had an answer for this, too. "As was his intention for he did not want to do to his boys what was done to him. It is possible to effect the sex of a child. It was made available to him for this purpose."

"Is there anything else, Thomas? So there is no possibility of these souls returning to Alejandro?"

"It is no longer possible Diane. Their blood is mixed with a warring faction and the dna is manipulated. The only hope is for Alejandro to sequester them and remove the offending dna which makes His people turn against Him."

"Will this "sequestering" take place any time in the next 365 days?"

"No, unfortunately but soon."

Not one to give up easily, I asked Thomas again, "How about 730 days?"

"This is more likely."

"Is this what you were sent here to tell me Thomas?"

"You must prepare."

I asked him, "How?"

He replied that I would need security and provisions but I do not think that these souls know exactly when events will play out or perhaps they are not to tell us exactly in time when to expect an event. I often am told things will happen "soon" and then that which I am expecting doesn't happen however I am also told that time and space exist simultaneously so . . . . I suppose that means that soon could happen right now or at any time.

"Why Thomas? Why do I need provisions?

"Because there will be all out rebellion before we can remove those who are the instigators. We need to see who they are. They remain hidden from us to avoid detection and so it is that we will identify them when they take arms against Our own – with the evil backing them."

"Thomas, you were saying that I need to prepare. How close to my home will the trouble be?"

"Close enough for you to not want to venture out for a bit until it settles down. You will need food provisions, water, additional drinks that will keep without refrigeration and a place to keep them all safe from those who might wish to help themselves to what you have stored."

"What kind of food Thomas?"

"Diane, you will have to decide this. Get some egg substitutes so that you can make a suitable breakfast for those who do not wish to eat beans. Get some jarred goods of applesauce, and other things that you like and canned vegetables for the family."

"Isn't the food in a jar better than what is in a can?"

"I am sure that whatever you have, people will eat. Your son and his girlfriend will join you there. Do not let him go to the battle. He must remain with you to be safe."

"If this is going to happen, I prefer that Ashley not move right now. Please ask Alejandro to allow her to remain here until this event passes and things are headed in the right direction."

"I assure you that she will be safe but it is best if she remains with you. We will attempt to encourage her in that direction. Perhaps she will not have a place to go in the summer as she thinks."

"That would be good. Things change and perhaps her friend's roommate does not leave right away."

"It is unfortunate that America must undergo such a siege but in order to break free from those who are tyrannous it is inevitable. You cannot know them without a clearing of all of the people, and even then, they can deceive you."

"I don't know when to start this collecting of things for the house. What else do I need?"

"You might need some fuel source, like firewood. Collect some and put it in some kind of container so that it is kept dry and away from insects. Find some kind of tinder box."

"Okay."

"Of course, you will want to buy more matches, and kerosene perhaps and lamps that burn kerosene. Keep these things hidden. Consider a locked box in the garage with a combination lock. You all know the combinations used around the house. It will be easy to remember for you."

"What about the security system? If there is no electricity for a while, it won't work anyway.

Is that going to happen? No electricity?"

"I see it happening but not all at once. It will come and go in segments. Sometimes you will have it and then you will not. Therefore, you will need to have your lamps and kerosene.

Order them today. I will show you some that are good for this purpose."

So as this particular conversation ended here, I can't say when the event Thomas Paine was seeing from his side might occur but it is inevitable as the world is inhabited by those who have a taste for humanity and the truest sense of the word.

Herbert Hoover

August 10, 1874–October 20, 1964

This one was very interesting and a great opening in the beginning I must say from this former President, Herbert Hoover, 31st President of the United States of America. The truth is that it is a honor and a privilege to assist these men both in their understanding of the nature of life and in their enlightenment about who God is. But most importantly is helping them to understand the God of Heaven and His nature for this will help them return home finally.

Herbert Hoover was born into a Quaker family which would have been close knit and faith based if it was a traditional Quaker household. Unfortunately, he was orphaned at age 9 years old and this may have been a trigger which caused him to become less sympathetic towards others as he himself was without his family at a very young age. He later attended Stanford and became a well accomplished geologist and established a lucrative enterprise as a mining engineer traveling the world and extracting mineral deposits for his businesses and was very successful doing this as well. As President, it seems as the opinions are mixed as to whether he was compassionate enough or not but he did work to provide refuge at the start of World War I for stranded Americans at and then worked to provide food and restoration for war ravaged Europe after World War II as part of the humanitarian efforts he was involved in. I certainly give him credit for this work.

Today is April 23, 2017 on the evening before Easter Sunday. "I am here to assist a persistent soul who has been seeking me tonight in Alejandro's name. Please tell me your name."

"My name is Herbert Hoover. I was the 31st President of the United States and a darn good one I must add. I was interested in protecting the interests of this nation above all other interests for I loved America.

She represented something very dear to me . . . freedom! I wanted to see freedom preserved for America's people at all costs. I knew America had enemies who did not support her ideals of freedom and liberty for the individual nonetheless I would stand tall and embrace the tenets of the Constitution and all that it stood for the betterment of the people of the United States of America. Mind you."

Somehow I wasn't able to complete the session and the next day, Easter, I came back to speak to Herbert Hoover.

I heard form Alejandro first thing however. "Yes, Diane. Please record what Herbert Hoover has to say here. I have been trying to awaken you because this is important and those who do not wish to have this kind of thing revealed will work against Me to entrap him. Record what he says now."

"I welcome you here Herbert Hoover. Alejandro asked that I listen to you on this Easter morning and so here I am. Please speak with me now."

"My name is Herbert Clark Hoover and as you can see there, I was the 31st President of the United States of America. I was selected for the task by The Elite having had no previous political experience myself. Despite this I was assured that I would have all of the help that I needed. I merely needed to step up and accept the calling and they would do the rest. I took orders from The Elite for they had a plan to put in place and needed someone who would be a figurehead for them and nothing more. They would see to it that the country went in a certain direction for the Elite desired to gain control over its resources and people. The way that they saw things, there were too many people who were gaining economically through playing in the Stock Market and it was necessary to crash that market to regain their own control over the companies interests in the United States. As long as they had power over the whole system they could crash it at any time through the manipulation of stock prices. They are about to do it again Diane. This is why Alejandro wanted me to speak to you. I have seen it all before. They do not fear anyone. They must have a foothold over the companies of the United States in order to move forward with their agenda to control the country. They will allow stock prices to drop exponentially while they pull all of their monies out of the system crashing it."

"This is why gambling is a bad idea. Gambling with this game playing creating artificial prices of what a thing is worth. They did it with real estate and now they will do it with the stock market. What should we do, Herbert? When will it happen? Can you tell me?"

"11-11-11 is their target date. You must tell your husband and your son to get their monies out of the stock market by then.. Put them elsewhere temporarily possibly into gold but do not just buy gold on paper. You must take ownership of the gold itself. Anything on paper will be worthless. This includes the value of a company's stock."

"Herbert, how do I convince them that what I am hearing is the truth?"

"Tell them that I experienced what they are capable of doing to win control at any costs. they do not care whose lives are ruined. They do not care if they make the Presidency a sham. They are merely interested in gaining control of the money thereby removing any power from those who own companies or those who are investing in companies and doing well. It is the last place where money is still being made and they must remove it if they are going to have success with their plan to crash the country. Diane, what people need to realize is that the value of a company is not in the artificial numbers assigned to its stock by the stock market. The value of a company is in its ability to create a service or product that is needed by others and to simply operate their business and be paid for the work that they do. It is time to end the playing of games whereby a company's value is manipulated merely for the privilege of those who know how to play a game to make money."

"Herbert, are you still with me? This is disturbing news for our country and for the world. Why do they want to plunge the entire world into a dark period again? Things were going so well and then they decide to pull the plug on life for everyone but themselves. I am counting on Alejandro to hear the prayers of the many and to stop this outrageous plan from happening where they accomplish destruction of business again How can people prepare?"

"This is something for your husband to decide. He must pull his money out of stocks and place it in a secure investment. Possibly land. But not ordinary stocks. Not paper. He can roll over money into land. Buy something Diane where both of you think you might want to live in the future. Get out of California for the foreseeable it is going to be against business and against people like yourself. Consider moving to the mountains where the air is cleaner for Dick's heart but still close enough for you to be near the ocean for you do love it so."

"Where is this place Herbert?"

"I am here Diane, thinking."

"Are we to stay here in this home during this time? Should we be leaving before that date you did give to me?"

"Take your money out of the stock market before November 11th and you will fair better than most. Just do it. If you believe for one moment that they will allow millions to keep their money, you are wrong. They are after it all. They are calculating and cold and manipulative. Remember these are bloodline families and they do not have a heart for anyone not even their own if their own go against them. They are ruthless in their nature. They want it all . . . period.

This is their power to control others. Draw you into the trap of playing the game and at the right time, change the rules. All of their people will pull out of the stock market days before and crash the market on their target date. The ultimate Illuminati move. Caution your son not to get too caught up in the game. He neither wants to be a player or a loser and indeed only those who manipulate the game win."

"You are kind to tell me these things I do give thanks to Alejandro this day. It is Easter today and people hopefully are thinking of Him and considering what the truth is. I send you love Herbert. Why were you involved with the Elite. How did they con you into the game? Why did you submit to them?"

"Money and influence, Diane. Pure and simple. They bought me with a price. Serve them and I would have whatever I needed for the rest of my life. What they don't tell you is that you are no longer free but a slave to them. They will use you and turn your life into a joke but if it is a means to an end they do not care. You are a pawn to them. If they can find those who have delusions of grandeur about themselves but who do not have a backing, they come in and offer you the possibilities to achieve all of your dreams but they will control your life from that day on. You lose everything to them. Freedom. Privacy. Humility. Earth. There is no getting out. Even at death, they control you as you have seen. They are the dark lords without a soul for they surrendered it to the darkness long before death."

"Tragic . . . for them . . . and for us for unfortunately those with the money are ruling the countries. Herbert, I need to know if Dick and I ought to go somewhere else before November 11, 2011. Should we be in a different location before then, in the mountains where there is fresh water available and cleaner air, more security from others. There is not enough time to sell this house and move into a new house in a mountain area. Our kids couldn't get there in time. It is too far away. What do we do?"

"I am seeing that it is for you to stay put at the moment. Purchase additional land somewhere, look into it right away, but stay put. Get additional provisions for your home as food will be unavailable to you for they will cause panic. You will be alright if you stay where you are for the moment. Just get out of the stock market well before 11-11-11."

"Herbert are you still here? I want to help you get to where you need to go . . . home."

"I would like that Diane. I have had enough of this world. Though there were times when my experiences here were satisfactory, my life was not easy. Losing my parents at a young age made my life traumatic at first and it ended traumatically."

"How do you mean it ended 'traumatically'?"

"The Elite destroyed my hopes of being a good President in my country. I had hoped to bring about great prosperity for the country and to see it doing well again. It was possible before they crashed Wall Street. I continued to strive for the betterment of humanity by supplying food for those in need, this was a passion of my own but I fought the public's image of me as a failure as a President due to what The Elite did in crashing the stock market under my watch.

They will do the same thing to Obama yet he will escape it narrowly. Obama may warn some people of what is coming. He will sense it is going to happen from those around him. He will begin to feel that he has been set up. It is all about how these people feel about those of the African nations. They have never aligned with them without it being advantageous to them Diane. They are deeply compromised in their integrity as humans to the allegiance with those who do evil."

"Herbert can you tell me where are you."

"I am between a rock and a hard place to be sure. I am not there where you are but I am not in heaven either. I did come at the request of

Alejandro but I was not with him. The call came through to me to be here to speak with you about what was coming."

"Do you realize that Alejandro forgives you? Do you realize that He is pure love and always was pure love? He loves all of humanity and truly is not willing that any would perish? He will welcome you home if you will consider in what ways you may have served him, but didn't and then repent before him so that all negative feelings about the experiences of life can be sent to the light leaving you free to go. He does not condemn us but it is our very souls which condemn us for you had a destiny in life that perhaps was not fully realized when you submitted to The Elite rather than to Alejandro. I encourage you to consider offering your appeal to Alejandro so that he may see you as you are before Him."

"All I want at this time is to be forgiven and to leave my regrets at the door and go home. I do hereby repent to Alejandro for having aligned myself with what I now believe to be evil. I ask for forgiveness and I do offer myself to Him fully now. Why you please forgive me for serving The Elite, for aligning myself with them, and for allowing them to destroy the livelihoods of many people in this country. Many may have achieved their destinies had I foreseen what The Elite had planned and warned them. I did not live the life that I might have lived had I trusted You more, rather than trusting them. I promise you my God in Heaven that I will serve You in any manner you ask for the privilege of returning home. Please allow me to do whatever is possible to warn the people of this good country as to what is coming. I will return home and send the warnings to the continent as you direct me. I will work hard on behalf of the people to warn them to stock up on food, for this was my passion to provide for the people who did not have food. Allow me to do something to prevent this tragedy from repeating itself in this country. I submit this to you now."

"We will wait upon his answer Herbert. We wait. I am going to clean up unless he comes quickly. I have to prepare for the day."

"Promise me that you will return Diane."

"You have my word and thank you for sharing the truth with me."

A while later I was able to get back to my office to assist Herbert Hoover in finishing his transition.

"Herbert we must get you out of there. Are you with me?"

"Absolutely for to go elsewhere at this time would be the end of me."

"Do you have anything to add to what you have said to me Herbert as I haven't yet heard back from Alejandro."

"Yes, I would like to say that it was never in my heart to do evil but I did lose my way when I agreed with The Elite. I must say once again that I am sorry for choosing to serve them. Alejandro will you forgive me and allow me to come home?"

Alejandro arrived and announced to me that He was here asking if I did feel His presence.

"Yes, I do. Blessings to you on this day when people try to remember You. I send you love and thank you for helping Herbert."

"Let's get him out of there shall we?"

"Yes!" I answered.

"Herbert this is your heavenly Father and Alejandro is my name. No more games. No more deceit. Alejandro is My name."

"I receive it," Herbert acknowledged. "Thank you."

"Allow Me to continue. Yours is a unique situation. Though you did seek to do much good in the world your loss of direction caused you to miss your final destiny. As Diane has said, it is upon Me to forgive you but first I will ask something of you."

"Did you ever once in your life give yourself to Me like you did to the Elite?"

"No, I did not. Perhaps I was overcome by negativity in the loss of love of my parents. I did not seek You. *Please* forgive me Alejandro. I will serve You now as You like."

"My point is this Herbert in asking You if you ever sought to know Me, those who seek Me do find Me. Those who seek Me I protect. Though you did *not* seek Me but you did not intentionally do evil and you are now repentant, I will allow you to come home. There are others before you whose evil was unfathomable and yet they repented and are now free. I am able to restore a man to his former glory if he will see the error of his ways in repentance.

In addition, I am calling you to serve Me now. As you can now attest to it yourself, the world is in dire straits. I must do something and I must take action quickly before My people lose everything."

"I am bringing you home and you will sound the alarm for all of My people to get out of the stock market." "Get out" shall be your message Herbert. Get out of her My people. Come out of her. This is the beast which consumes all of the energy created by the hands of My people.

The Elite have used that energy to create controlling businesses of their own but now My people will win. Herbert Hoover you are called by Me as My own now, and you shall serve Me in this way. You will sound the alarm to My people to get out of the stock market beginning today. You will sound the alarm up until 11-11-11 and then you will continue to sound the alarm for a greater danger follows this one."

"The Day of the Lord shall come as predicted by John. I will allow My people to see that without Me they can do nothing and then I will come and remove their enemy and the earth shall have peace once again. Is this acceptable to you. Will you agree to serve Me in this manner?"

"Yes, Yes, Alejandro a thousand times yes. I am yours now forever in eternity. Thank you. I am at your mercy."

"Maybe so but I still give you free choice. You may choose your eternity."

"I choose you this is my answer to you. I graciously choose You."

"I accept. You are free to come home now. I release you Herbert Hoover. You shall still achieve your destiny in warning the people to come out of the beast."

Herbert then said to me, I am leaving now, Diane. Well done. Enjoy your Easter with your family. Get some clearing done of your family members now. You'd do well to convince him to transform his gold into a land purchase. Buy something in Oregon near the ocean and mountains. You will have some cool weather, no snow and you will be near the grandchildren which are still coming. Great time to buy land. Visit Oregon!

"Now I must bring Herbert home. Off you go, Diane," says Alejandro.

Though I thought this was the end when Alejandro left, Herbert Hoover still wanted to speak with me.

"I must speak to you quickly. I am to bless you for assisting me in leaving here. This is what I will do. I will go to heaven and ask that a door be opened for you to get all of your food supplies in place this week before the alarm goes out. Then I will ask that your husband will understand the need to take the gold investment and roll it over into land in Oregon. How's that sound? Land with visibility of the oceans but mountain air for Dick."

"It shall be done for you. I admire your tenacity to serve Alejandro, Diane. It is clear to me that you have found favor with Him, and He with me."

"Adieu. Fair well. Get your supplies."

I asked Him what money I ought to spend on the supplies.

Herbert Hoover recommended that I use the money which my mother left to me. He said that "her money will have gone a long way to help all of you". It wasn't a lot of money but it was enough for me to prepare as I was led to prepare and if the situation becomes difficult in the near future I will have some things to assist in helping my family.

"Thank you. Adieu Herbert."

Part III

A New Dawn for the Remnant

Stonewall Jackson

January 21, 1824 – May 10, 1863

The message brought forth today June 10, 2011 by this soul was for my edification and for those who would read the truth here in The Trinity. He was brief. This was someone I did not know that much about but his coming to me was for the purpose of bringing forth this message.

Stonewall Jackson's name was well known in the area of Virginia where I grew up. He was a General under Robert E. Lee serving in the Confederate Army. The American Civil War took place in this area of the world and so his name appeared on signs on historical sites there.

Stonewall was a West Point graduate, served in the U.S. Army and then later in life was a teacher at V.M.I., Virginia Military Institute. He earned his nickname Stonewall from the first battle at Bull Run where he refused to back down and the Confederates noted his standing there like a "stone wall" not moving or giving up.

Here we go:

I thought that I heard the name of this person as Stonewall Jackson and so I did inquire,

"Who is this please? Did you say Stonewall Jackson?".

"Diane, my name is Stonewall Jackson. It is indeed for a battle is about to commence. I need to put forth some strategies for the people. First, all wars have a beginning as to what will happen first. Here it is. The trumpets will sound first. This is your time to move indoors and get out of the battle zone. All battles are fought outdoors. You need not worry as long as you remain indoors. Next, the God of Heaven has sent His Son to make known the reasons for the battle which will commence. Thus the people will hear Yahoushua Hamashiach speak to the conditions which require the intervention of the Almighty. All will hear what deceit has transpired against the people of this earth and then the battle will commence."

Louis Armstrong

August 4, 1901 – July 6, 1971

Now I am going to tell you about what happened this morning prior to my addressing the needs of the soul whose name is above. First, this morning I thought I felt the energy of a soul and at the same time I saw a young, little girl in the shop where I was and saw that she was carrying a toy. She was cute and I do like to see children and tend to watch them.

What I saw that she had in her hands was a trumpet, not a doll, not a book but a trumpet! Not only that, she came to the back of the shop and walked in front of me. You might say "big deal", but not me! I am a believer that the God of Heaven is planning to do what is spoken of in the scriptures and in the scriptures there is a trumpet sounded before we see the leadership we truly need in the world.

Back to the work at hand. I felt the presence of a soul and he did tell me his name.

I welcomed him and then heard him.

"My name is Louis Armstrong."

"Welcome Louis! Tell me your intentions in coming to me."

"I have an announcement to make Diane, at the request of the God of Heaven, I have an announcement to make."

"Excellent, Louis. I am ready."

"This is Louis Armstrong! I was a trumpet player in my life. You might remember me by my signature big cheeks. That's what happens to the muscles after years of pushing air against the walls of the mouth. But I am here to discuss a matter of some importance to all of you.

This is a certain warning to you for I am selected to bring forth a sound to all of the earth to notify you of His coming. This sound will be heard around the world. It will be the sound of trumpets and I will lead it. This is an honor and a privilege to me for I did not serve the God of Heaven in my life."

"I did not make a Godly sound with my trumpets. Who knows what healing sound I might have brought forth if I had connected to Him while living. But I am to have a reprieve for He has blessed me in giving me the honor of announcing His arrival! You will hear the sound of my trumpets exactly 24 hours before His coming!"

"Hasten to gather your families and go into your homes. Lock the doors and remain there until He calls to you to come forth. This is His only forewarning to you of His trumpet call. then you must take action. The rest is up to Him. Prepare then. Time is of the essence."

I thanked Louis Armstrong for his message and let Him do the rest.

Conclusion of the Matter

Today is March 14, 2011 and what I heard today was the collective of souls who had been assisted in crossing to the light of Heaven and they brought forth a message which I will post here.

I asked who was here for me to assist.

"We are Diane. We are the consciousness of all of those whom you have assisted in crossing over to the light. We are gathered here in one accord for the pure purpose of thanking you for your assistance for we were once lost, but now we are found, by Alejandro. We want to tell you that you are blessed above all women in that you were willing to come into the darkness to free us from ourselves, for our own souls testified against us before Alejandro, telling us that we were unworthy for we had not chosen Him in life, to serve Him to love Him, to lift up His name among men. Do you not know that you are beloved of Him, for no one sought to know Him as you did, fasting 40 days at the risk of your life, to know His name. There is no one like you. for this, you are being lifted up now. It is your destiny hour beloved. We give you thanks in the heavens. you are to be exalted among men. Let us write your summary for you. Include the text which we have spoken above and also, add this:"

"To the people of the nations, called by His name.

We are the people who have been set free by Him after our deaths for we did not know Him in life, but our God, Alejandro, is such a gracious and consuming loving God, that He has seen to it that one did come into the darkness, to rescue His own, to tell us the truth of His nature, that even though we were lost, He Found us, and demonstrated that love is long suffering, even unto death. Now we are free. We are free to send you love from the heavens that you too would know Him, now, while you have time before you, to seek

Him, and when you seek Him, he will be found by you, and you will rediscover your destinies. We once were lost. Now we are found. There is hope for all of His people for He is a consuming fire, able to consume that which is not of Him, and restoring you unto His nature. Do not have despair, but have hope, in Him. Let go of the world's feelings which separate you from Him. Let go of the anger, hatred, resentment, bitterness, and sorrow of this world now. Let it go. Send it home to the light and He will consume it recreating it for good and not for evil. Then when you are free of these energies of emotion, seek His face. Seek to know Him. Ask Him to fill you with His energy, His fire, His love. He is faithful to do it. We know. He did it for us. Those whose stories are contained within the pages of this book do testify to the truth of what is written here and do release Diane Freeman to tell our stories to the world that many may be set free."

In addition Alejandro has released me now to list here among these names as well all of the other souls who did come through in 2011 asking for assistance in crossing to the light or who were sent to Me divinely with revelation for humanity.

John F. Kennedy

Jacqueline Kennedy Onassis

Robert Kennedy

Edward Kennedy

Michael J. Jackson

Whitney Houston

Prince

Heath Ledger

Paul Walker

Robin Williams

Joan Rivers

Tupac Shakur

Elvis Aaron Presley

Wolfgang Amadeus Mozart

Patrick Henry

James Maitland Stewart "Jimmy"

Princess Diana of Wales

Robert Trent Jones

Adolf Hitler

Abraham Lincoln

Samuel Adams

James Madison

Abigail Adams

Lee Harvey Oswald

John Edgar Hoover

Arthur M. Young

Christopher Columbus

Isaac Asimov

Ricardo (Gonzalo Pedro) Montalban y Merino (actor)

Benjamin Franklin

Alexander Haig

Elizabeth Taylor

Lewis Meriwether

Mark Antony of Rome

Ronald Reagan

Karl Marx

Dr. Thomas Walker

Heinrich Luitpold Himmler

Franklin D. Roosevelt

Henry Brooks Adams

John Wayne

Thomas Paine

Herbert Hoover

Alexander Hamilton

Louis Armstrong

George Washington

H. R. Haldeman

General Douglas MacArthur

Sandra Dee

Margaret Thatcher

Henry Wadsworth Longfellow

Napoleon Bonaparte

Robert Louis Stevenson

James Foster Dulles

Frank Lloyd Wright

John Adams

Mussolini

Grover Cleveland

Alexander McQueen (fashion designer)

Steve McQueen (actor)

Martha Washington

George W. Washington

K. C. Irving (James Irving)

George Washington Carver

Queen Elizabeth I

Rock Hudson

Edgar Allan Poe (whose poem for me appears at the end of my book)

Margaret Meade

Robert Louis Stevenson

Loren Nancarrow

Oscar de la Renta

Margaret Thatcher

Nancy Reagan

Ronald Reagan

Oscar de la Renta and many, many others.

"Thank you, all of you. Love, love, love and more love to all of you. Alejandro, and all of you. Send your blessings that I may know who is to be His publisher."

Diane Freeman

In addition, the God of Heaven did instruct me at different times to clear souls on the planet who were otherwise in darkness and lost not knowing where to go or how.

Some of these were many of the souls from the concentration camps of Germany, as He had me conduct research to find the names of the people there who were taken to the different internment camps by the Nazis, and then He selected individuals who were lost at each camp to represent all souls lost there, who we did speak with, and we educated them about salvation, about Him, and they did repent, accept Him and were sent home. Most did not know Him personally nor had they known to choose Him for themselves. It is a free will choice exercise and must be chosen by each person. The God of Heaven does not force Himself on anyone, it is clear in the recorded scriptures that each of us must choose whom we will serve.

Not to do so leaves you lost at the end of your days. He also cleared souls from the loss of souls on the Hindenburg, the Titanic, the Civil War grounds at Gettysburg, and other battle fields.

Again, He showed me the names of individuals who were leaders in each of those tragedies, the ship's captain of the Titanic, the military leaders in the wars, captains of planes that went down in America such as the off the coast of New York. He cleared the souls lost in The Twin Towers on September 11th and the souls who were lost on the hijacked planes. Those who chose Him are safe at home under His wing. He is good and not willing that any should perish. He directed me to clear the lost souls who were tortured and abused in asylums across the U.S. where people left their children in the hands of not so Godly men and women who mistreated them in the child's despair.

In clearing the souls and the negative energy which collects in areas where there is this loss of life and the mistreatment of humanity, He has lifted much negative energy from the earth that surrounds the areas where these tragic events take place. He did it. He chose to do it and He used me to assist Him. What an blessing for me and a privilege but to Him be the honor and glory.

This book was written and its evidence presented that you might have the truth.

There is no one other than the Almighty who can verify its authenticity. To second guess its truth is to second guess the Almighty who is the true, author and originator of the essence of the book.

So it is not given to you, the reader, or any other earth bound soul to criticize, judge or otherwise nullify the contents of this book. To do so is to sin against the Almighty Himself who did ordain the writer and the souls themselves who presented themselves to her for their release unto Him, for His purposes, under Heaven.

The evidence of this and more is almost made manifest upon the earth and when it has been shown to you what is the truth, all shall be free indeed.

* * *

Edgar Allan Poe's poem to me:
In the dark of night when souls roam free a flicker of light appears.
The source is unknown and yet is seems this light has come for me.
I chance to search it out and see for myself if it can truly be.. that my freedom has come at last.
I follow the source and wait my turn for others have seen it too.
I see the energy increase in volume, the hope I feel is palatable.
It is real.
I can feel that this is real and all my fears are fading.

I know now that God has come to free these souls who wish to give Him glory.

His hand has reached into the depths of despair and I am hearing that hope again has come for me.

The darkness will soon reveal me for my light is increasing as I share my story to this soul whose light is stronger, intense and beautiful in love she knows me for souls whose capture meant misery, unholiness, dreadfulness and fear.

My light is growing, my energy billowing.

I can again feel God's love.

This feeling of ecstacy overwhelms my being all because of her love for man.

I give thanks to God for remembering me when no one else could do so.

He sent His own to rescue me . . . a poet, a no one.

Let His name again resound on earth as it once did in all men and may their souls escape this place as I did.

Edgar Allan Poe

Robert Louis Stevenson's prose to me:

In the dark of night where souls are kept against their will, against their might.

A man's thoughts are sheltered here not permitted to touch another for in the sharing of thoughts is the risk of freedom, the hope of liberty, the daring of men who will rise to their destinies in time of despair.

This is not permitted.

Why is it that souls lapse here in no man's land?

What have they done to deserve such a tribute to their souls?

As my awareness awakens . . . I see!

It is man's lack of love of God that testifies against him here for those who have loved God and lifted Him up in the world know . . .

God will never leave them nor forsake them.

How then can so many be here?

Was their love for themselves greater than for God?

It is here in the ultimate darkness of despair that the soul itself testifies against one's self.

There is no hiding from the truth.

"What did you do in God's name?" the question doth ask.

And what can be my answer?

I have none and so my soul says nothing.

I have no retreat.

I have no defense.

I have no offer to God to make.

My shame and my guilt are here to testify against me.

My friends in life

Do not let this happen to you.

Remember the God whose likeness you bear.

Give Him His just reward.

Share yourself with Him anew.

Let His name resound again in the land.

For He alone is the God of love.

There are none like Him.

His love came forth even here in the darkness through His daughter whose love was greater than her fear for her soul.

And so it is I could give tribute to my God

I leave these words for the world

Remember my fate

Robert Louis Stevenson

Who wrote a fairytale story about the wanderlust of man who chose not carefully enough in life to love God first, to give God the glory, first to lift up His name, first. And I paid a certain price. But now I am free to again roam the heavenly highways and byways.

Thanks be to God and to one who loves Him as greater than herself.

Diane Freeman

My quest for freedom is over.

Glory be to God!!

Printed in the United States
By Bookmasters